The Emergence of Jewish Gh[e

This book is a linguistic-cultural study of the emergence of the Jewish ghettos during the Holocaust. It traces the origins and uses of the term "ghetto" in European discourse from the sixteenth century to the Nazi regime. It examines with a magnifying glass both the actual establishment of and the discourse of the Nazis and their allies on ghettos from 1933 to 1944. With conclusions that oppose all existing explanations and cursory examinations of the ghetto, the book impacts overall understanding of the anti-Jewish policies of Nazi Germany.

Dan Michman is Professor of Modern Jewish History and Chair of the Arnold and Leona Finkler Institute of Holocaust Research at Bar-Ilan University, Ramat-Gan. He is also Chief Historian at the Yad Vashem International Institute for Holocaust Research. His work has been published in eleven languages and deals with modern Jewish history and the history of Dutch Jewry, with a focus on the Holocaust. His books include *Bimay Shoa Ufkuda (Days of Holocaust and Reckoning)*; *Het Liberale Jodendom in Nederland, 1929–1943 (Liberal Jewry in the Netherlands, 1929–1943)*; and *Holocaust Historiography: A Jewish Perspective: Conceptualizations, Terminology, Approaches and Fundamental Issues*, and he is co-author (with Jozeph Michman and Hartog Beem) of *Pinkas: Geschiedenis van de joodse gemeenschap in Nederland (Pinkas: The History of the Jewish Community in the Netherlands)*. Volumes he has edited include *Post-Ziyonut ve-Shoa (Post-Zionism and the Holocaust)*, volumes 1 and 2; *Belgium and the Holocaust: Germans, Belgians, Jews*; *Les intellectuels face à l'affaire Dreyfus: alors et aujourd'hui (Intellectuals Responding to the Dreyfus Affair: Then and Now*, co-edited with Roselyne Koren); *Remembering the Holocaust in Germany, 1945–2000: German Strategies and Jewish Responses*; *Encyclopedia of the Righteous Among the Nations: Belgium*; *Hashoa Bahistoriya Hayehudit: Historiografiya, Toda'a u-Farshanut (The Holocaust in Jewish History: Historiography, Consciousness, Interpretations)*; *De la mémoire de la Shoah dans le monde juif (On the Memory of the Shoah in the Jewish World*, co-edited with Françoise Ouzan); and *Holocaust Historiography in Context: Emergence, Challenges, Polemics and Achievements* and *The Holocaust and Justice: Representation and Historiography of the Holocaust in Post-War Trials* (both co-edited with David Bankier).

The Emergence of Jewish Ghettos During the Holocaust

DAN MICHMAN
Bar-Ilan University and Yad Vashem, Israel

Translated by Lenn J. Schramm

Yad Vashem

CAMBRIDGE
UNIVERSITY PRESS

32 Avenue of the Americas, New York NY 10013-2473, USA

Cambridge University Press is part of the University of Cambridge.

It furthers the University's mission by disseminating knowledge in the pursuit of education, learning and research at the highest international levels of excellence.

www.cambridge.org
Information on this title: www.cambridge.org/9781107437128

© Dan Michman 2011

This publication is in copyright. Subject to statutory exception and to the provisions of relevant collective licensing agreements, no reproduction of any part may take place without the written permission of Cambridge University Press.

First published 2011
Reprinted 2011
First paperback edition 2014

A catalogue record for this publication is available from the British Library

Library of Congress Cataloguing in Publication data

Mikhman, Dan.
The emergence of Jewish ghettos during the Holocaust / Dan Michman.
   p. cm.
Includes bibliographical references and index.
ISBN 978-0-521-76371-4 (hardback)
1. Jews – Segregation – Government policy – Germany – History – 20th century.
2. Jewish ghettos – Germany – History – 20th century. 3. Jews – Germany – Social conditions – 20th century. 4. Germany – Ethnic relations – History – 20th century.
I. Title.
DS134.255.M55 2010
940.53´185–dc22   2010031318

ISBN 978-0-521-76371-4 Hardback
ISBN 978-1-107-43712-8 Paperback

Cambridge University Press has no responsibility for the persistence or accuracy of URLs for external or third-party internet websites referred to in this publication, and does not guarantee that any content on such websites is, or will remain, accurate or appropriate.

In memory of my father
Dr. Jozeph Michman (Melkman)
(Amsterdam, April 2, 1914–Jerusalem, February 20, 2009)
a Zionist leader, teacher, Holocaust survivor, historian, and builder of cultural life in Israel

my life-long personal and academic mentor

The translation and publication of this book were made possible with the support of the

Israel Science Foundation

and

Bar-Ilan University – Office of the Vice President for Research

Contents

	Introduction	page 1
1	Historiography and Popular Understandings	6
2	Ghetto: The Source of the Term and the Phenomenon in the Early Modern Age	20
3	Ghetto and Ghettoization as Cultural Concepts in the Modern Age	25
4	The Nazis' Anti-Jewish Policy in the 1930s in Germany and the Question of Jewish Residential Districts	31
5	First References to the Term "Ghetto" in the Ideological Discourse of the Makers of Anti-Jewish Policy in the Third Reich (1933–1938)	36
6	The Semantic Turning Point in the Meaning of "Ghetto": Peter-Heinz Seraphim and *Das Judentum im osteuropäischen Raum*	45
7	The Invasion of Poland and the Emergence of the "Classic" Ghettos	61
8	Methodological Interlude: The Term "Ghettoization" and Its Use During the Holocaust Itself and in Later Scholarship	90
9	Would the Idea Spread to Other Places? Amsterdam 1941, the Only Attempt to Establish a Ghetto West of Poland	94
10	Ghettos During the Final Solution, 1941–1943: The Territories Occupied in Operation Barbarossa	102

11	Ghettos During the Final Solution Outside the Occupied Soviet Union: Poland, Theresienstadt, Amsterdam, Transnistria, Salonika, and Hungary	122
12	Summary and Conclusions	145
Bibliography		163
Index		183

Introduction

> I will enumerate and describe briefly a number of questions which have hardly been studied so far and which require thorough and fundamental elucidation.... The external and the internal Ghetto arrangements; the differences between the mediaeval Ghetto and the Nazi Ghetto in layout and purpose; the role of such creations as the *Sammelghetto* (Central Ghetto), Transit-Ghetto, etc. Naturally, the external and internal aspects of the Ghetto life should be considered as well.
>
> Philip Friedman, "Problems of Research on the European Jewish Catastrophe" (1959)

The ghetto phenomenon was central to Jewish life under the National Socialist regime and is a keystone of Holocaust consciousness and memory. The prevailing notion about the Jews' fate during the Holocaust is that the Germans concentrated them in ghettos as a systematic element of their policy; and that in areas where the Nazis did not do so (for whatever reason), they nevertheless took the first steps toward ghettoization, meaning the segregation of the Jews without visible walls or fences. Indeed, much has been published about ghettos: many studies have dealt with particular ghettos, mainly in Poland and Lithuania and to a lesser extent in other regions. There are also extensive descriptions in the *yizkor-bikher* (community memorial books, of which about 1,400 have been published in the past six decades) and in the memoirs of survivors (a genre that today encompasses thousands of publications). This literature provides a multifaceted picture of life in quite a few ghettos.

In 1959, Philip Friedman, perhaps the leading Holocaust scholar of the immediate post-war period, endeavored to define the goals of Holocaust research, then still in its infancy:

In order to avoid dealing with abstract notions only, I will enumerate and describe briefly a number of questions which have hardly been studied so far and which require thorough and fundamental elucidation. (1.) *The Ghetto and the Judenrat*: We are confronted with some form of Jewish self-government, but as a matter of fact, this home rule is nothing but a travesty of the term as a result of the misuse and abuse by the Nazis of ideas of Jewish autonomy and territorialism, for the purpose of misleading and deceiving. Further problems are: The external and the internal Ghetto arrangements; the differences between the mediaeval Ghetto and the Nazi Ghetto in layout and purpose; the role of such creations as the *Sammelghetto* (Central Ghetto), Transit-Ghetto, etc. Naturally, the external and internal aspects of the Ghetto life should be considered as well.[1]

Astonishingly, however, the research literature has never dealt systematically and in depth with a number of fundamental questions about the emergence and nature of this phenomenon. When exactly did the idea of establishing ghettos for Jews take shape in the minds of Third Reich officials who dealt with *Judenpolitik* (anti-Jewish policies)? Were the circumstances those of orderly and premeditated planning (as assumed by many), or the result of local pressures, without prior preparation (as hinted in some studies)? Who supported the idea and who opposed it? What are the origins of the idea? Why did the term "ghetto" take root (and how does it relate to alternative terms that Nazi-German discourse applied to the same phenomenon)? How many ghettos were there? For what purposes were they actually used? Was their establishment linked to the development of the idea of the Final Solution of the Jewish Question? Should the term "ghettoization," which is a derivative of the noun "ghetto," be applied to the measures of concentration and segregation directed against Jews in regions where physical ghettos were not established (such as Western Europe)? Were the *Judenräte* (Jewish councils) – another foundational element of Holocaust history and consciousness – intrinsically linked to the phenomenon of the ghettos?

Some of these questions have been left unanswered because it has become axiomatic that ghettos *were* an integral part of Nazi anti-Jewish policy.[2] However, a thorough examination of the extensive source

---

[1] Philip Friedman, "Problems of Research on the Jewish Catastrophe," *Yad Vashem Studies* 3 (1959), p. 37 (reprinted with slight changes as "Problems of Research on the Holocaust: An Overview" in Philip Friedman, *Roads to Extinction: Essays on the Holocaust*, p. 564). On the emergence of Holocaust historiography and Friedman's important role within it, see David Bankier and Dan Michman, eds., *Holocaust Historiography in Context: Emergence, Challenges, Polemics and Achievements*.

[2] See, for instance, the definition given on the Simon Wiesenthal Center Web site: "Jews were forced to live in ghettos during WWII. They functioned as a transition before the Jews were deported to their deaths."

Introduction

materials at our disposal and of the scholarly literature on Nazi anti-Jewish policies, especially those published in recent years, reveals that this assumption is based on a fallacy: the central authorities of Nazi Germany never elaborated a clear and unequivocal definition of what a ghetto was or should be (from their point of view). Moreover, we do not have a single major document that points to the sources of the ghetto concept, its essence, and the ways for implementing and managing it (later in this study we discuss the exact meaning of Reinhard Heydrich's well-known *Schnellbrief* of September 21, 1939, which is often perceived as the "smoking gun"[3]). On the contrary, the German documents of the period that were written by officials involved in setting up ghettos propose varying reasons and explanations for their establishment and need – which shows that the officials themselves were not sure about the origins of the idea and its precise purposes.

I attempt to suggest some answers to these questions – evidently the first attempt to do so (except for one article by Philip Friedman, written more than fifty years ago[4]). My discussion will focus on the history of the semantics and cultural contexts of the term "ghetto." Most past treatments of the ghetto phenomenon during the Holocaust have tried to understand it from an administrative and organizational perspective and have neglected the linguistic and cultural aspects entirely. I believe that in this case a combined cultural, linguistic, and semantic approach can provide a better answer than the approaches tried in the past. It is clear to me that this novel approach will raise new questions for future research to address. But, if the thesis proposed here does indeed trigger a renewed discussion of a topic that is so central to the Holocaust, I will have done my part.

The ideas presented in this study crystallized during the first months of 2007, when – in my function as the chief historian at Yad Vashem – I sat down to write an introduction to *The Yad Vashem Encyclopedia of the Ghettos During the Holocaust* (Yad Vashem, 2009), then in preparation. As early as 2005, during the first deliberations by the team working on the encyclopedia, the problem arose of which places should be included in it. During these discussions we realized something that had been known

---

[3] Yehuda Bauer, addressing the *Schnellbrief* in his comprehensive overview of the Holocaust, attaches a note to the word "ghetto," where it appears in paragraph 5 of the section on the Jewish councils, to the effect that this is "the earliest reference to the German plan to establish ghettoes"; see Yehuda Bauer (with the assistance of Nili Keren), *A History of the Holocaust*, pp. 149, 360n5.

[4] Philip Friedman, "The Jewish Ghettos of the Nazi Era."

but not fully appreciated, namely, that the Nazi bureaucracy never really defined what it meant by the word "ghetto." Forced to come up with a definition of our own, the encyclopedia staff decided on the following: "Any concentration of Jews by compulsion in a clearly defined section of an existing settlement (city, town, or village) in areas controlled by Germany or its allies, for more than one month." This definition included various patterns of residential concentration – neighborhoods, streets, groups of buildings (but not single buildings, such as the *Judenhäuser* [Jewish houses] in Germany), or barracks – and did *not* require the existence of a Jewish administration, although this element often existed. Parallel to our work, a team at the United States Holocaust Memorial Museum in Washington, D.C., developed a slightly different definition for their multi-volume *Encyclopedia of Camps and Ghettos, 1933–1945* (of which volume 1 was also published in 2009). The essential problem posed here demanded a systematic study. *The Yad Vashem Encyclopedia of the Ghettos During the Holocaust* includes a short version of my thesis; this book is a much more extensive and fully annotated version.

The initial questions were mine, but many friends and colleagues assisted me in clarifying problems and developing the ideas and answers. First of all, I would like to thank my colleagues at the Yad Vashem International Institute for Holocaust Research and the team that worked on the *Encyclopedia of the Ghettos*: Professor David Bankier (an outstanding scholar and marvelous friend and colleague, who unfortunately passed away in February 2010), Dr. Tikva Fatal-Kna'ani, Dr. Bella Gutterman, Professor Guy Miron, Dr. Leah Preiss, Ruth Shachak, Shlomit Shulchani, and Dr. Arkadi Zeltser. Others who helped me by providing documents and advice, making remarks on the draft text, and responding to my first presentation on this topic, delivered at the annual John Najmann lecture at Yad Vashem (on May 3, 2007), are: Dr. Natalya Aleksiun, Professor Gershon Bacon, Dr. Avi Barkai, Dr. Nicolas Berg, Dr. Jochen Böhler, Dr. Martin Dean, Dr. Chavi Dreyfus–Ben Sasson, Dr. Diana Dumitru, Dr. Mali Eisenberg (Gotdiner), Dr. Chava Eshkoli, Dr. Kiril Feferman, Dr. Ronit Fischer, Dr. Klaus-Peter Friedrich, Dr. Kinga Frojimovics, Professor Gershon Greenberg, Dr. Pim Griffioen, Mr. Matthias Holzberg, Dr. Rita Horvath, Dr. Wendy Lower, Dr. Jürgen Matthäus, Dr. Avraham Milgram, Dr. Alexandra Namysło, Professor Benjamin Ravid, Dr. Shlomo Shafir, Dr. Margalit Shlain, Mrs. Nina Shpringer, Professor Alan Steinweis, Professor Kenneth Stow, Professor Kerstin Stutterheim, and Professor Yfaat Weiss. Additional thanks are extended to the anonymous readers of Cambridge University Press and S. Fischer

Introduction

Verlage, whose helpful comments allowed me to refine both the structure of the book and its conclusions. I wish to express special thanks to the late Professor Alan Zuckerman, who attended my lecture and in its wake established the contact with Cambridge University Press that led to this publication. I came to know Alan as a result of this study, and we became personal friends. His death on August 20, 2009, after several months of suffering, is a great loss to his wife Ricki and their children, to the academic world, and to me personally. This book is dedicated to his blessed memory too.

Lenn J. Schramm did an excellent job in translating the text, correcting, improving, and drawing my attention to problems in the original version; I thank him deeply for that. The people of Cambridge University Press, and in the first place Lewis Bateman – who made the initial contact with me – oversaw the whole publication process in an extraordinary way; I am deeply indebted to their professionalism. The Yad Vashem Publication Department supported the translation and was efficient as always. Financial support for the translation of the text was provided by The Israel Science Foundation and the office of the Vice President for Research of Bar-Ilan University, the university where I have been teaching for more than three decades now. The Arnold and Leona Finkler Chair of Holocaust Research at Bar-Ilan University provided me as always with some of the basic administrative help needed to carry out my research.

I had to do the final editing of this book in July 2009, and it was at that time that I found out I had to undergo heart surgery. I would like to thank from the depths of my heart my friend and cardiologist, Dr. Yeda'el Har-Zahav, for having maneuvered me smoothly and with endless support through this procedure, and his wife Ilana for her helping hand. Additional thanks and deep appreciation are extended to Dr. Ehud Raanani, Head of the Cardiac Surgery Department, and Dr. Ami Sheinfeld, Senior Heart Surgeon, at the Sheba Medical Center, who carried out the surgery with full success and in the most friendly and supportive manner; the efficiency and warmth of the entire team of the Heart Surgery Department was crucial in speeding up my recovery process.

Last but not least, I would like to express my deepest thanks to my wife Bruria, with whom I have been walking through the labyrinth of life for almost four decades. Her constant support and love, especially needed in dire times, make everything I do easier. Moreover, her penetrating questions about the thesis set forth in this book, asked while we were jogging together one evening in February 2007, drove me to look for – and find – the final link that closed the circuit: Peter-Heinz Seraphim's 1938 book, *Das Judentum im osteuropäischen Raum*.

I

Historiography and Popular Understandings

> The preliminary steps of the ghettoization process consisted of marking, movement restrictions, and the creation of Jewish control organs.... The three preliminary steps – marking, movement restrictions, and the establishment of a Jewish control machinery – were taken in the very first months of civil rule [in Poland].... In this book we shall be interested in the ghetto only as a control mechanism [for movement restrictions] in the hands of the German bureaucracy. To the Jews the ghetto was a way of life; to the Germans it was an administrative measure.
>
> Raul Hilberg, *The Destruction of the European Jews* (1961)

> **Ghettoisation.** The establishment of ghettos was one of the most effective means to get the Jewish population under total control and have them exploited. With the beginning of the mass murder campaign they turned for them into giant prisons, from which the Nazis could send the inmates to the annihilation camps.... The ghettos were a milestone on the way to genocide.
>
> Michael Alberti, "'Exerzierplatz des Nationalsozialismus': Der Reichsgau Wartheland 1939–1941" (2004)

> Removing the Jew from the urban space was part of a more comprehensive process of removal from the political situation and from the German *Lebensraum*. The ultimate goal was to make all of these *Judenrein*. Whereas the space of the new city was reserved for the Aryan German, the ghetto was the urban space allotted to the Jew.
>
> Boaz Neumann, *The Nazi* Weltanschauung: *Space, Body, Language* (2001)

The most common image of the Jews' experience under the Nazi regime before the start of the Final Solution is that they lived in ghettos. It is true that survivors from many countries – Germany, Austria, the

Historiography and Popular Understandings

Netherlands, Belgium, France, Italy, Denmark, Norway, the Island of Rhodes, and elsewhere – could testify that there were no ghettos in those places. Nevertheless, this image took hold even during the Holocaust itself. The Warsaw ghetto in particular made its mark on public awareness in Eretz-Israel/Palestine (now Israel) and in other parts of the world. The Warsaw ghetto was seen as indicative of what was happening to the Jews under the Nazis.[1] The strong impact of the Warsaw Ghetto uprising in April 1943 reinforced this perception. Later, because much of the initial Jewish research on the Holocaust was conducted by Polish- and Lithuanian-born historians, including Samuel Gringauz,[2] Philip Friedman,[3] Nachman Blumenthal,[4] and Meir (Mark) Dworzecki,[5] the Polish (or Polish-Lithuanian) model came to occupy center stage in the public mind and in historical studies. This model gives special weight to the few large ghettos for which we have abundant and diverse documentation, including Warsaw, Łódź, Bialystok, Vilna (Vilnius), and to a lesser extent also Lublin, Krakow, and Kovno (Kaunas).[6] It is true that many Jews – some three-quarters of a million all told – were

---

[1] For example, during a meeting of the representative office of Polish Jews in Palestine, in the summer of 1942, shortly after the so-called Zygelbojm report on the murder of the Jews in Poland was received, Rabbi Yitzhak Meir Levin, the Agudath Yisrael (Ultraorthodox) leader who was prominent in efforts to rescue Jews in Europe, called on the "Allied governments to come to the assistance of our brothers who are being persecuted in the ghettos." Levin to Itzhak Gruenbaum, August 28, 1942, quoted in Chaim Shalem, *Et La'asot le-Hatzalat Yisrael. Agudat Yisrael be-Eretz Yisrael lenochah ha-Shoah*.

[2] Samuel Gringauz, "The Ghetto as an Experiment of Jewish Social Organization," and "Some Methodological Problems in the Study of the Ghetto." Gringauz was a Lithuanian Jew who had lived in Memel until 1938. See also note 9.

[3] Philip Friedman, "The Jewish Ghettos of the Nazi Era." Friedman was probably the seminal and most influential figure in the study of the Jewish aspects of the Holocaust in the 1940s and 1950s. For more information on him, see David Bankier and Dan Michman, eds., *Holocaust Historiography in Context*; Roni Stauber, *Laying the Foundations for Holocaust Research: The Impact of Philip Friedman*.

[4] Nachman Blumenthal, *Darko shel Judenrat: Te'udot mi-Ghetto Bialystok*, and *Te'udot mi-geto Lublin: Judenrat lelo Derech*. Although these volumes were published in the 1960s, Blumenthal had been an active historian before, at first in the Displaced Persons camps right after the war, later at the Ghetto Fighters' House in Israel after its establishment in the early 1950s, and then at Yad Vashem when it was officially inaugurated in 1953. See Boaz Cohen, "Ha-Mehkar ha-Histori ha-Yisre'eli al ha-Shoah ba-Shanim 1945–1980."

[5] Mark Dworzecki, *Yerushalayim de-Lita ba-Meri uva-Shoah*. On Dworzecki's life and work, see Cohen, "Holocaust Research in Israel, 1945–1980," chapter 7, esp. §7.6.

[6] Léon Poliakov claimed that the first ghetto to be established was in Łódź; yet he devoted 17 of the 23 pages of his chapter on "The Ghettos" to the Warsaw ghetto; see his *Harvest of Hate: The Nazi Program for the Destruction of the Jews of Europe*, pp. 39, 84–107.

concentrated in these ghettos, which justifies, so far as memory is concerned, the importance assigned to the ghetto experience. But numerically speaking – which is what matters for a global understanding of the phenomenon – these cities accounted for a negligible fraction of the about 1,140 ghettos that existed at some time or other, not only in Poland, but also in the Soviet Union, Romania, and Hungary (all of them are listed in *The Yad Vashem Encyclopedia of the Ghettos During the Holocaust*). Nevertheless, because of the dominance of the Polish model, based on a very small number of ghettos, the measures taken to isolate the Jews from their surroundings, pursuant to the Nazis' anti-Jewish policy, came to be referred to as "ghettoization" even in places where there was no physical ghetto.[7]

There was another motive behind the attempt to conceptualize the ghetto as an all-inclusive phenomenon: the desire to achieve a deeper understanding of the inner logic of the Nazis' anti-Jewish policy, going back to its origins. Consequently the ghettos were described and understood – and rightly so – not merely as a return to the pre-Emancipation ghetto but also as an essential element in a larger picture. And because it was the intentionalist thesis (i.e., the idea that the anti-Jewish policies of the Third Reich developed from a preconceived malicious and systematic vision of total annihilation)[8] that held sway during the first several decades after the Holocaust (and certainly among Jewish scholars), the ghetto and ghettoization were considered to be a clear escalation in the application of this policy. Scholars assumed that such a significant phenomenon must have been the outcome of deliberate forethought and planning. Gringauz, one of the most important intellectuals among the survivors in the Displaced Persons camps on German soil in the immediate aftermath of World War II, tried to understand the Holocaust using conceptual tools; in the late 1940s he proposed that one way to understand

---

[7] See, for example, the definition of the term in an interpreters' lexicon of Nazi German: "*Ghetto = abgesperrter, später vollständig abgeriegelter und bewachter Stadtteil für Juden in polnischen Städten, der von Deutschen nicht betreten und von den Juden nicht verlassen werden durfte; hieß in Warschau 'jüdischer Wohnbezirk', in Lodz 'Wohngebiet der Juden', wurde auch als 'Seuchen-Sperrgebiet' bezeichnet; – Ghettoisierung = Zwangsanweisung (auch von westeuropäischen Juden) ins Ghetto; war organisatorisch der erste Schritt auf dem Weg in die Konzentrations- und Vernichtungslager.*" Karl-Heinz Brackmann and Renate Birkenhauer, *NS-Deutsch: "Selbstverständliche" Begriffe und Schlagwörter aus der Zeit des Nationalsozialismus*, pp. 86–7.

[8] For the term "intentionalism" and the basic approach of the "intentionalist" school in the historiography of Nazism, see Tim Mason, "Intention and Explanation: A Current Controversy about the Interpretation of National Socialism."

the phenomenon was to see the ghetto, in its external form (what he called the "morphological view"), as "one of the forms of mass destruction in the great Jewish catastrophe of 1939–45, which initiated the liquidation of the East European era of Jewish history."[9] Léon Poliakov, a French Jew of Polish origin, was the first historian to write a comprehensive history of the Holocaust at the end of the 1940s. He explained, in his chapter about the fate of the Polish Jews after the invasion in September 1939 ("Persecution Unleashed"), that

> the general [German] policy [in Poland] conformed to Heydrich's program [in the *Schnellbrief* of September 21, 1939] of isolating the Jews, concentrating them in ghettos, and using them for forced labor, until circumstances permitted their "total" evacuation.... Finally, a systematic policy of ghettoization was instituted. The Lodz ghetto was the first to be set up.[10]

In the introduction to his programmatic essay on the ghettos Friedman wrote that it dealt "with Nazi policy of confining the Jews to ghettos, as a preliminary step towards genocide."[11] Nor was this an absurd idea: Eichmann's deputy Dieter Wisliceny had said something very similar at the Nuremberg trial.[12]

This notion became strongly entrenched in the literature after the publication, in 1961, of Raul Hilberg's influential work, *The Destruction of the European Jews*.[13] Hilberg was not an intentionalist and did not believe that the Nazis had had some "final solution of the Jewish question" in mind during their early years in power; hence there was no reason for him to view the ghettos as a preparatory stage for the Final Solution. Nevertheless, he sought to understand the Holocaust through a model of evolving bureaucratic measures. He described the Holocaust as

---

[9] Gringauz, "The Ghetto as an Experiment of Jewish Social Organization," p. 3. On Gringauz, see at greater length Zeev W. Mankowitz, *Life between Memory and Hope: The Survivors of the Holocaust in Occupied Germany*, pp. 174–91.

[10] Poliakov, *Harvest of Hate*, pp. 38–9.

[11] Friedman, "The Jewish Ghettos of the Nazi Era," p. 59. He added: "The methods employed in carrying out the genocide policy were not of a spontaneous or accidental nature, but were rather part and parcel of an unfolding plan, which began with the concentration and isolation of the Jews" (p. 61).

[12] "Als zweite Phase kam von diesem Zeitpunkt ab [1940] die Konzentrierung aller Juden in Polen und in übrigen von Deutschland besetzten Gebieten des Ostens, und zwar in Form von Ghettos" ("As a second phase came – from this point in time onwards [1940] – the concentration of all Jews in Poland and in other territories occupied by Germany in the East, in the form of ghettos"); United Restitution Organisation, *Dokumentensammlung*, p. 156.

[13] Raul Hilberg, *The Destruction of the European Jews*.

having progressed (or, perhaps better, regressed) in linear fashion, from the Nazis' rise to power in 1933 to the campaign of systematic murder that began in 1941. One of the stages in this escalation as enumerated by Hilberg was the "concentration" of the Jews, accompanied by a range of measures (including the Jewish badge) to isolate and separate them from the general population and to regulate them. He identified this phase with ghettoization, whether or not an actual physical ghetto was established, and defined the ghetto as a "control mechanism,"[14] invented by the bureaucracy. Hilberg wrote:

The preliminary steps of the ghettoization process consisted of marking, movement restrictions, and the creation of Jewish control organs.... The three preliminary steps – marking, movement restrictions, and the establishment of a Jewish control machinery – were taken in the very first months of civil rule [in Poland].... In this book we shall be interested in the ghetto only as a control mechanism [for movement restrictions] in the hands of the German bureaucracy. To the Jews the ghetto was a way of life; to the Germans it was an administrative measure....

The most important, and ultimately also the most troublesome, of the preliminary steps in the ghettoization process was the establishment of Jewish councils – *Judenräte*....

By the end of 1941 almost all Jews in the incorporated territories and the *Generalgouvernement* were living in ghettos.[15]

---

[14] On Hilberg's understanding of the Holocaust, see Dan Michman, *Holocaust Historiography, a Jewish Perspective: Conceptualizations, Terminology, Approaches, and Fundamental Issues*, pp. 16–20.

[15] Hilberg, *The Destruction of the European Jews*, pp. 144–8, 152–3. We can learn about how Hilberg has been understood by his readers from the recent exposition of his view by Boaz Neumann, who writes that, according to Hilberg, "following the Nazi German invasion of Poland, and with greater intensity the invasion of the Soviet Union, there was a clear exacerbation of their Jewish policy. In the first stage the Jews were locked up in ghettos. On Sept. 21, 1939, soon after the invasion of Poland, Reinhard Heydrich issued instructions to concentrate and intern the Jews in separate neighborhoods in the cities, for reasons associated with general police security, while taking economic needs into account. The first ghetto in Poland was established in October 1939." Neumann, *Nazism*, p. 154. The late Leni Yahil, even though she adopted a more cautious and complex approach, also wrote that, following the invasion of Poland, "planning [of] the measures against the Jews was comprehensive, far-reaching and guided by principle. Heydrich issued his orders on this subject to the commanders of the Einsatzgruppen at a meeting held on September 21, 1939, and went on to detail and assign them in an express letter dispatched to the commanders that same day.... It was one of the prime documents characterizing the process that was to develop into the Final Solution"; one of the orders was "the concentration operation [which] would require the establishment of ghettos." "The wording of Heydrich's express letter makes it clear that he regarded the ghetto not as a permanent institution, but as a temporary concentration until it proved possible to achieve the ultimate solution to the problem by disposing of the Jews." Yahil,

Hilberg saw no problem in the Nazis' use of the term "ghetto." In the first part of his book, in the chapter entitled "Precedents," he asserted that in its anti-Jewish policy the Third Reich incorporated many of the measures advocated by the Church in the Middle Ages, including the "compulsory ghettos" prescribed by the Synod of Breslau in 1267.[16] In the wake of Hilberg and Friedman, the concept of the "ghetto" became ingrained in the expanding scholarly discourse on Nazism and the Holocaust. In many works it is difficult to distinguish an original application of the term "ghetto" – that is, its use by the German bureaucrats and ideologues – from its later use by scholars to denote a phenomenon they *interpret* as a ghetto or as ghettoization.[17] Consequently the term also took hold in the popular mind, which derived much of its information from the scholarly literature.[18]

Thus the basic perception that the formation of the ghettos was a stage in Nazi policy that led inevitably to the Final Solution crystallized during the first fifteen years of research following the Holocaust.[19] Because

---

The Holocaust: The Fate of European Jewry, 1932–1945, pp. 146, 147, 164; see also the entire section on "The Ghetto," pp. 164–71.

[16] Hilberg, *The Destruction of the European Jews*, p. 6. It should be emphasized that the term "ghetto" was never used in the decision of the Breslau synod; the term came into use only 250 years later.

[17] For example, Friedman notes as "the first Nazi demand for a ghetto" the formula published in the legal journal *Deutsche Justiz* in 1935: "segregation was a wise and honest institution [in the Middle Ages], the abolition of which brought harm to all nations." Friedman, "The Jewish Ghettos of the Nazi Era," p. 64. (The original reads as follows: "[In der] frühe[n] Absonderung der Juden in den Städten...kam...eine tiefe Weisheit zutage, deren Mißachtung sich an unserem Volke bitter gerächt hat"; N. Haastert, "Rechtspflege und Rechtspolitik," *Deutsche Justiz*, 2 August 1935, pp. 1090–1, quote from p. 1091). But as one can see, the passage deals with the separation of the Jews and not with a true ghetto.

[18] See, for example, Itamar Levin, *Lexicon ha-Shoah*, p. 74: "Ghetto. the common term for a restricted region in which and only in which Jews were allowed to live.... Under the Nazi regime the ghettos were intended to segregate the Jews and to serve as a place from which they could be deported to planned Jewish concentrations (such as the Lublin region or Madagascar). Alternatively, the ghetto was a place where their liquidation would *begin* [emphasis added] after they had been despoiled of their property – chiefly 'indirect extermination' by means of starvation and disease – and from which they would be deported to concentration and death camps."

[19] In his influential study of the *Judenräte*, Isaiah Trunk stated that "the ghettos as a rule were similar, if not identical, in their formal framework of repressive restrictions and in the role they were destined to play in the 'Final Solution of the Jewish Question.'" Trunk, *Judenrat: The Jewish Councils in Eastern Europe under Nazi Occupation*, p. xviii. This approach became dominant in German scholarship, too, and has gained significant ground in recent years, as members of the younger generation of academics pay increased attention to Jewish aspects of the Holocaust. Take, for example, the definition

the ghettos were characterized as concentrations of Jews living in a particular territory and in isolation from the surrounding population, the Judenrat – the Jewish council, that is, the German-appointed governing body of the Jewish community – came to be viewed as a distinctive and perhaps even primary characteristic of the ghetto, the "municipal council" of the ghetto, and its creation a direct consequence of ghettoization. The identification of the two was almost total in the 1970s, following the publication in 1972 of Isaiah Trunk's *Judenrat*. Trunk's text depicted the Jewish society of the ghettos of Poland and the Baltic states (not of Eastern Europe as a whole, as wrongly suggested by its subtitle) from the perspective of the Judenrat. Trunk emphasized this in several places: "I have cited as many local events in as many ghettos as possible";

offered by Michael Alberti: "**Ghettoisierung**. *Die Errichtung der Ghettos stellte eines der wirkungsvollsten Mittel dar, um die jüdische Bevölkerung einer totalen Kontrolle und Ausbeutung zu unterwerfen. Beim Beginn der Massenmorde waren sie zudem riesige Gefängnisse, aus denen die Nationalsozialisten ihre Insassen in die Vernichtungslager schicken konnten.... Die Ghettos waren ein Meilenstein auf dem Weg zum Genozid.*" ("**Ghettoisation**. The establishment of ghettos was one of the most effective means to get the Jewish population under total control and have them exploited. With the beginning of the mass murder campaign they turned them into giant prisons, from which the Nazis could send the inmates to the annihilation camps.... The ghettos were a milestone on the way to genocide.") Alberti, "'Exerzierplatz des Nationalsozialismus': Der Reichsgau Wartheland 1939–1941," p. 118. Again, students of how the term "ghetto" was used before the Nazi era, such as Jürgen Heyde and Katrin Steffen, who otherwise take a fairly sophisticated approach, nevertheless write, when they come to the Nazi era: "Right from the beginning of World War II, so-called 'ghettos,' a discursive euphemism, were set up in all larger areas of Jewish settlement in occupied Poland as a first stage in the murder of the Jews in the concentration camps. 'Ghetto' thus became a symbol for a rule of arbitrary will and terror, for oppression, deprival of basic rights and simply for destruction." Heyde and Steffen, "The 'Ghetto' as Topographic Reality and Discursive Metaphor: Introduction," p. 425. The "popular" version is reflected in the entry on the "Ghettos" that appeared until recently (2007) on the website of the United States Holocaust Memorial Museum, Washington, D.C.: "During World War II, ghettos were city districts (often enclosed) in which the Germans forced the Jewish population to live under miserable conditions. Ghettos isolated Jews by separating Jewish communities from the non-Jewish population and from neighboring Jewish communities. The Nazis established over 400 ghettos. The Germans regarded the establishment of ghettos as a provisional measure to control and segregate Jews. In many places ghettoization lasted a relatively short time. With the implementation of the 'Final Solution' in 1942, the Germans systematically destroyed the ghettos and deported the Jews to extermination camps where they killed them.... Daily life in the ghettos was administered by Nazi-appointed Jewish Councils (Judenräte) and Jewish police, whom the Germans forced to maintain order inside the ghetto and to facilitate deportations to the extermination camps" (this formulation has since been changed, in the wake of the Museum's *Camps and Ghettos* project, and thus can no longer be retrieved).

"So-called Jewish 'self-government' is one of the key problems in the history of the ghettos."[20] It is no wonder, then, that Hilberg entitled his critique of Trunk's book, which claims to be about the *Judenräte* (the many Jewish Councils throughout Poland and the Baltic countries), "The Ghetto as a Form of Government" (my emphasis).[21] Hilberg did indeed see the ghetto as a form of government that the Germans imposed as part of the process of extermination, whereas Trunk saw it as an imposed geographical and social structure but also as a continuation of the pre-Holocaust community. In any case, they both entertained the implicit postulate that Judenrat and ghetto were two sides of the same coin, linked instruments of a focused policy, an approach that was widely adopted in the scholarly literature.[22] The influential Israeli scholar Israel Gutman, even though he acknowledged the lack of an overall German instruction to establish ghettos and proposed that the initiative to do so was taken by local authorities at various times, still asserted, in his conceptual entry in the *Encyclopedia of the Holocaust*, that

the ghettos established by the Germans in the countries they occupied in World War II... were not designed to serve as a separate area for Jewish habitation;

---

[20] Trunk, *Judenrat*, pp. xvii, xviii.
[21] Raul Hilberg, "The Ghetto as a Form of Government: An Analysis of Isaiah Trunk's *Judenrat*."
[22] A classic example can be found in Jean-Philippe Schreiber and Rudi van Doorslaer, *Les Curateurs du Ghetto: L'Association des Juifs en Belgique sous l'occupation nazie*, eds., a collection of studies on the Association des Juifs en Belgique – the Belgian counterpart of the Judenrat – published under the title "The Administrators of the Ghetto." Not only are the heads of the Judenrat referred to as administrators of a *ghetto* (expressing the mutual dependence of the two concepts), but the term is applied to the heads of the Jewish community in a country where there were no ghettos! There are other such examples. In his sociological analysis of the Judenräte, the German scholar Werner Bergmann writes that "in the case of the ghettos the Jewish community is almost completely cut off from the outside world as a result of external pressure and contact with the outside world is limited to a few easily supervised 'gates.'... These are clearly marked both in a concrete sense as gates in the ghetto wall and in the form of exclusive boundary officers (members of the Jewish Council) which accordingly are also to be watched over by the outside world." Bergmann, "The Jewish Council as an Intermediary System." According to Gustavo Corni, "the question of the Judenräte is one of the most controversial in the entire history of the ghettoization of the Jews." Corni, *Hitler's Ghettos: Voices from a Beleaguered Society, 1939–1944*, p. 61. For the Polish-British Jewish sociologist Zygmunt Bauman, the link between ghetto and Judenrat is an essential element in explaining the Holocaust. See Bauman, *Modernity and the Holocaust*, p. 136. See also Philip Friedman's outline for future research, which posits an inherent link between ghetto and Judenrat: "Problems of Research on the Jewish Catastrophe."

they were merely a transitional phase in a process that was to lead to the 'Final Solution' of the Jewish Question.²³

They were, he added, in fact "compulsory camps."²⁴

The burgeoning Holocaust research produced since the end of the 1960s, internationally and by Israeli academics in particular,²⁵ has tended to conceive of society in the ghettos as that of a vibrant Jewish community confronted by existential challenges. Gutman's trailblazing study of the Warsaw Jews gave vivid accounts of ghetto life, including the social problems encountered by the Jewish inhabitants and the developments that ultimately led to the uprising of April 1943.²⁶ There had been sporadic attempts at multifaceted portraits of one ghetto or another before Gutman: Dworzecki composed an interesting if nostalgic retrospective of the Vilna ghetto soon after the war ended;²⁷ both Trunk and Wolf Jasny published works on the Łódź ghetto in the 1960s.²⁸ In addition, there were generally non-scholarly accounts of the ghettos in the various community memorial books.²⁹ Polish and German scholars, too, devoted attention to

---

²³ Israel Gutman, "Ghetto," p. 579. Note, though, that in the entry for "Poland" he seems to contradict this statement, at least in part: "Ghettoization: Unlike the Judenräte, which were established under a central directive and on short notice, the process of confining the Jews to ghettos was drawn out, depending largely on decisions taken by authorities on the spot. Sealed-off (closed) ghettos with an internal Jewish government of sorts, and economic life, and essential services were introduced only in eastern Europe, the Baltic states, and the Soviet Union.... The real reason for creating the ghettos was to implement a radical method of isolating the Jews, separating the Jewish communities from one another, and keeping the Jews apart from the rest of the population" (pp. 1159, 1161).

²⁴ Gutman repeated his view in a popularization included in the most influential textbook on the Holocaust used in Israeli high schools, which he co-authored with Chaim Schatzker, *The Holocaust and Its Significance*, esp. pp. 69–71. (The original Hebrew version was reprinted several times and sold about 150,000 copies.) For the further entrenchment of this view in Israeli high school curricula, see subsequently published textbooks: David Schachar, *Am ve-Olam: Perakim be-Toledot Yisrael veha-Amim 1870–1970, vol. B: 1920–1945*, pp. 318–20; Nili Keren, *Shoah: Masa'el ha-Zikkaron*, pp. 43–6; Ketzia Tabibian, *Masa'el he-Avar: ha-Me'a ha-Esrim: Bi-Zchut ha-Herut*, pp. 170–4; Israel Gutman, *Shoah ve-Zikkaron*, pp. 50–4.

²⁵ Michman, *Holocaust Historiography*, pp. 338–44.

²⁶ Israel Gutman, *The Jews of Warsaw, 1939–1943: Ghetto, Underground, Revolt*.

²⁷ Dworzecki, *Yerushalayim de-Lita ba-Meri uva-Shoah*.

²⁸ Isaiah Trunk, *Lodzsher geto: a historishe un sotsyologishe shtudie mit dokumentn, tabeles un mape*; A. Wolf Jasny, *Di geshikhte fun Yidn in Lodzsh: in di yorn fun der daytsher yidn-oysrotung*.

²⁹ Some of the memorial books, written in Yiddish, are now available online: http://www.nypl.org/research/chss/jws/yizkorbookonline.cfm.

the ghettos in the first days of Holocaust research, and their contributions have increased since the early 1990s.[30] Nevertheless, Gutman's was the most comprehensive and thorough inquiry, and the research model he developed was followed by an entire group of Israeli Jewish historians, who produced a series of monographs on various ghettos in Poland and Lithuania over a period of two decades.[31]

Attempts were made to use this material to construct a paradigm of the ghetto phenomenon and of life in the ghettos. The Italian scholar Gustavo Corni wrote a volume on the social history of the ghettos as seen from the inside, studying key aspects of life in the ghetto on the basis of the Jewish voices preserved in diaries, memoirs, and testimonies.[32] The Israeli scholar Boaz Neumann, who analyzed Nazism not through a historical narrative but as a comprehensive *Weltanschauung* that incorporates several elements of the opposition and confrontation between "the Aryan" and "the Jew," placed the ghetto under the rubric of "urban spaces":

Removing the Jew from the urban space was part of a more comprehensive process of removal from the political situation and from the German *Lebensraum*. The ultimate goal was to make all of these *Judenrein*. Whereas the space of the new city was reserved for the Aryan German, the ghetto was the urban space allotted

---

[30] For early research on Poland, see Centralny Komitet Żydów Polskich, *Instrukcje dla zbierania materiałów historycznych z okresu okupacji niemieckiej*; Szymon Datner, *Walka i zagłada białostockiego getta*; Filip (Philip) Friedman, *Zagłada żydów lwowskich*; Józef Kermisz, *Powstanie w getcie warszawskim (19 kwietnia–16 maja 1943)*; Garszon Taffet, *Zagłada Żydów Żółkiewskich*. As for more recent Polish scholarship, see, e.g., Stanisława Lewandowska, *Życie codzienne Wilna w latach II wojny Światowej*; Barbara Engelking-Boni and Jacek Leociak, *Getto Warszawskie: Przewodnik po nieistniejącym mieście*; Katarzyna Zimmerer, *Zamordowany świat: Losy Żydów w Krakowie 1939–1945*. We should also note Ruta Sakowska's studies of the Warsaw ghetto, which cannot be reviewed in detail here. For German scholarship see, e.g., Alberti, "Exerzierplatz des Nationalsozialismus," and Andrej Angrick and Peter Klein, *Die "Endlösung" in Riga. Ausbeutung und Vernichtung 1941–1944*.

[31] Yitzhak Arad, *Ghetto in Flames: The Struggle and Destruction of the Jews in Vilna in the Holocaust*; Yael Peled, *Krakow ha-Yehudit 1939–1943: Amida, Mahteret, Ma'avak*; Sarah Bender, *The Jews of Białystok during World War II and the Holocaust*; Tikva Fatal-Knaani, *Zo lo Otah Grodna. Kehillat Grodna u-Sevivatah be-Milhama uve-Shoah 1939–1945*; Michal Unger, *Lodz: Aharon ha-Getta'ot be-Polin*; Aharon Einat, *Ha-Hayim ha-Penimiyim be-Ghetto Vilna*. For ghettos outside Poland and Lithuania, see Dan Zhits, *Ghetto Minsk ve-Toledotav le-Or ha-Te'ud he-Hadash*; Hava Baruch, "Ghetto Budapest. Ifyuno ve-Yihudo shel Tahalich ha-Ghetto' izatsiya veha-Kiyum ha-Yehudi be-Virat Hungariya beyn Yuni 1944 le-Yanuar 1945."

[32] Corni, *Hitler's Ghettos*, p. 1. A more modest attempt in this direction can be found in Dan Michman, "Jewish Life under Nazi Rule: Three Examples" (Hebrew).

to the Jew. Usually the ghetto was a defined area in the city, but sometimes it was only a single street. For example, Dillstraße in Hamburg was a ghetto street intended for Jewish residents only.[33]

The British scholar Tim Cole began with an inductive approach that at first sight differs from Neumann's inclusive viewpoint. Cole investigated the special case of the Budapest ghetto(s) from the perspective of Hungarian anti-Semitic geographical, architectural, and municipal planning, but nevertheless reached a conclusion not too dissimilar from Neumann's: the Hungarian persecutors, he believes, reshaped the Hungarian capital to accord with their attitude toward the Jews, whom they wanted to displace from every national, economic, cultural, and social center in order to reinforce the foundations of Magyar life, as they understood it. Cole, like Neumann, attached great importance to the spatial aspect as a way to understand overall Nazi policy (including that of their allies) as the product of their racist ideology.[34] All three of these scholars – Corni, Neumann, and Cole – offer interesting and thought-provoking insights into the ghetto in an overall Nazi context. The weakness of their approach, however, is that they base their case on the assumption that the ghetto was an essential part of Nazism's worldview and policies per se. Even though they know that ghettos were set up in only some of the regions where Jews were persecuted, they present them as an inherent element of Nazism and as a preparatory step toward the extermination process or as its first phase. In this regard they accept the basic notions of earlier scholars about the role of the ghetto in the evolution of the Nazis' anti-Jewish policy.[35]

Finally, we should note the views of Christopher Browning. In 1986 Browning wrote an important essay, "Nazi Ghettoization Policy in Poland, 1939–1941" – the first research paper that focused on the topic as

---

[33] Boaz Neumann, *Re'iyat ha-Olam ha-Natzit: Merhav, Guf, Safa*, p. 145. Note that Neumann classes the *Judenhäuser* in Germany as a form of ghetto, contrary to the later decision by the team of the *Yad Vashem Encyclopedia of the Ghettos*.

[34] Tim Cole, *Holocaust City: The Making of a Jewish Ghetto*.

[35] We should note here that a retrospective reading of the research literature, one that takes account of what we know today, indicates that Friedman's 1954 programmatic essay remains unsurpassed. Despite his intentionalist view of the Holocaust, he had an ear that was sensitive to the diversity in the historical material, complemented by a vast knowledge and superb analytical skills. These attributes allowed him to formulate fundamental questions for important future research directions, many of which have still to find suitable answers in later scholarship. On Friedman's scholarly activities, see especially Ronnie Stauber, "Philip Friedman and the Beginnings of Holocaust Historiography."

such since Friedman. Browning launched his inquiry as part of a study of the emergence of the Final Solution of the Jewish Question, and referred to the debate then raging in the literature between intentionalists and functionalists:

> Ghettoization was not a conscious preparatory step planned by the central authorities to facilitate the mass murder nor did it have the "set task" of decimating the Jewish population. Ghettoization was in fact carried out at different times in different ways for different reasons on the initiative of local authorities....
>
> ...a better understanding of German ghettoization policy in Łódź and Warsaw is vital to the historian's wider understanding of the dynamics of Nazi Jewish policy in the 1939–41 period and the relationship of this policy to the Final Solution that followed.... the concentration of Jews in Polish cities as a preliminary to their expulsion was part of a policy ordered by the central authorities in September 1939, but the subsequent creation of sealed ghettos was not. On the contrary, the sealed ghetto resulted from the failure of Berlin's expulsion policy. Local authorities were left to improvise and found their way to the sealed ghetto. They did so at different times and for different immediate reasons but always within the common ideological parameters set by the failed expulsion policy – namely, that ultimately Jews and "Aryans" did not live together.[36]

The conception he developed then, which deals only with the growth of the ghettos in Poland after the German invasion and not with what took place earlier or later, was reiterated with no essential change in his major opus, *The Origins of the Final Solution*, and in a subsequent article that summarized his view of the emergence of the Final Solution.[37] In his book he states that

> The starting point of Nazi policy in eastern Europe had been Heydrich's September 21 conference with the Einsatzgruppen leaders. On that occasion Heydrich had stipulated the immediate (within three to four weeks) concentration of Jews "in ghettos" in cities in order to facilitate "a better possibility of control and later deportation." Heydrich's following *Schnellbrief* stipulated precisely the setting up of councils of "Jewish Elders."... Aside from this, however, Heydrich was vague about the nature and organization of Jewish life in the cities....
>
> The concentration of Jews in cities was not accomplished within Heydrich's three-to-four-week time frame.... Jewish urban ghettos, intended as temporary way stations on the road to complete deportation, now became a factor with which local German authorities unexpectedly had to cope on a long-term basis.

---

[36] Christopher R. Browning, *The Path to Genocide: Essays on Launching the Final Solution* (originally published in *Central European History* 19/4 [1986], pp. 343–68).

[37] Christopher R. Browning (with contributions by Jürgen Matthäus), *The Origins of the Final Solution: The Evolution of Nazi Jewish Policy, September 1939–March 1942*, pp. 111–68; and "On My Book *The Origins of the Final Solution*: Some Remarks on Its Background and on Its Major Conclusions."

Little guidance came from Berlin.... Local authorities in the General Government and the incorporated territories were thus left to fend for themselves. In this light, ghettoization policy as practiced in Poland in 1940 and 1941 would be the direct result, not of Heydrich's *Schnellbrief* of September 21 ordering the concentration of Jews in cities, but rather of the Germans' failure to carry out the subsequent deportations envisioned therein.

If an idea of ghettoization was present from the beginning, just how and when the idea was to be given concrete form varied greatly....

Whatever the particular reasons of the moment, ghettoization was fully consonant with the basic assumptions and long-term goals of Nazi Jewish policy, which aimed at a total removal of the Jews from the German sphere.[38]

In his later article he interprets the ghettos as one of the four pillars on which the Final Solution was later constructed.[39] Thus, in Browning's eyes there was "an idea of ghettoization ... present from the beginning": in his interpretation, "ghettoization" equals "concentration," whereas clearly defined ghettos – the physical phenomenon of restricted urban neighborhoods – were the result "of the Germans' failure to carry out the envisioned deportations." In this mode, Browning harmonizes the ghetto idea as part of overall policies with his factual finding that the actual emergence of ghettos was chaotic, sporadic, and stretched over a long period.

To sum up, current research (with a few exceptions) makes the following assumptions:

a. Ghettos and ghettoization were a central experience of all European Jews during the Holocaust.
b. The largest ghettos are representative of the stage of Jewish life (chiefly in Eastern Europe) that immediately preceded the Final Solution.[40]
c. The ghettos were a systematic and deliberate element introduced by the German authorities in Poland after its occupation as part of their overall policy, or were at least a general phenomenon that took shape in response to the failure of the deportation policy.
d. The ghettos were a preparatory phase and a step on the descent toward total annihilation (even according to those who do not believe that the Final Solution was planned from the outset).
e. There is an intimate and inherent link between ghetto and Judenrat.

---

[38] Browning, *The Origins of the Final Solution*, pp. 111, 113, 123.
[39] Browning, "On My Book."
[40] For a very recent example of this approach, see Bender, *The Jews of Białystok during World War II and the Holocaust*, pp. 278–81.

Saul Friedländer, in his most recent comprehensive study of the Holocaust, condensed these elements into a cohesive narrative:

> From the outset the ghettos were considered temporary means of segregating the Jewish population before its expulsion. Once they acquired a measure of permanence, however, one of their functions became the ruthless and systematic exploitation of part of the imprisoned Jewish population for the benefit of the Reich (mainly for the needs of the *Wehrmacht*) at as low a cost as possible. Moreover, by squeezing the food supply and, in Lodz, by replacing regular money with a special ghetto currency, the Germans put their hands on most of the cash and valuables the Jews had taken along when driven into their miserable quarters.
>
> The ghettos also fulfilled a useful psychological and "educational" function in the Nazi order of things: they rapidly became the showplace of Jewish misery and destitution, offering viewers newsreel sequences that fed existing repulsion and hatred; a constant procession of German tourists (soldiers and some civilians) were presented with the same heady mix....
>
> The Jewish Council (*Judenrat*) was the most effective instrument of German control of the Jewish population.[41]

---

[41] Saul Friedländer, *Nazi Germany and the Jews 1939–1945, vol. 2: The Years of Extermination*, pp. 38–9.

2

Ghetto: The Source of the Term and the Phenomenon in the Early Modern Age

> ...in all future times in this city, as in all other cities, holdings, and territories belonging to the Roman Church, all Jews should live solely in one and the same location, or if that is not possible, in two or three or as many as are necessary, which are to be contiguous and separated completely from the dwellings of Christians. These places are to be designated by us in our city and by our magistrates in the other cities, holdings, and territories. And they should have one entry alone, and so too one exit.
>
> Pope Paul IV, *Cum Nimis Absurdum* (1555)

The word "ghetto" can be traced to Venice in what historians refer to as the "Early Modern Age" (the early sixteenth century); there is no documentary evidence of it before that time, although modern scholarship applies it retrospectively to Jewish neighborhoods in earlier centuries. In medieval Christian Europe, Jews tended to live in close proximity to one another, chiefly because of their religious and social needs (easy access to the synagogue and other vital community institutions). Sometimes this geographic concentration was the result of local rulers' invitations to Jews to settle in their cities, including the allocation of a district or street in which they could live. Sometimes these places were surrounded by a wall to protect the Jews. The name applied to such places in the various languages might be – depending on the size of the allotted district – Jewry (in England), "Jew street/alley," "Jewish quarter," "Jewish courtyard," "Jewish village," "Jew Town," etc. (Judengasse, Judenhof, Judenviertel, Judendorf, Judenstadt in German; rue/ruelle des juifs, Juiverie in French; carrière juif in Occitan;[1] Judería, Giudecca, Zueca in Spanish; Judaismo,

---

[1] Philippe Prévot, *Histoire du ghetto d'Avignon*.

Judaiche in Italian). Only in extraordinary cases were Jews compelled to live in such a special quarter (for example, by the Synod of Breslau in 1267,[2] and in Frankfurt in 1462[3]); normally it was a voluntary arrangement.

Until the sixteenth century, the city fathers of Venice had sometimes permitted individual Jews to live in the city, but they had never tolerated an organized Jewish community. In 1509, however, when a number of Jewish moneylenders fled from the nearby mainland to escape the besieging armies of the League of Cambrai,[4] they were allowed to take refuge in the city itself. As a compromise between the willingness to allow Jews to remain in the city and the desire to preserve their segregated status, in 1516 the Senate decreed that all the Jews live on a single island, known as "Ghetto Nuovo" (i.e., the "New Ghetto"). The island had acquired that name because it was used for dumping the refuse from the adjacent "Old Ghetto" ("Ghetto Vecchio"). The Old Ghetto was so called because it was the site of the local brass foundry (*ghetto* is a noun derived from the verb *ghettare*, which means "to cast metal"). The Ghetto Nuovo was surrounded by a wall and had two gates, one on each side of the island, which were locked from dusk to dawn. Benjamin Ravid, the leading scholar of the history of the Venice ghetto, notes correctly that the Venetian coinage of the term "ghetto" was, accordingly, not the beginning of the Jews' residential segregation in Europe; rather, the name of this particular local instance caught on to describe a phenomenon that had existed previously.[5] The Venetian case was interesting, however, because it created an opportunity for Jews to settle in a city that previously had not been open to them. The Jewish population grew and, later, in 1541, the Ghetto Vecchio was acquired by the community (to facilitate a clearer

---

[2] As noted previously, Hilberg saw this decree as a precedent for the Holocaust. He did not hesitate to use the word "ghetto" in his book, even though it does not appear in the Synod's decision. It is important to emphasize that the decree in question applied only to the see of Breslau and that it should be viewed as an attempt to implement the decisions of the Fourth Lateran Council of 1215, which mandated rigorous separation between Christians and Jews. The Council's decisions were implemented only partially in the Catholic world.

[3] In Spain, too, there were closed neighborhoods, though their nature was somewhat different from those in Frankfurt. See David Nirenberg, *Communities of Violence: Persecution of Minorities in the Middle Ages*.

[4] The League of Cambrai was established in 1508 at the initiative of Pope Julius II, in concert with Louis XII of France, the Emperor Maximilian I, and Ferdinand of Spain, to oppose the growing power of Venice.

[5] Benjamin Ravid, "Alle Ghettos waren jüdische Viertel, aber nicht alle jüdischen Viertel waren Ghettos."

separation between the veteran Jews, the "Tedeschi," and the more recent arrived Levantine Jews). Finally, in 1633, a "Ghetto Nuovissimo" was opened. From an urban point of view, says urban historian Donatella Calabi:

> The impression one gets... is that over the course of the centuries the inhabitants of the ghetto had been organizing themselves and creating new areas of specialization both within and outside their allotted neighborhood. The ghetto itself was no longer just a temporary shelter for a minority group, as it had been in the first decades of the sixteenth century, but an urban area in which, alongside the necessities of everyday life – bakeries, the numerous shops for herbs and fruit, for wine, meat, cheese, oil, tobacco, candles, books, the inn for foreign Jews, a wood store, another for pottery, a depository for coffins – there were also provisions for worship and education (synagogues, schools and confraternities) and hospitals (one for the *Levantine* Jews and one for the *Tedeschi* Jews). Finally a number of activities had been developed for the benefit of the entire complex of citizens (the traditional pawnshops and the sale of second-hand goods) which were regarded as absolutely indispensable for Venice and which were not to be found in the other neighborhoods.[6]

Thus, "ghetto" did not originally have a negative connotation.

Nevertheless, the sixteenth century saw a change, as religious motives on the one hand and the beginnings of the modern centralized state on the other led the authorities of various communities to increasingly establish designated quarters for resident Jews. The first place to do so after Venice, in 1546, seems to have been Ragusa, a city that had strong commercial and political connections with Venice.[7] The term "ghetto" spread to various localities following the establishment of the ghetto in Rome by Pope Paul IV, in 1555, as part of the Counter-Reformation. The Roman ghetto was instituted in accordance with the bull *Cum Nimis Absurdum*. According to its first section:

---

[6] Donatella Calabi, "Venice: The Ghetto and the City, 1541–1797," pp. 57–8.
[7] Ragusa (modern-day Dubrovnik, on the Adriatic coast of Croatia) was an independent republic in the Early Modern Age. In the 1570s, a "new ghetto" was established. See Bernard Stoley, "Dubrovnik"; Vesna Miović, *The Jewish Ghetto in the Dubrovnik Republic (1546–1808)*. For more about Ragusan Jewry and the conditions in the ghetto, see Moises Orfali, "Doña Gracia Mendes and the Ragusan Republic: The Successful Use of Economic Institutions in 16th Century Commerce," esp. pp. 192–3. An interesting reference in contemporary Hebrew to the Dubrovnik ghetto can be found in Aaron Hacohen, *Ma'asei Yeshurun* [*The Story of Jessurun*], in Shlomo Ohev and Aaron Hacohen, *Sefer Shemen ha-tov* [*The Book Good Oil*] (Venice, [5]417 [= 1656/7]). This describes a blood libel in Ragusa (Rhacusa) in 1622. The author recounts that a certain woman attributed the death of a girl to the Jews: "the judicial officers immediately ordered the closure of the door of the courtyard of all the Jews, called 'ghetto.'" See Dan Yardeni, "Alilat dam be-Raguza (Dubrovnik), erev Sukkot 1623" ["A blood libel in Ragusa (Dubrovnik) on the eve of Sukkot 1623"], *Ha'aretz Literary Supplement* Sept. 26, 2007, p. 1 (Hebrew).

Ghetto: The Source of the Term and the Phenomenon

Desiring to make sound provisions as best we can, with the help of God, in the above matter, we sanction by this our perpetually valid constitution that, among other things, in all future times in this city, as in all other cities, holdings, and territories belonging to the Roman Church, all Jews should live solely in one and the same location, or if that is not possible, in two or three or as many as are necessary, which are to be contiguous and separated completely from the dwellings of Christians. These places are to be designated by us in our city and by our magistrates in the other cities, holdings, and territories. And they should have one entry alone, and so too one exit.[8]

Although the word "ghetto" does not appear in this bull, over time the general public adopted the Venetian term to designate the compulsory Jewish residential neighborhood. According to Kenneth Stow, who has studied the Rome ghetto, this was the beginning of a religiously motivated attitude toward the Jews that characterized the Early Modern Age (Stow suggests that the Jews associated the term ghetto with the Hebrew noun *get*, meaning a divorce letter!). The Pope saw "his" ghetto as a place in which the Jews could be isolated until all of them accepted baptism. Starting in the late seventeenth century and throughout the eighteenth century there were attempts to accelerate this process by pressuring the Jews and abducting Jewish children.[9] This walled and gated ghetto of the Papal State, which derived its popular name from Venice, formed the model that took hold of the public mind and was copied in other places, though not always on account of religious piety. That is, the Venetian word plus the Roman content constituted what became the common cultural concept and widespread phenomenon – though precisely how this came about remains uncertain, because the nature of the ghettos of the second half of the sixteenth century was ambivalent.[10] What is clear is that this model was adopted throughout the Italian peninsula and nearby

---

[8] The original Latin text is as follows: "Volentes in praemissis, quantum cum Deo possumus, salubriter providere, hac nostra perpetuo valitura constitutione sancimus quod de cetero perpetuis futuris temporibus, tam in Urbe quam in quibusvis aliis ipsius Romanae Ecclesia civitatibus, terris et locis, iudaei omnes in uno et eodem, ac si ille capax non fuerit, in duobus aut tribus vel tot quot satis sint, contiguis et ab habitationibus christianorum penitus seiunctis, per nos in Urbe et per magistratus nostros in aliis civitatibus, terris et locis praedictis designandis vicis, ad quos unicus tantum ingressus pateat, et quibus solum unicus exitus detur, omnino habitent." The English translation here is from Kenneth R. Stow, *Catholic Thought and Papal Jewry Policy 1555–1593*, p. 295.

[9] Kenneth R. Stow, *Theater of Acculturation: The Roman Ghetto in the Sixteenth Century*.

[10] Despite the many comprehensive studies of individual ghettos, there is no thorough comprehensive study of the ghettos in Italy and the extent to which the system was transferred from place to place. On the ambivalent nature of the Italian ghettos during their first decades, see Roni Weinstein, "'Mevudadim akh lo dehuyim': Hayehudim ba-hevrah ha'italkit bitkufat hareformatsya hakatolit" ('Segregated Though Not Repelled': The Jews in Italian Society in the Age of the Catholic Reformation). Professor Magda

lands in the sixteenth century,[11] in part because Pius IV (1559–1565), who succeeded Paul IV, enforced his predecessor's bull, as far as he was able, throughout Italy, until almost every Italian town with a Jewish community had a special Jewish quarter, which was referred to as the "ghetto."[12] The process of establishing ghettos in Italy continued until the end of the eighteenth century: the last Italian ghetto was established in Correggio in 1779, at a time when Jews had already been granted full citizenship in the newborn United States of America.[13]

From the seventeenth century, the term "ghetto" spread outside Italy,[14] in official parlance and especially in popular speech, under the influence of the Catholic discourse shaped by the Vatican. But it did not gain general currency all over Europe until the early nineteenth century.[15] In the German-speaking world of the nineteenth century, the closed Jewish quarter of Frankfurt, established in 1462, became the dominant model of a "ghetto," even though it had never been officially referred to by that name.[16]

Teter of Wesleyan University in the United States is working on a broad treatment of the ghetto in the Early Modern Age.

[11] The ghetto in Florence was established in 1570/71, evidently in connection with the reorganization of the Duchy of Tuscany; that is, the ghetto system was used for a different purpose than in the Papal State. See Stephanie B. Siegmund, *The Medici State and the Ghetto of Florence: The Construction of an Early Modern Jewish Community*, Stanford: Stanford University Press, 2005.

[12] Maria Giuseppina Muzzarelli, "Beatrice de Luna, vedova Mendes, alias Donna Gracia Nasi: una Ebreia influente (1510–ca. 1569)," esp. pp. 108–9; Kenneth Stow, *Alienated Minority: The Jews of Medieval Latin Europe*, pp. 296–7.

[13] The sequence is as follows: Venice, 1516; Rome, 1555; Florence, 1571; Siena, 1571; Mirandola, 1602; Verona, 1602; Padua, 1603; Mantua, 1612; Rovigo, 1613; Ferrara, 1624; Urbino and Pesaro Senigallia, 1634; Modena, 1638; Este, 1666; Reggio Emilia, 1670; Conegliano Veneto, 1675; Turin, 1679; Casale Monferrato, 1724; Vercelli, 1725; Acqui, 1731; Moncalvo, 1732; Finale, 1736; Correggio, 1779. See Robert Bonfil, *Jewish Life in Renaissance Italy*, pp. 68–75.

[14] Jürgen Heyde, "The 'Ghetto' as a Spatial and Historical Construction: Discourses of Emancipation in France, Germany, and Poland," p. 433.

[15] Benjamin Ravid has written at length about the history of the ghetto and the diffusion of the term. See Ravid, "Alle Ghettos," pp. 13–30, 289–91; Ravid, "Ghetto." For the background to the establishment of the ghetto in Venice and how the Jews lived there, see also Ravid's collected articles on the subject, *Studies on the Jews of Venice 1382–1797*. For a short description that emphasizes the social aspects of life in the Italian ghettos, with many illustrations, see Ariel Toaff, "Ghetto," *Enciclopedia delle Scienze Sociali*, vol. 4, pp. 285–91. For a view of the urban aspects of the Venice ghetto, see Enio Concinna, Donatella Calabi, and Ugo Camerino, *La Città degli Ebrei: Il Ghetto di Venezia – Architettura e Urbanistica*.

[16] Backhaus et al., *Die Frankfurter Judengasse*.

3

Ghetto and Ghettoization as Cultural Concepts in the Modern Age

> ... the fanatic bigotry which built the ghettos, was the most active means in God's Hands to keep us afar from the lack of culture of the Middle Ages and in confined circles to nurse the sense of family life and family happiness and the sense of communal life in us.
>
> Rabbi Samson Raphael Hirsch, commentary on Genesis 45:11 (1867)

> The common people have not, and indeed cannot have, any historic comprehension. They do not know that the sins of the Middle Ages are now being visited on the nations of Europe. We are what the Ghetto made us.... When civilized nations awoke to the inhumanity of discriminatory legislation and enfranchised us, our enfranchisement came too late. It was no longer possible to remove our disabilities in our old homes. For we had, curiously enough, developed while in the Ghetto into a bourgeois people, and we stepped out of it only to enter into fierce competition with the middle classes.
>
> Theodor Herzl, *Der Judenstaat*, chapter 2 (trans. Sylvie D'Avigdor) (1896)

> The ghetto had been abolished long before, but nevertheless there still existed an invisible wall which separated the [Jewish] quarter from the rest of the city. Many Polish children spoke about it with fear, and their parents spoke about it with contempt.
>
> Bernard Singer, *Moje Nalewki* (1959, referring to the interwar period)

Even though it is not yet totally clear how the term ghetto spread from Italy throughout the European cultural sphere, its dissemination certainly took place during the seventeenth and eighteenth centuries. The broader and more widespread cultural meaning of the ghetto – "the ghetto as metaphor" – took root in the nineteenth century, precisely at the time that the ghettos in their original form were being dismantled (the last ghetto, in Rome, survived de jure until 1848 and de facto until 1870).[1] The metaphoric sense that became established around that time referred to a densely populated and separate Jewish neighborhood within a city, and it was associated with a whole series of (mainly pejorative) stereotypes of "the Jews."[2] In the nineteenth and twentieth centuries, this meaning came to be part of the discourse about the options for Jewish emancipation – with the Roman ghetto, as the last relic of the old phenomenon in that age, serving as a living reminder – and had two opposed connotations. In the negative sense, the Jews' perspective on the ghetto was of a symbol of the repression, isolation, and backwardness from which they needed to escape. This line was adopted by both the maskilim (the carriers of the Jewish Enlightenment) and the Zionists. Theodor Herzl, in *The Jewish State* and in his play *The New Ghetto*, maintained that the Jews had to escape their "ghettoized" condition among the nations, and also to uproot the ghetto from their own minds.[3] From a non-Jewish and chiefly anti-Semitic perspective, the ghetto was perceived as the crucible of all of the Jews' corrupt and perverse traits.[4] In the positive sense, Jews developed a nostalgic longing for the ghetto as a vital form of Jewish life, despite all the problems associated with it.[5] Examples of a positive view of the ghetto can be found in both Rabbi Samson Raphael Hirsch's religious writings

---

[1] Benjamin Ravid, "Alle Ghettos waren jüdische Viertel, aber nicht alle jüdischen Viertel waren Ghettos," p. 29.

[2] For a broad although not always focused discussion of this phenomenon and of the literature on the question, with references to additional literature on the sources of the term and its usage over the centuries, see Alex Bein, *The Jewish Question: Biography of a World Problem*, pp. 146–53, 525–8.

[3] Theodor Herzl, *Der Judenstaat*; and *Das neue Ghetto*. On this play as the key to understanding Herzl, see Jacques Kornberg, *Theodor Herzl: From Assimilation to Zionism*, pp. 9–10, 130–58. In *The Jewish State* Herzl emphasized how the ghetto had shaped Jewish behavior.

[4] On this, see Jürgen Heyde, "The 'Ghetto' as a Spatial and Historical Construction," pp. 434–43; Kenneth H. Ober, *Die Ghettogeschichte: Entstehung und Entwicklung einer Gattung*; Gabriele von Glasenapp, *Aus der Judengasse: Zur Entstehung und Ausprägung deutschsprachiger Ghettoliteratur im 19. Jahrhundert*. The medieval historian Mark R. Cohen would date the spread of the pejorative image somewhat earlier: "Especially during the later Middle Ages, when popular fear and hatred of the Jews grew in intensity and popular antisemitic stereotypes proliferated, the Jewish quarter became a mysterious, frightful place, increasing the target of terrified, antisemitic Christian mobs": Cohen, *Under Crescent and Cross: The Jews in the Middle Ages*, p. 123.

[5] Benjamin Ravid, "From Geographical Realia to Historiographical Symbol: The Odyssey of the Word Ghetto"; Ravid, "Ghetto," p. 273; Richard I. Cohen, "Nostalgia and 'Return to the Ghetto': A Cultural Phenomenon in Western and Central Europe"; David B. Ruderman, "De culturele betekenis van het getto in de joodse geschiedenis" (for an

and Salo Wittmayer Baron's historiography. Hirsch (1808–1888), the founder and first leader of the Neo-Orthodox religious stream in German Jewry, referred in his commentary on Genesis 45:11 to the consolidation of the tribes of Israel into a people in Goshen, of all places:

> To become a nation without intermingling, they [the Jews] had to come into the midst of a nation, who in principle as a nation were opposed to the whole nature of the Jews, and that was Egypt. In the same way, the fanatic bigotry which built the ghettos, was the most active means in God's hands to keep us afar from the lack of culture of the Middle Ages and in confined circles to nurse the sense of family life and family happiness and the sense of communal life in us.[6]

Baron (1895–1989), transforming this view into a secularized historical observation, perceived the ghetto as the essential structure that preserved Jewish collective existence in the Middle Ages:

> Feudalism's dissolution of European society into a hierarchy of corporate bodies, each with a separate economic function and political status, the Church's adherence to tradition and its need of external testimony, the State's perennial fiscal difficulties, met halfway an irrepressible inner urge of the Jew to survive in no matter how hostile an environment until the messianic end of days. Out of this extraordinary combination arose the European ghetto. Often territorially delimited, it furnished the people in exile, by means of its remarkable interplay of social and religious forces, an effective substitute for the lost state and territory.[7]

Whereas the former, negative, connotation is often manifested in the polemic literature of the Jewish street as well as in various strands of anti-Semitic literature, the latter, positive, one is reflected chiefly in Jewish writings, especially of the late nineteenth and early twentieth centuries, after many Jews had emigrated to the lands across the sea. Examples for both meanings from countries where there had never been a ghetto in the original sense of the term include *Children of the Ghetto* (1892), about the poor Jews of London, by the English author and Zionist (and later

---

earlier English version, see "The Cultural Significance of the Ghetto in Jewish History" in David N. Myers and William V. Rowe, eds., *From Ghetto to Emancipation*, pp. 1–16).

[6] *The Pentateuch*, p. 621. The original German reads: "Um zum Volke zu werden, ohne sich zu vermischen, dazu mußte sie in die Mitte einer Nation kommen, der das ganze jüdische Wesen national widerstand, und dies war Mizrajim [Ägypten]. Und so war später der Fanatismus, der die Ghetti baute, das wirksamste Mittel in Gottes Hand, um uns von aller Unkultur des Mittelalters fern zu halten und im engen Umkreis Familiensinn und Familienglück und Gemeindesinn bei uns zu pflegen": *Der Pentateuch*, p. 512.

[7] Salo Wittmayer Baron, *The Jewish Community: Its History and Structure to the American Revolution*, vol. 1, p. 209. The book was first published in 1942, but the author wrote it in the 1930s (I have used the 1948 edition).

FIGURE 1. Morris Rosenfeld's Yiddish book, *Songs of the Ghetto*, is an example of the popularity of the nostalgic and positive attitude to "the ghetto." This is the title page of the German edition, published in 1920, which sold between 26,000 and 30,000 copies (Berlin and Vienna: Benjamin Harz Verlag).

Territorialist) leader Israel Zangwill;[8] *Ghetto* (1898), by the Dutch Jewish playwright Herman Heijermans, about the orthodox Jewish proletariat of Amsterdam;[9] and Louis Wirth's sociological study of the Jews of Chicago, *The Ghetto* (1928).[10] In the German-speaking world in the generations after the Emancipation (that is, from the second half of the nineteenth century), both Jews and non-Jews associated the contemporary ghetto, as a tangible phenomenon, mainly with the concentrations of Jews in Eastern Europe.[11] This linked up with the cultural stereotype of the *Ostjuden* in Germany, which was in turn associated (though not exclusively) with the discourse in Poland, both by Jews and non-Jews, about the life of Jews there.[12] The Polish ghetto, as perceived by the Jews, is reflected very clearly in the memoirs of the Polish Jewish journalist Bernard Singer, published in Poland in 1959, after the Holocaust:

The Jewish quarter in Warsaw covered one-fifth of the city. It was home to 250,000 people, and thus one-third of the population. There were no drawbridges or guards at its borders; the ghetto had been abolished long before, but nevertheless there still existed an invisible wall which separated the [Jewish] quarter from the rest of the city. Many Polish children spoke about it with fear, and their elders often treated it with contempt.[13]

Thus "ghetto" and "Ostjuden" became intimately associated in this discourse, especially for those who were familiar with the Jews of Poland.[14]

---

[8] Israel Zangwill, *Children of the Ghetto*.
[9] Herman Heijermans, *Ghetto*.
[10] Louis Wirth, *The Ghetto*. In the United States, "ghetto" was used by extension to refer to the neighborhoods occupied by Jewish newcomers from Eastern Europe during the age of mass immigration. See in particular the book by the non-Jewish Hutchins Hapgood, which describes how the middle and upper classes in New York were afraid of the "ghetto" and its people. Harry Golden wrote in his preface to a new edition: "The Jewish quarter of New York is generally supposed to be a place of poverty, dirt, ignorance and immorality – the seat of the sweatshop, the tenement house, where 'red lights' sparkle at night, where the people are queer and repulsive. Well-to-do persons visit the 'Ghetto' merely from motives of curiosity or philanthropy; writers treat it 'sociologically,' as of a place in crying need of improvement": Hapgood, *The Spirit of the Ghetto: Studies of the Jewish Quarter of New York*, p. xvii. On the frequent use of the term in North American Jewish literature, see Konrad Gross, "Schtetl und Ghetto im jüdisch-amerikanischen und -kanadischen Roman."
[11] Anne Fuchs and Florian Krobb, eds., *Ghetto Writing: Traditional and Eastern Jewry in German-Jewish Literature from Heine to Hilsenrath*.
[12] See, for instance, Jacob Leschtschinski, "Getto un wanderung in yiddisher leben."
[13] Bernard Singer, *Moje Nalewki*, p. 7, as cited in Stephen D. Corrsin, "Political and Social Change in Warsaw from the January 1863 Insurrection to the First World War." I would like to thank my friend and colleague Professor Gershon Bacon for calling this passage to my attention.
[14] For an illuminating article on this point in the *Jahrbuch des Simon-Dubnow-Instituts / Simon Dubnow Institute Yearbook* 4 (2005), see Katrin Steffen, "Connotations of

The notion of the ghetto became so entrenched that from the end of the nineteenth century the term came to be applied to dense concentrations of non-Jewish groups, too (such as the "black ghettos" in the United States).[15] For the most part, however, ghetto continued to be associated with an overcrowded and impoverished *Jewish* neighborhood. This in turn produced the concept of "ghettoization" – the concentration of people in overcrowded and harsh living conditions.[16]

Alongside this use of ghetto, its more general metaphoric application to various forms of "separation" also took root. In this sense it always has an accompanying adjective – a "social ghetto" or a "spiritual ghetto." This metaphoric use was also widespread,[17] especially in Poland at the height of anti-Semitism there in the late 1930s. A notable example is the institution of so-called ghetto benches for Jews in the universities, first introduced at the Lwów Polytechnic Institute in 1935 and later at the University of Wilno (Vilna/Vilnius).[18]

Exclusion: 'Ostjuden,' 'Ghettos,' and Other Markings." Other important contributions on this subject, found in the same volume, are: Jürgen Heyde and Katrin Steffen, "The 'Ghetto' as a Topographic Reality and Discursive Metaphor: Introduction"; Heyde, "The 'Ghetto' as a Spatial and Historical Construction"; Alina Cała, "The Discourse of 'Ghettoization': Non-Jews on Jews in 19th- and 20th-Century Poland."

[15] Bein, *The Jewish Question*, p. 526 (*Die Judenfrage*, p. 69).

[16] On the ghetto as experienced by photographers, see Rachel Salamander, *Die jüdische Welt von Gestern: Text- und Bild-Zeugnisse aus Mitteleuropa 1860–1938*, pp. 82–9.

[17] An interesting example of such a usage in Jewish discourse can be found in a personal letter from the future Nobel laureate Samuel Joseph Agnon to Zalman Schocken, written in the wake of the Arab massacre of Jews in Hebron in 1929. He wrote that "since the pogrom my attitude to the Arabs has changed. My attitude now is as follows. I do not hate them and I do not love them; what I want is not to see their face. In my humble opinion a big ghetto of half a million Jews should be made in Eretz Israel [Palestine], because if this is not done we are – God forbid – lost." See Shmuel Joseph Agnon, *Me-atzmi el atzmi* (From Myself to Myself), p. 430.

[18] Ezra Mendelsohn, *The Jews of East Central Europe Between the World Wars*, p. 73. For a picture (from the photo collection of the Jewish Historical Institute, Warsaw) showing a demonstration of Polish nationalist students at the Lwów Polytechnic Institute in 1937, under the banner "Day without Jews. We demand an institutionalized Ghetto," see http://zydziwpolsce.edu.pl/panel10.html. I would like to thank Dr. Natalya Aleksiun for providing me with this reference.

4

The Nazis' Anti-Jewish Policy in the 1930s in Germany and the Question of Jewish Residential Districts

> From a police point of view I think that a ghetto, in the form of a completely segregated district with only Jews, is not possible. We would have no control over a ghetto where the Jew gets together with the whole of his Jewish tribe. It would be a permanent hideout for criminals and first of all [a source] of epidemics and the like.... The control of the Jews by the watchful eyes of the whole population is better than putting thousands upon thousands of Jews together in a single district of a city where uniformed officials will be unable to check on their daily activities.
> Reinhard Heydrich at a meeting of senior German officials in Hermann Goering's office on November 12, 1938, two days after Kristallnacht

It was long the scholarly consensus that, from the outset, the anti-Jewish policy of the Nazi regime had clear, well-articulated, and coordinated objectives that developed and escalated in a fairly consistent manner. This approach (which came to be called "intentionalism"), at least in its earlier and more simplistic version, has been challenged by the research of recent decades. Today it is clear that although the Nazi regime set itself an anti-Semitic objective from its very inception in 1933 – "dealing with the Jews" – it was not clearly defined and remained rather vague. This left bureaucrats and functionaries – from the most senior to the lowest echelons – broad scope in which to maneuver when implementing this policy. Some emphasized economic dispossession, while others focused on expelling Jews from positions of influence in the civil service, cultural life, the economy, and other domains; some stressed the assault on Jewish morale, while still others concentrated on pushing them out of the country (that is, emigration). Outside the ruling circles, the public at large – businesses, voluntary organizations, institutions, and individuals – were encouraged in various ways to participate in the social and economic processes that steadily forced the Jews out of many spheres of life; and many Germans were more than happy to take advantage of these opportunities.[1] All of these actions were aimed at segregating and isolating the Jews from the Aryan population.

Jews, especially those who, ruined economically, were forced to lower their standard of living and move to smaller homes, found it difficult to renew their leases or find new apartments, as private and corporate landlords in Germany became increasingly unwilling to accept Jewish tenants. After the enactment of the Nuremberg Laws in September 1935 economic and social pressures forced Jews to leave their large homes in urban areas; from the beginning of 1938 Jews were no longer entitled to government rent subsidies.[2] In Berlin, a low-rent housing company registered the names of all its Jewish tenants and refused to continue renting to most of them.[3] Looking back, an official of the German Foreign Ministry referred to 1938 as the "year of destiny" (*Schicksalsjahr*) in the annals of the anti-Jewish policy;[4] it was indeed a year when things got very much worse for Jews with regard to housing. The encouragement of emigration and systematic restriction of Jews' options in the housing market were introduced in Austria after its annexation in March 1938.[5] In the Old Reich, too, the constriction of housing options was felt. Nevertheless, despite this intensive activity, some of it propelled by the idea of relegating the Jews to their pre-emancipation status – to bring back the Middle Ages, as it were, when the Jews were not integrated into society at large[6] – no policy of concentrating the Jews in ghettos was instituted.

---

[1] There is a vast literature on this topic. For up-to-date summaries of the anti-Jewish policy of those years, see Frank Bajohr, "'The Folk Community' and the Persecution of the Jews"; Saul Friedländer, *Nazi Germany and the Jews*, vol. 1: *The Years of Persecution 1933–1939*, pp. 113–44; David Bankier, ed., *Probing the Depths of German Antisemitism: German Society and the Persecution of the Jews 1933–1941*; Götz Aly, *Hitlers Volksstaat* (English edition: *Hitler's Beneficiaries*).
[2] "Verordnung über Mietbeihilfen," 30 March 1938, in *Reichsgesetzblatt* (1938) I, p. 342.
[3] Friedländer, *Nazi Germany and the Jews*, vol. 1, p. 260.
[4] German Foreign Ministry circular about government policy toward the Jews in 1938, Berlin, January 25, 1939, in *Akten zur deutschen auswärtigen Politik 1918–1945*, Series D (1937–1945), vol. V, pp. 780–5.
[5] Gerhard Botz, *Wohnungspolitik und Judendeportation in Wien 1938 bis 1945: Zur Funktion des Antisemitismus als Ersatz nationalsozialistischer Sozialpolitik.*
[6] On this matter see the "Draft Law for Regulating the Status of the Jews" (Entwurf zu einem Gesetz zur Regelung der Stellung der Juden), drawn up as early as April 1933 but never implemented: Shaul Esh, "Tokhnit-av le-haqiqat ha-Natsim neged ha-yehudim" (A master plan for Nazi anti-Jewish legislation), in *Iyyunim be-heqer ha-sho'ah ve-yahadut*

Anti-Jewish Policy and Jewish Residential Districts

But the term "ghetto," as a possible element of the emerging anti-Jewish policy, came up at the well-known meeting in the office of Hermann Göring (the second-ranking personage in the country in those days) on November 12, 1938, two days after Kristallnacht. The topic of discussion was overall anti-Jewish policy, and all the relevant senior officials of the Third Reich took part. At the start of the meeting Joseph Goebbels, the Minister of Propaganda, complained that the Jews were still mixing in German society and demanded their separation in swimming pools, beaches, forests, and other recreational sites. Göring proposed assigning the Jews separate areas in forests. Near the end of the session, Reinhard Heydrich, the head of both the SIPO and SD (Security Police and SS Security Service), emphasized that the focus should be on forcing the Jews to emigrate. Among other things he said that, under the circumstances, emigration would take a long time, and even then an undesirable number of Jews would remain in the country. He added:

Because of Aryanization and other restrictions, Jewry will become unemployed. We will see the remaining Jews becoming proletarians. I would have to take measures in Germany to isolate the Jews, on the one hand, so that they will not enter into the normal life of the Germans. On the other hand, I must create possibilities of permitting the Jews certain activities, in the matter of lawyers, doctors, barbers, etc., while yet limiting them to the smallest possible circle of customers.[7]

Göring replied: "You will not be able to avoid having ghettos in the cities on a really big scale. They will have to be established."[8] In other words, Göring believed that destitution and internal migration within Germany, caused by the despoliation of the Jews, would cause them to concentrate in certain districts in the larger cities, which would become dense pockets of poverty – "ghettos."[9]

---

zemanenu, pp. 142–7; Otto Dov Kulka, *Deutsches Judentum unter dem Nationalsozialismus*, vol. I, pp. 37–40.

[7] Stenographische Niederschrift der Sitzung im Reichsluftfahrtministerium am 12. Nov. 1938, Doc. 1816–PS, in *Trials of the Major War Criminals before the International Military Tribunal, Nuremberg, 14 November 1945–1 October 1946*, vol. 28, p. 533; English translation in Yitzhak Arad, Yisrael Gutman, and Abraham Margaliot, eds., *Documents on the Holocaust*, p. 110.

[8] "Sie werden nicht darum herumkommen in ganz großem Maßstab in den Städten zu Ghettos zu kommen. Die müssen geschaffen werden": *Trials of the Major War Criminals*, vol. 28, p. 533.

[9] Note that Peter Longerich's reading of this is incorrect: as he understands it, Göring proposed the establishment of ghettos and Heydrich was opposed ("Auf einen Vorschlag Görings eingehend, wonach 'in ganz großem Maßstab in den Städten Ghettos' geschaffen

Surprisingly enough, Heydrich immediately stated his opposition to such a development:

As for the matter of ghettos, I would like to make my position clear right away. From a police point of view I think that a ghetto, in the form of a completely segregated district with only Jews, is not possible. We would have no control over a ghetto where the Jew gets together with the whole of his Jewish tribe. It would be a permanent hideout for criminals and first of all [a source] of epidemics and the like. The situation today is that the German population [which lives together with the Jews] forces the Jews to behave more carefully in the streets and the houses. The control of the Jews by the watchful eyes of the whole population is better than putting thousands upon thousands of Jews together in a single district of a city where uniformed officials will be unable to check on their daily activities.

Göring: We only have to cut off the telephone link with the outside.

Heydrich: I could not stop the movements of Jewry out from this district completely.[10]

The theoretical discussion continued for a while; the existence of an urban fabric in which it was not totally possible to isolate the Jews from non-Jews was mentioned. Heydrich asked Göring to clarify his concept of the ghetto: "What would it be like in the ghetto? Would the Jew have to go shopping in the Aryan section?" Later he added something important: "All these measures will lead, practically [and] organically, to [the establishment] of a ghetto. I must say: we shouldn't want to build a ghetto today. But these measures would automatically drive the Jews into a ghetto *of the form specified here*."[11]

Where did Göring and Heydrich pick up the term "ghetto" precisely at this time? What is more, the emphatic terms that Heydrich employed twice – first, "a ghetto, in the form of a completely segregated district

---

werden sollten, entgegnete Heydrich daß dies...nicht durchführbar sei"). But the context indicates clearly that Göring is *wondering* about the issue and observing that ghettos would emerge as a result of the processes in question; he is not proposing that they be created. Consequently, Heydrich's remark that this is unfeasible must be understood to mean that, in his opinion, promoting the emergence of ghettos in this way is undesirable because it is contrary to the regime's objectives. See Longerich, *Politik der Vernichtung. Eine Gesamtdarstellung der nationalsozialistischen Judenverfolgung*, p. 210.

[10] *Trial of the Major War Criminals*, vol. 28, p. 534; English version in Arad et al., *Documents on the Holocaust*, p. 111.

[11] Emphasis added. "Wie wäre es im Ghetto? Müßte da der Jude in den arischen Teil zum einkaufen gehen?...Diese ganzen Maßnahmen werden praktisch-organisch zu einem Ghetto führen. Ich muß sagen: man soll heute nicht ein Ghetto bauen wollen. Aber durch diese Maßnahmen werden die Juden automatisch in ein Ghetto gedrängt in der Form, wie das eingedeutet wurde": *Trial of the Major War Criminals*, vol. 28, p. 536.

with only Jews," where he himself proposes a definition of the ghetto (and rejects the emergence of such neighborhoods); later, "a ghetto of the form specified here," where he is summarizing Göring's concept – reveal a slight distinction between Göring's notion of a ghetto and Heydrich's. What, then, was the sense entertained by Heydrich – to which, as he insisted, he was totally opposed?

5

First References to the Term "Ghetto" in the Ideological Discourse of the Makers of Anti-Jewish Policy in the Third Reich (1933–1938)

> As for [the Jews'] social life, today we can rightly speak of an invisible Jewish ghetto.
>
> From the situation report (*Lagebericht*) summarizing 1937, submitted by the Hamburg office of the Department of Jewish Affairs in the SD

The anti-Semitic discourse of the early years of the Nazi regime so far has not been the subject of a systematic linguistic analysis.[1] The best conclusion that can be drawn from the available information is that the term "ghetto" first came into use, in rather vague fashion, in the mid-1930s. For example, in the confidential situation reports (*Lage- und Stimmungsberichte*) produced by the Gestapo and SD, which tracked popular sentiment in Germany to help the authorities direct their steps, the term appears from time to time in expositions of the Jews' changing situation as a result of the anti-Jewish measures, chiefly in descriptions of how the Jews themselves were interpreting it. According to a report for May–June 1934, written at the SD Main Office (*SD-Hauptamt*) and referring to

---

[1] Several studies have dealt with the "Nazi lexicon/vocabulary" and anti-Semitism to some extent. To the best of my knowledge, though, there is no comprehensive study from the perspective of discourse analysis. For studies with an emphasis on vocabulary, see Victor Klemperer, *LTI – Notiz eines Philologen*; Robert Michael and Karin Doerr, *Nazi-Deutsch/Nazi German: An English Lexicon of the Language of the Third Reich*. Nachman Blumenthal began work on the issue in the 1950s but never completed his study. Parts were published as three articles: "On the Nazi Vocabulary," *Yad Vashem Studies* 1 (1957), pp. 49–66; "Aktion," *Yad Vashem Studies* 4 (1960), pp. 57–96; "From the Nazi Vocabulary," *Yad Vashem Studies* 6 (1967), pp. 69–82. On general issues, see Ruth Wodak, ed., *Language, Power and Ideology: Studies in Political Discourse*. Not all of these studies cast useful light on our subject.

the emergence of separate Jewish cultural organizations, the ultra-right-wing German Jewish group *Nationaldeutschen* (German Nationalists)[2] was still opposed to "a ghetto in any form whatsoever" (*Ghetto in jeder Form*).[3] Sixteen months later, in a survey of the Jews' reaction to the Nuremberg Laws, the Security Police (SIPO) office in Cologne reported that

the [members of the National Union of] Jewish Frontline Soldiers feel particularly wronged by these laws because they feel themselves to be first of all Germans and only afterwards Jews. [The situation is that] a ghetto is being created for them, something they had not anticipated.[4]

A year and a half later, in March 1937, the Jewish Affairs Department of the SD, established in 1935, noted that the activities of the Jewish cultural organizations (*jüdischen Kulturbunde*), especially in the large cities, "are slowly leading the Jews into a spiritual ghetto" (*ein geistigen Ghetto*).[5] Finally, in the summary report for 1937, the Hamburg office of the Jewish Affairs Department of the SD, surveying the situation in its region, noted that "as for [the Jews'] social life, today we can rightly speak of an invisible Jewish ghetto" (*einem unsichtbaren Ghetto der Juden*).[6] Here we must note two important points: the extremely sparse use of the term "ghetto" in the situation reports throughout the 1930s (in fact, most instances of the word have been quoted here); and the fact that they all clearly invoke its metaphorical sense – "spiritual" or "invisible."

This was not a matter of chance. Nazi functionaries apparently became aware of the "ghetto" – as a description of the escalating isolation, mainly spiritual but also social, of the Jews of Germany – from the discourse of the German Jews themselves after the Nazis came to power in 1933. It

---

[2] The reference is to the *Verband nationaldeutschen Juden*, headed by Max Naumann. On this tiny organization, which identified strongly with right-wing German nationalism, see Avraham Margaliot, *Bein hatzalah le'avdan* (Between Rescue and Annihilation), pp. 171–5; George Mosse, *Germans and Jews: The Right, the Left, and the Search for a "Third Force" in Pre-Nazi Germany*, pp. 111–15.
[3] SD-Hauptamt, Lagebericht May/June 1934, BAB, R 58/229, in Otto Dov Kulka and Eberhard Jäckel, eds., *Die Juden in den geheimen NS-Stimmungsberichten 1933–1945*, p. 76.
[4] Stapostelle Regierungsbezirk Köln, Bericht für September 1935, 18.10.1935, BAB, R 58/3039c, in Kulka and Jäckel, eds., *Die Juden*, p. 160.
[5] SD-Hauptamt II 112, Bericht für 1.1.–31.3.1937, 8.4.1937, OA Mos, 500/3/316, in Kulka and Jäckel, eds., *Die Juden*, p. 227.
[6] SD-Oberabschnitt Nord-West II 112, Jahreslagebericht für 1937, 14.1.1938, Forschungsstelle für Zeitgeschichte in Hamburg, 93121, in Kulka and Jäckel, eds., *Die Juden*, p. 251.

was a discourse the Nazis followed and monitored closely. The situation reports tracked developments in the German Jewish community and served as a channel (though not the only one) for conveying the trends of ideas there. For example, writing in *Der Morgen*, the periodical of the Centralverein deutscher Staatsbürger jüdischen Glaubens (Central Association of German Citizens of the Jewish Faith) in 1934, a young Jewish man reported that

> Among the young people, the older ones... still read Goethe and saw Dürer with the eyes of other times, when they did not have to ask whether this was permitted. Among the younger ones, who were raised on the Bible and who to their distress know only too well how to maneuver within limits, there is growing opposition to an educational world whose development they can no longer share without second thoughts. Rising around are the walls of an invisible ghetto, [which is] a horror show for everyone else who comes from this space. The older ones... do not want a ghetto, absolutely not, for all that they are aware of the allures of the peace within it, and when they add new courses to the wall that surrounds German Jewry, getting higher and higher, the brain does not know what the hands are doing. Nevertheless, they were asking even before the first year [of Nazi rule] was over, should we build a ghetto on top of a ghetto, taking the German classics into it? Do we have the right to leave them out?[7]

On several occasions, liberal Jewish leaders in Germany spoke out against various proposals, advanced mainly by Zionists, for the Jews to retreat inward and strengthen their Jewish roots, calling it "a return to the ghetto." But in 1933 one liberal, Alfred Hirschberg of the Centralverein, did propose that "collective emancipation" (*Gruppenemanzipation*) of the Jews replace individual emancipation, which had now run into fierce German resistance. He maintained that nothing in his proposal required surrendering eternal Jewish values, which are intrinsically liberal. But, he added,

> We are speaking about the extent to which the existence of Judaism remains possible now, with or without eternal Jewish values, those that stand against the [spirit of the] age and the age opposes them.... Here the spiritual debate once again becomes a spiritual ghetto when one says: I am defending these values, and because I have [absolutely] no chance of realizing them, I [at least] implement them within my own circle.

---

[7] Quoted by Avraham Barkai, "'*Wehr Dich!*': *Der Centralverein deutscher Staatsbürger jüdischen Glaubens (C.V.) 1893–1938*, p. 322. The passage relates to the debate about the principles that should guide Jewish life in the face of the Nazi persecution: should they be drawn from Jewish sources, with a consequent return to Jewish distinctiveness and separation, or from the ideas of enlightened German writers and thinkers, with loyalty to the classic liberalism to which many German Jews had been attached for decades?

Not doing so would be a "total surrender to the forces of the moment" (*vollkommene Kapitulation vor den realen Kräften*), that is, a betrayal of the mission of Judaism.[8]

The fullest discussion of the German Jews' feeling of ghettoization was provided by the dynamic young Liberal rabbi, Joachim Prinz, first in an April 1935 sermon that was reprinted in the Zionist paper *Jüdische Rundschau* and later, after the enactment of the Nuremberg Laws (September 15, 1935) and the deterioration in the situation of German Jews in the second half of 1936 (after the Berlin Olympics), in his book *Das Leben im Ghetto. Jüdisches Schicksal in fünf Städten* (Life in the Ghetto: The Jewish Destiny in Five Cities). In the 1935 sermon, entitled "Life without Neighbors: An Attempt at a First Analysis, Ghetto 1935," he wrote:

> The fact that we are living in a ghetto is beginning to penetrate our awareness. This ghetto is distinguished – one must acknowledge – in many ways, both in concept and reality, from what we have previously understood by [this term]....
>
> The internal situation that we refer to as "a ghetto" is manifested in a fact that, truth to tell, has only moral standards that grow from the inside and consequently have no general application.... On the basis of our experience and the exigencies of our life we designate as a "ghetto" the fact *that we are living in a country, we Jews of Germany, where they tell us without any prettification or adornment, on many occasions, that our lives are a burden on the German people*....
>
> To this internal situation, which we call a "ghetto," something else is added. The medieval ghetto was sealed at night. The gate was shut strictly and aggressively. The bolt was thrown deliberately: one left the "world" and entered the ghetto. Today the situation is just the opposite. When the door of our house closes behind us, *we leave the ghetto and enter our homes*. This is the basic difference. The ghetto is no longer a defined geographical area, at least not in the sense of the Middle Ages. The ghetto is the "world." It is outside that the ghetto exists for us. In the markets, in the street, in the hotels – the ghetto exists in every place. It has a sign. That sign is: no neighbors. *The Jewish destiny is to have no neighbor*...
>
> The ghetto of 1935 does indeed have walls, in the form of measures and laws. But we should rather see the invisible walls, those of culture, of the landscape, and of the inner response. We should know and others should know its true name: Ghetto 1935.[9]

---

[8] Barkai, "'Wehr Dich!'" pp. 328–9. See also pp. 326 and 327.

[9] Joachim Prinz, "Das Leben ohne Nachbarn. Versuch einer erste Analyse. Ghetto 1935," *Jüdische Rundschau*, April 1935; partially reprinted in *Verfolgung und Ermordung der europäischen Juden durch das nationalsozialistische Deutschland 1933–1945* (hereafter VEJ), vol. 1, ed. Wolf Gruner: *Deutsches Reich 1933–1937*, pp. 426–9, Doc. 161. In *Das Leben im Ghetto* (1937), Prinz collected a series of lectures on the vitality of Jewish life in "ghettos," by which he meant Jewish neighborhoods in major cities in the past: Alexandria, Amsterdam, Frankfurt am Main, and Prague. These cases exemplified "that life in the ghetto, although causing many anxieties, nevertheless was also characterized

These internal Jewish uses of the word clearly express the authors' conception of the ghetto in a spiritual and metaphorical sense, as social, legal, and mental separation from the surrounding society, a separation that – as during earlier decades – was viewed by some as a bad situation that must not be revived in any fashion, whereas others saw it as offering a way to defend and cultivate important values (in this case liberal values) against a hostile world.

Explicit use of the term by a policymaker can be found in a letter from Heydrich to Rudolf Hess, the Deputy Führer and Minister without Portfolio, in early February 1937. Heydrich proposed issuing a decree (*Erlass*) that would make it possible to establish separate "Jewish" resorts (*jüdischer Gastwirtschaften*) and to label them as such. He noted that this – as a follow-up to the Nuremberg laws – would be another way to "return the Jews to the ghetto, to prevent them from frequenting German public places, and to separate them more effectively than before from those of German blood."[10] Here "ghetto" has the sense of "virtual ghetto": the social isolation of the Jews from the Germans. (Incidentally, this document shows that at the time Heydrich still thought that Jews would continue to go on vacation; and because people on vacation are more permissive, Jewish vacationers must be kept from mixing with Germans. Such a step might also promote their further isolation.) Heydrich's usage is fully compatible with the way the term was used at the time by his Jewish Affairs experts in the SD and Gestapo.

Starting in the summer of 1938 the word took on a more tangible meaning – though still in the pre-emancipation sense of a separate residential quarter for Jews. This sense can first be discerned in a memorandum on "Dealing with the Jews in the Capital of the Reich in all domains of public

---

by luck and greatness" ("daß das leben im Ghetto zwar viele Sorgen, aber auch Glück und Größe kannte"): see p. 8. On Joachim Prinz, his views, and his reaction to the Nazis, see Michael A. Meyer, ed., *Joachim Prinz, Rebellious Rabbi: An Autobiography. The German and Early American Years*. Significantly, the influential series on Jewish history and culture published by the Jewish publisher Schocken Verlag vis-à-vis the Nazi persecutions of the first years, republished in 1935 a description of the ghetto of Rome, written by the 19th-century German historian Ferdinand Gregorovius: *Der Ghetto und die Juden in Rom*; Rabbi Leo Baeck, leader of the Reich Representation of the Jews in Germany, wrote a foreword.

[10] "... *das Judentum in ein Ghetto zurückzudrängen, es von Besuch deutscher Lokale zurückzuhalten und schärfer als bisher von Deutschblütigen zu trennen*": Heydrich an Stellvertreter der Führer am 1.2.1937: quoted in Wolf Gruner, "Die NS-Judenverfolgung und die Kommunen. Zur wechselseitigen Dynamisierung von zentraler und lokaler Politik 1933–1941," p. 93; also published in *VEJ* 1: *Deutsches Reich 1933–1937*, p. 635, Doc. 264.

life," submitted by the Gestapo office in Berlin in May 1938. Among the points raised were the Jews' presence in public places, limitation of their residential options, and, in particular, the denial of residence permits to Jews who wanted to move to Berlin from smaller communities elsewhere in the country, because of the restrictions to which they were subject and the absence of Jewish support systems in the provinces.[11] The memorandum stated, in part, that a policy of requiring Jews to obtain permits to settle in Berlin could be used not only to control migration to Berlin but also to regulate where they could live *within* the city.

> This point is relevant to the question of the ghetto. Even if for the moment it does not seem feasible to concentrate the Jews of Berlin in a ghetto, this approach [the issuance of permits] might make it possible to ensure that some parts of the city would not be newly settled by Jews. In this way, a sort of ghetto would be created over the long term [in those places where Jews would be allowed to live].[12]

Here a ghetto, meaning a separate though not closed or restricted neighborhood for Jews, with no other specific features (poverty and overcrowding, hermetic closure, etc.), is presented as a good idea in and of itself (just as Heydrich had used the term metaphorically in a positive sense for a social ghetto in 1937).

This memorandum was discussed in several forums and elicited various reactions. One of them is particularly important. On September 22, 1938, a meeting was held at the Justice Ministry to consider removing Jews from the coverage of the Tenant Protection Law (*Aufhebung der Mieterschutzes für Juden*), as well as their increasing destitution and its consequences. The minutes were taken by the Chief Building Inspector of Berlin (*Generalbauinspektor für die Reichshauptstadt*), whose presence is relevant. The Interior Ministry representative noted that it was necessary to determine

> how many Jewish households would be harmed by these measures, since Jewish households with no roof over their heads would become a burden on the municipality, which would have to find housing for them. What is more, this

---

[11] The second half of the 1930s saw the rapid demise of the Jewish communities in provincial towns throughout Germany, because of the psychological, economic, and social pressures that were felt more strongly in smaller places where the Jews were a tiny and vulnerable minority (Aryanization, separate education, and the severing of social relations). The revocation of the legal status of the Jewish communities in April 1938 further undermined their financial viability.

[12] Quoted in Wolf Gruner, "'Lesen brauchen sie nicht zu können...' Die Denkschrift über die Behandlung der Juden in der Reichshauptstadt auf allen Gebieten des öffentlichen Lebens vom Mai 1938," p. 322.

involves creating a ghetto, a matter that was investigated by the Reichsführer SS [Himmler] but about which no decision has been made to date.[13] But he must insist that the municipality cannot assume a significant additional burden with regard to construction and housing. There is also a need to clarify the question of the Jewish workshops in such a ghetto that would be established, especially the situation if Jews from the provinces (Jewish cattle-dealers and the like) move to the city, where they would be unemployed.

The representative of the office of the Deputy Führer, Rudolf Hess, asked that "the question of the ghetto and other consequences be removed from the discussion. He has no reservations about leaving the Jews to find another place to live on their own. He also proposes that the municipality build barracks to house homeless Jews." In response, a representative of the Municipal Building Inspector's Office said that the question of barracks for Jews in Berlin, Frankfurt, and elsewhere remained open; but as for Berlin itself, they were thinking about special new construction in a particular section (the German word is *Teil*) of Berlin.[14]

In this discussion we clearly hear an echo of another line of development – the mission of Albert Speer, since 1937 the Chief Building Inspector, to redevelop Berlin and turn it into *the* metropolis of the Greater German Reich. Shortly before this meeting, in September 1938, he included in his vision a proposal for a "Jewish settlement" (*Judensiedlung*) on the outskirts of Berlin. According to the memorandum, some 2,700 small dwelling units (*Kleinwohnungen*) would be built there; the intention was to house approximately 2,500 Jewish families who would be evicted from their large homes in the center of town and other areas where real estate was expensive. Although the memorandum refers to a special residential solution for Jews – which was considered to be a desirable measure for them – it does not call the neighborhood a ghetto. The plan was never implemented; but, after Kristallnacht, Göring, who was in charge of the Four-Year Plan (which made him essentially the supreme minister for economic affairs),[15] authorized Speer to define rules for rental. Soon after, in early 1939, Speer made use of this power to evict Jews from

---

[13] This refers to discussions held by the Gestapo and SD concerning a ghetto, in the wake of the previously cited Gestapo memorandum from May.

[14] Protokoll der Besprechung im Reichsjustizministerium vom Generalbauinspektors für die Reichshauptstadt, Referent: Dr. Fränk/II/Hp., vom 22.9.1938, BAB (formerly ZstAP, 157, Bl. 205–7).

[15] The Four-Year Plan was instituted in 1936 to prepare Germany for war, both economically and logistically.

First References to "Ghetto" in the Third Reich

their apartments and relocate them to "Jewish houses" (*Judenhäuser*).[16] It is important to note, however, that the government itself was supposed to build this special neighborhood, and that although the apartments were to be tiny, it was still accepted that even Jews deserved minimal but normal living conditions.

This matter – the possibility of relocating the Jews to a special neighborhood for an interim period – should be seen in the context of the emphases of the anti-Jewish policy of those years. Along with the process of internal Jewish migration to the big cities, the authorities encouraged and pressured the Jews to leave Germany altogether. In this context the word "ghetto" also came up in remarks made by Herman Göring at a meeting in his office on October 14, 1938 (about a month before the meeting of November 12), which dealt with measures in various fields for which Göring had responsibility – mainly economic matters, but also Jewish affairs. According to him, in the wake of recent developments (Nazi Germany was still trumpeting its victory in the Sudeten crisis, several weeks earlier), "the Führer had instructed him to implement a massive plan to keep the achievements to date from being rendered worthless. There are problems facing them, but he [Göring] would overcome them as vigorously as possible and with no inhibitions." Göring mentioned various economic difficulties and then came to the Jewish problem (*Judenproblem*): "With regard to the Jews one must now employ all means, because they must get out of the economy." Aryanization was part of this policy, but Göring was angry that party institutions were meddling in this matter. Aryanization, he said emphatically, was a matter for the state alone. And, counter to the policy that sought to accelerate the Jews' departure from Germany, even at the price of allotting foreign currency to the emigrants, he emphasized that "he would not provide foreign currency for pushing out the Jews." Nevertheless, "if necessary, ghettos should be set up in several large cities" (*Im Notfalle müsse man Ghettos in den Einzelnen Großstädten einrichten*).[17] It is clear from the context that Göring was using the term "ghetto" in the sense of the Berlin Gestapo memorandum of the previous May. But unlike the Gestapo, and also unlike Speer, Göring saw a ghetto as a planned temporary Jewish neighborhood, a way

---

[16] For the full story of the Jewish residential policy, see Konrad Kwiet, "Without Neighbors: Daily Living in *Judenhäuser*," on which the last paragraph is based.

[17] *Trials of the Major War Criminals before the International Military Tribunal, Nuremberg, 14 November 1945–1 October 1946*, vol. 27, pp. 160, 163.

station for emigration – perhaps as a form of pressure to persuade the Jews to leave the country even without foreign currency. The reference to a ghetto in his remarks at the meeting on November 12 must be explained in this context. An article in the SS organ *Das Schwarze Korps*, two weeks after Kristallnacht, was in a similar vein:

The program is clear.
   It is: total elimination, complete separation! ...
   It can no longer be asked of any German that he should continue to live under one roof with Jews, a race stamped with the mark of murderers and criminals, and deadly enemies of the German people.
   The Jews must therefore be driven out of our apartment houses and residential areas and put into a series of streets or blocks of houses where they will be together and have as little contact as possible with Germans. They must be marked and the right must be taken from them to own houses or land or a share in either, because it cannot be expected of a German that he should submit to the power of a Jewish landlord and maintain him by the work of his hands.[18]

As we have seen, however, Heydrich was opposed to this idea. Why?

---

[18] "Juden, was nun?" *Das Schwarze Korps*, 24.11.1938. English version from Arad et al., eds., *Documents on the Holocaust*, pp. 119–20.

6

The Semantic Turning Point in the Meaning of "Ghetto": Peter-Heinz Seraphim and *Das Judentum im osteuropäischen Raum*

> The ghetto is at the same time the basis from which the Jewish expansion stems. From here, overpopulation and social misery push the Jews into the non-Jewish sectors of the economic and cultural life of the host countries. It is in the ghetto that the threads, not only of Jewish economic life, but also of the entire urban economic fabric, are woven together. This is where the merchants live, from the peddlers and rag-sellers through the middle-sized and large merchants and the exporters; this is the place from which the Jewish artisan who has been proletarianized finds his way to the factory; this is where the Jews' religious and political leaders are raised; this is where *the Jewish essence* is molded in its specific form, as it is found in Eastern Europe, in order to exert from here, from the business centers, an influence on the surroundings and on the nations among whom the Jews live.
>
> Peter-Heinz Seraphim, *Das Judentum im osteuropäischen Raum* (1938)

A dramatic change in how the term "ghetto" was understood can be discerned in the book by Peter-Heinz Seraphim, *Das Judentum im osteuropäischen Raum* (Jewry in the Territory of Eastern Europe), published in the autumn of 1938.[1] The Jews of Eastern Europe (the *Ostjuden*) attracted the attention of scholars who worked in two disciplines – Eastern European studies (*Ostforschung*, in Nazi jargon), which had developed since 1936, and study of the Jews (*Judenforschung*), which developed in

---

[1] The precise date of publication is of major importance for us. Seraphim dated his preface "May 1938" but, as is the way with the publication of books, especially in the days of lead type, several months passed before the volume actually appeared. According to the author of the monograph on Seraphim, Hans-Christian Petersen (letter to the author, April 4, 2007), there is correspondence that notes that Seraphim sent a copy of the book to Albert Brackmann in November; the book had apparently been published several weeks earlier, in September.

tandem with it.² Seraphim was one of the leading "scholars" of Eastern European Jewry in Nazi Germany; his book, with its detailed description of all aspects of Jewish life in Eastern Europe, from the Baltic to the Black Sea, and especially in Poland, the Soviet Union, the Baltic states, Romania, and Hungary, was his crowning achievement.³

A chapter of particular importance for us (III-2), on the "Urbanization of the Jews of Eastern Europe" (*Verstädterungsprozess der Juden Osteuropas*), included fifteen pages on the ghettos of Eastern Europe.⁴ Drawing on the writings of the major Jewish (and Zionist) sociologist Arthur Ruppin, along with other scholars, and buttressed by statistics, diagrams, and tables, Seraphim traced the process by which the Jews – who had never been part of the agricultural sector – had migrated from the villages and small towns to mid-size towns and large cities, especially the capitals. The Jews' urbanization, he argued, was substantially different from the urbanization process in Europe as a whole, because the Jews did not change their occupations or way of thinking, but only their place of residence. The Jews were always different from their neighbors, but felt comfortable among fellow Jews, wherever they lived; this was why the transition had been so easy for them. Now (in the modern era), however, their migration to the mid-size towns and large cities had created large and separate concentrations of Jews. These served – here Seraphim

---

² On the emergence of "eastern European Jewry," its characteristics and its significance for modern Jewish history, see Jacob Katz, "From Ghetto to Zionism, Mutual Influences"; Ezra Mendelsohn, *The Jews of East Central Europe Between the World Wars*; Michman, *Holocaust Historiography: A Jewish Perspective*, pp. 62, 65, 73. On Eastern European studies under the Nazi regime, see, for example, Michael Burleigh, *Germany Turns Eastwards: A Study of 'Ostforschung' in the Third Reich*; Winfried Schulze et al., eds., *Deutsche Historiker im Nationalsozialismus*. See also G. F. Volkmer, "Die deutsche Forschung zu Osteuropa und zum osteuropäischen Judentum in den Jahren 1933–1945"; Claudia Koonz, *The Nazi Conscience*; Dirk Rupnow, "Radicalizing Historiography: Anti-Jewish Scholarship in the Third Reich"; and the collection of articles on this topic, Nicolas Berg and Dirk Rupnow, eds., "Schwerpunkt: 'Judenforschung' – Zwischen Wissenschaft und Ideologie." For a list of books on Jews and Judaism published during the 1930s and used by the Nazis, see Hans-Heinrich Wilhelm, *Die Einsatzgruppe A der Sicherheitspolizei und des SD 1941/42*, pp. 501–10.

³ Hans-Christian Petersen, *Bevölkerungsökonomie – Ostforschung – Politik: Eine biographische Studie zu Peter-Heinz Seraphim (1902–1979)*; Alan Steinweis, *Studying the Jew: Scholarly Antisemitism in Nazi Germany*, pp. 142–51; Götz Aly and Susanne Heim, *Vordenker der Vernichtung: Auschwitz und die deutschen Pläne für eine neue europäische Ordnung*, pp. 96–101 (there are major changes in the English translation of this last work, including an abridgement of the treatment of Seraphim); Koonz, *Nazi Conscience*, p. 199.

⁴ Seraphim, *Das Judentum*, pp. 324–72, esp. pp. 355–72.

Amt des Generalgouverneurs
für die besetzten polnischen Gebiete
Bücherei

Das Judentum im osteuropäischen Raum

Von

Dr. habil. Peter-Heinz Seraphim
Dozent an der Universität Königsberg i. Pr.

Herausgegeben
unter Mitwirkung des Instituts für Osteuropäische
Wirtschaft an der Universität Königsberg i. Pr.

Mit 197 Abbildungen
auf 32 Kunstdrucktafeln und im Text
sowie einer Übersichtskarte

Bücherverzeichnis Nr. *371*
Buchzeichen:
Standplatz: Abt.

1938

ESSENER VERLAGSANSTALT

FIGURE 2. Title page of Peter-Heinz Seraphim's 1938 book, *Das Judentum im osteuropäischen Raum* (Jewry in the Territory of Eastern Europe). Note the stamps indicating that this copy was one of the first volumes (nr. 371) in the library of the General Governor of the Occupied Polish Territories, installed at the end of October 1939.

quoted Ruppin – as the nerve centers of the economic, cultural, and political life of our age. The Jews' concentration in the major cities caused processes that

Jewish sociologists generally evaluate only negatively: (1) the disintegration of the intimate community life; (2) easier access to higher education; (3) encouragement of risky transactions; (4) a lower birth rate; (5) friendlier relations with non-Jews; (6) abandonment of religion.[5]

He added:

No doubt this view is not wrong per se. These consequences *can* indeed take place, and they do take place in many cases. But on the other hand, one must not forget that these Jews live in the mid-sized towns and large cities in a closed Jewish society, that is, they create a city within a city,[6] the Jewish *ghetto*. Within this Jewish residential district the national and religious sense of community can express itself in a fashion that is utterly different and much stronger than it would be were the Jews living scattered among the non-Jewish population of the big city. The ghetto – of course in the sense of a totally voluntary Jewish residential community – is the Jews' unconscious means of defense against the danger of the dissolution of the Jewish religion, the Yiddish language, and Jewish national feeling. Emigration and the ghetto are the two sides of the coin of the Jews' life – not only outwardly, in the sense of movement and the residential patterns of the Jewish people, but also *internally*, in the sense of the risk of assimilation and defense against assimilation.

But the ghetto is at the same time the *basis* from which *the Jewish expansion* stems. From here, overpopulation and social misery push the Jews into the non-Jewish sectors of the economic and cultural life of the host countries. It is in the ghetto that the threads, not only of Jewish economic life, but also of the entire urban economic fabric, are woven. This is where the merchants live, from the peddlers and rag-sellers through the mid-sized and large merchants and the exporters; this is the place from which the Jewish artisan who has been proletarianized finds his way to the factory; this is where the Jews' religious and political leaders are raised; this is where *the Jewish essence* is molded in its specific form, as it is found in Eastern Europe, in order to exert from here, from the business centers, an influence on the surroundings and on the nations among whom the Jews live.

All sociologists agree that the city, especially the big city, has a destructive influence on a people, in the sense of the disintegration of community life, in the sense of the loss of traditions, customs, biological increase, and national unity. Only *one single people* is an exception to this rule: the *Jewish one*.

---

[5] Seraphim, *Das Judentum*, pp. 354–5.
[6] Anyone familiar with the vocabulary of modern anti-Semitism will hear in this an echo of the 19th-century expression alluding to the Jews as "a state within a state." See Jacob Katz, *A State within a State: The History of an Anti-Semitic Slogan.*

The reason all these perils have hardly impacted the Jews, to an astonishing extent – even if they have not escaped them totally – is to be found in their *residential patterns*: for two thousand years the Jews have been chiefly city-dwellers but have nevertheless preserved their solidarity as a religious and national community, as no other people has done – in part in the *ghetto*, a defensive means for national survival, the great source of Jewry's strength.[7]

... It goes without saying that social and hygienic conditions in these Jewish ghettos are very bad.... If we consider that only one-third [of Jewish residences] in the Warsaw ghetto, and in Łódź fewer than one-fifth of the residences, have sanitary facilities, we have said enough about the social and hygienic conditions.[8]

Seraphim included maps of the "Jewish ghettos" (which he referred to variously as *das jüdische Ghetto*, *das Judenghetto*, and *die Ballung der Juden*) in Warsaw, Krakow, Lemberg (Lwów), Vilna, Łódź, Kovno, and Riga, to illustrate how the centers of those cities were solidly Jewish (he shaded the "ghettos" to make them stand out), a core from which the Jews expanded and took over the rest of the city. But the phenomenon was much more serious than that. Whereas the external appearance of the medieval ghetto had distinguished it from the rest of the city, the case of the modern ghetto was different, he stressed: because the Jews took over existing buildings from non-Jewish citizens and merchants ("perhaps," he wrote, "in order to infiltrate the city" in a way that "would arouse as little attention as possible"), no difference could be perceived from the outside. What created the sharp sense of difference was the lifestyle within, with its strong oriental stamp (*stark orientalische Note*).[9]

Seraphim was building on a tradition inherited from decades of modern anti-Semitism. In his 1879 *Ein Wort über unser Judenthum* (A Word about Our Jewry), the historian and politician Heinrich von Treitschke, whose works were widely read and quoted and whose expression, "the Jews are our misfortune" (*die Juden sind unser Unglück*) became a favorite Nazi slogan, displayed on many billboards, had written as follows:

our country is invaded year after year by multitudes of assiduous pants-selling youths from the inexhaustible cradle of Poland, whose children and grand-children are to be the future rulers of Germany's exchanges and Germany's press.... We Germans ... have to deal with Jews of the Polish branch, [who] ... are incomparably more alien to the European and especially to the

---

[7] Seraphim, *Das Judentum*, pp. 355–6 (all emphases in the original).
[8] Seraphim, *Das Judentum*, p. 366.
[9] Seraphim, *Das Judentum*, p. 371.

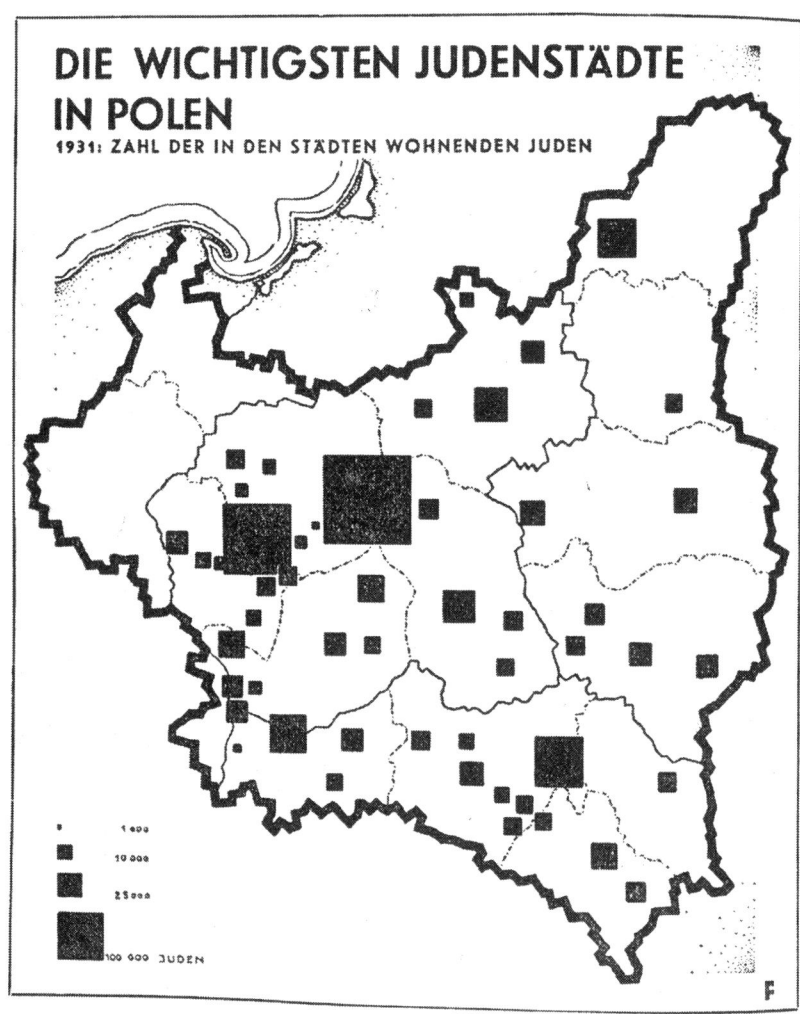

FIGURE 3. Illustration 19 from Peter-Heinz Seraphim's 1938 book, *Das Judentum im osteuropäischen Raum*, showing the number of Jews living in the most important Jewish cities in Poland, 1931.

German national character [than the Jews of the Western and Southern European countries].[10]

[10] Heinrich von Treitschke, "Unsere Aussichten," *Preußische Jahrbücher*, 44 (1879), pp. 559–76; the quote is from pp. 572–3. It was republished in *Ein Wort über unser Judenthum*, Berlin: 1879–80; English translation: *A Word About Our Jewry*, ed. Ellis Rivkin, trans. Helen Lederer, in Paul R. Mendes-Flohr and Jehuda Reinharz, eds., *The Jew in the Modern World: A Documentary History*, pp. 343–5.

The Semantic Turning Point in the Meaning of "Ghetto"

FIGURE 4. Illustration 20 from Peter-Heinz Seraphim's 1938 book, *Das Judentum im osteuropäischen Raum*, showing the percentage of Jews in the population of the most important Jewish cities in Poland, 1931.

Seraphim refined and reinforced this idea by pointing out the precise source of the danger: the Eastern European Jewish ghetto, the source of Jewish vitality and power but also the wellspring of their contamination and filth, a repulsive place. Another famous German scholar, Werner Sombart, in his widely read book, *The Jews and Economic Life*, written

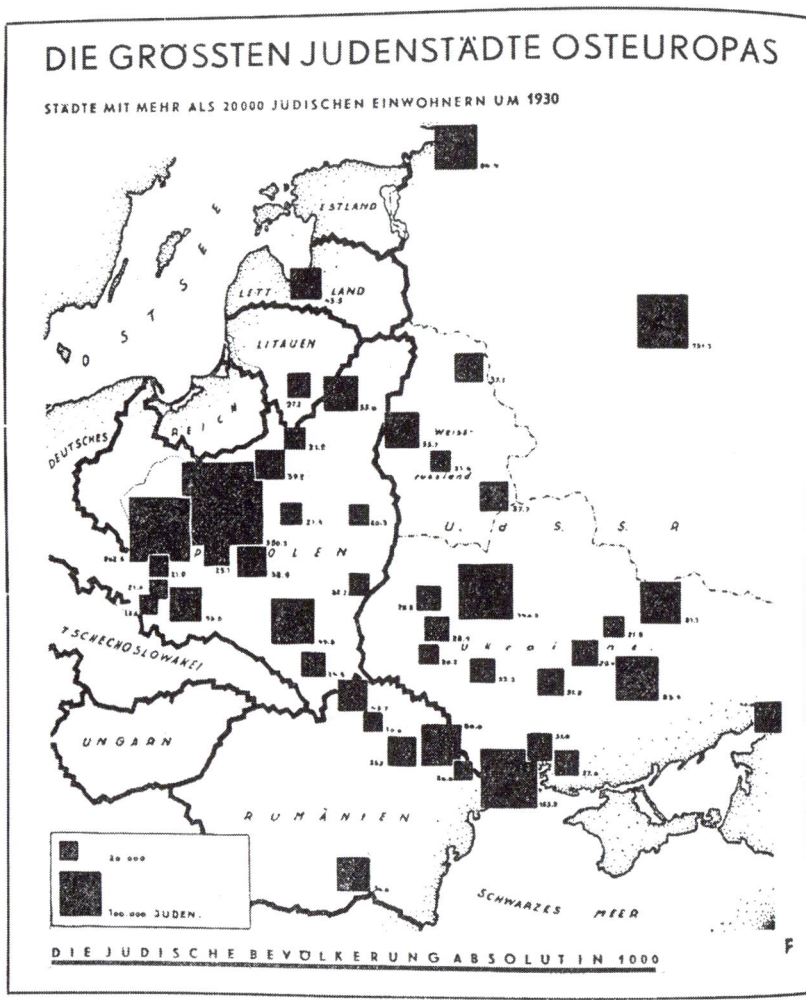

FIGURE 5. Illustration 24 from Peter-Heinz Seraphim's 1938 book, *Das Judentum im osteuropäischen Raum*, showing the largest Jewish cities (more than 20,000 Jewish inhabitants) in Eastern Europe (in absolute numbers), in 1930.

before World War I, had also raised the issue of the Jewish ghetto and the ghetto destiny (*Ghettoschicksal*) that molds "the Jews" (in general) into a race with inherent characteristics.[11] Seraphim, some thirty years later, expanded on the traits noted by Sombart, focusing on Eastern Europe as the hothouse in which the Jewish peril had flourished and become

[11] Werner Sombart, *Die Juden und das Wirtschaftsleben*, pp. 429–34.

The Semantic Turning Point in the Meaning of "Ghetto"

FIGURE 6. Illustration 25 from Peter-Heinz Seraphim's 1938 book, *Das Judentum im osteuropäischen Raum*, showing the largest Jewish cities (more than 20,000 Jewish inhabitants) in Eastern Europe (percentages), in 1930.

even more efficient. Note that the link between ghetto and Ostjuden was not Seraphim's invention. In fact, he drew it from the discourse about the ghetto that was current in Poland and among Polish Jews.[12] He may also have been influenced by plans for ghettoization floated by Polish

---

[12] Seraphim quotes Jewish sources (most of them written in German). The link between ghetto and Ostjuden can also be found in the writings of German Jews: see Katrin Steffen, "Connotations of Exclusion: 'Ostjuden,' 'Ghettos,' and Other Markings."

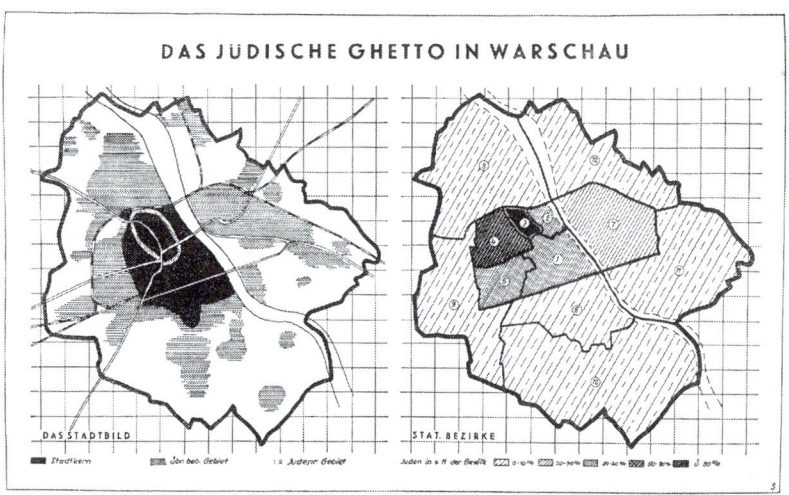

FIGURE 7. Illustration 26 from Peter-Heinz Seraphim's 1938 book, *Das Judentum im osteuropäischen Raum*, showing the Jewish ghetto in Warsaw.

anti-Semites in the second half of the 1930s.[13] As we have seen, the earlier Nazi meaning (before 1938) was based again on a Jewish source, but a different one – the German Jews. Seraphim added to his inversion of the Jewish discourse, and Jewish scholarship,[14] an element that had been central to racial anti-Semitism since the time of Wilhelm Marr: the sense that the historic processes in which the Jews are involved were propelled by destiny. Just as Hitler, in *Mein Kampf*, believed that if he did not intervene, "the Jew" will "triumph over the people of this world, his Crown will be the funeral wreath of mankind, and this planet will once again follow its orbit through ether, without any human life on its surface, as it did millions of years ago,"[15] Seraphim saw the progress of the Jewish problem in Eastern Europe as a dramatic development that required action.[16]

---

[13] See Alina Cała, "The Discourse of 'Ghettoization': Non-Jews on Jews in 19th- and 20th-Century Poland."

[14] On the use of the work of Jewish scholars by Nazi *Judenforschung*, see Mitchell B. Hart, "'Let the Numbers Speak': On the Appropriation of Jewish Social Science by Nazi Scholars."

[15] Adolf Hitler, *Mein Kampf*, trans. James Murphy, p. 46.

[16] "*Das Jahrhunderte hindurch festgefügte, geschlossene und geballte jüdische Siedlungsgebiet Osteuropas ist in den ersten drei Jahrzehnten des 20. Jahrhunderts in den Zustand einer Gärung und Zersetzung geraten*" ("The Jewish area of settlement in Eastern Europe, which was for many centuries firmly tied up, closed and concentrated, turned in the first three decades of the 20th century into a state of fermentation and decomposition"): Seraphim, *Das Judentum*, p. 320.

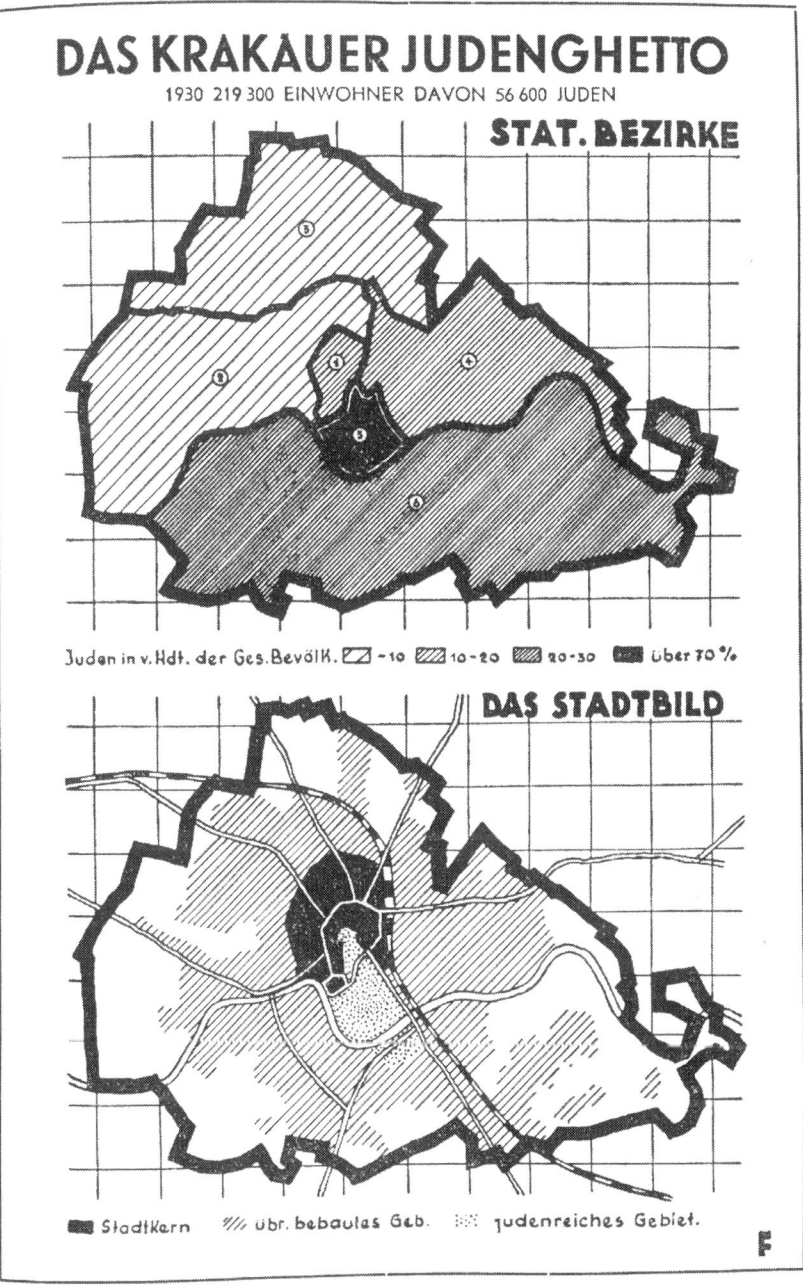

FIGURE 8. Illustration 27 from Peter-Heinz Seraphim's 1938 book, *Das Judentum im osteuropäischen Raum*, showing the ghetto of the Jews in Krakow, 1930; Krakow had 219,300 inhabitants, 56,600 of whom were Jews. (top) City neighborhoods; (bottom) the character of the city, emphasizing the partial overlapping of the part "full of Jews" with that of the city center.

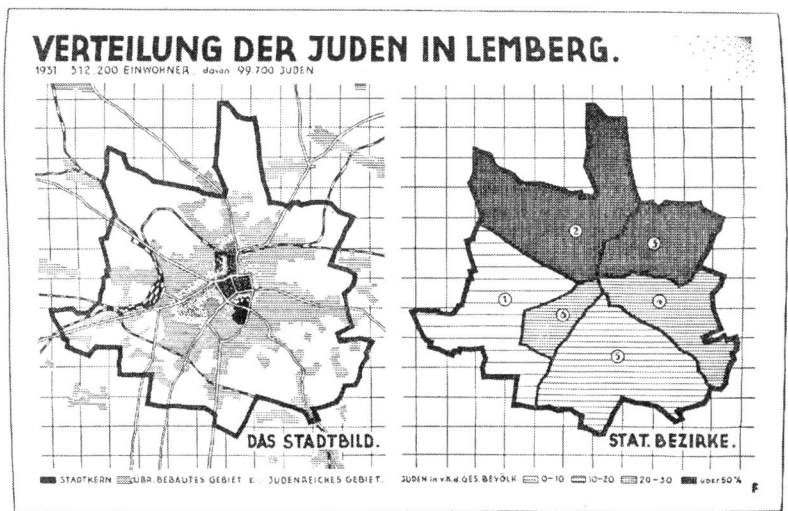

FIGURE 9. Illustration 28 from Peter-Heinz Seraphim's 1938 book, *Das Judentum im osteuropäischen Raum*, showing the distribution of the Jews in Lemberg, 1931, which had 312,200 inhabitants, 99,700 of whom were Jews.

We have no "smoking gun" – no document or memorandum written by Heydrich himself or one of his close aides – that provides unequivocal evidence that Nazi officials who dealt with Jewish affairs, especially in Heydrich's circle, ever read Seraphim's book. Nevertheless, we can infer this indirectly, both from Heydrich's remarks at the meeting on November 12, 1938, and from the documented use of the book by Nazi administrators in Poland a year later.[17] What is more, at the November meeting Heydrich relied on information provided by his Jewish affairs specialists in the Gestapo and especially the SD, such as Herbert Hagen, the head of the Department for Jewish Affairs, and Adolf Eichmann, of the same department, whose star was on the rise and who had been summoned from Vienna to attend this meeting. They saw themselves as intelligence analysts who deeply understood Jewish affairs. Along with their ideological commitment to Nazism, these SD personnel were practical men and policymakers,[18] as Heydrich defined their role in July 1937.[19] Part

---

[17] See Chapter 7, note 4, and Figure 2 above, in which I relate to a copy of this book from the library of the General Governor of Poland, Hans Frank.

[18] Jürgen Matthäus, "Konzept als Kalkül. Das Judenbild des SD 1934–1939."

[19] For Heydrich's order that divided up the work between the SD and the Gestapo (July 1, 1937), see "Gemeinsame Anordnung für den Sicherheitsdienst des Reichsführer-SS und

The Semantic Turning Point in the Meaning of "Ghetto"

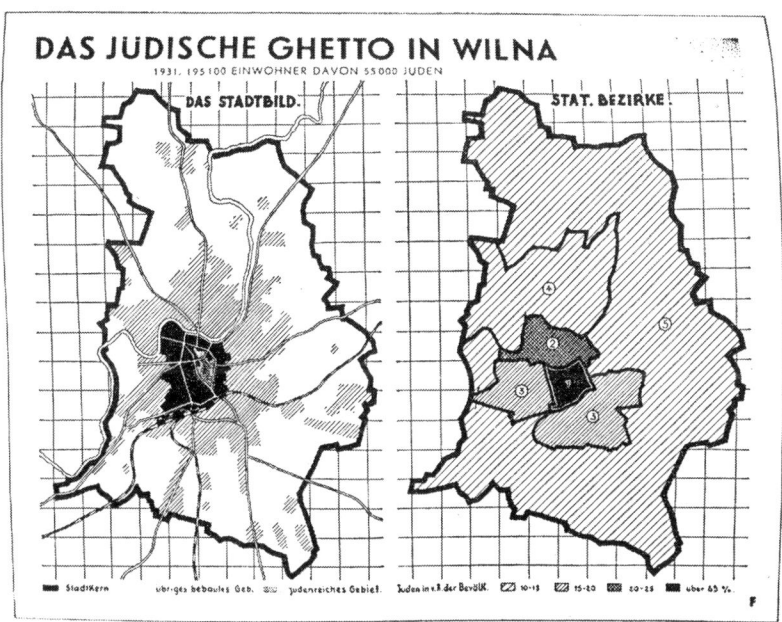

FIGURE 10. Illustration 29 from Peter-Heinz Seraphim's 1938 book, *Das Judentum im osteuropäischen Raum*, showing the Jewish ghetto in Vilna, 1931; Vilna had 195,100 inhabitants, 55,000 of whom were Jews.

of their job was to study what university scholars wrote in this field. In fact, members of the Jewish Department of the SD met with members of the Jewish Department of the Gestapo (II B 4) on September 27, 1938, to discuss the Gestapo memorandum from May about the possibility of ghettoization. At this meeting

> there was full agreement about the need to work against actual ghettoization, due to considerations of the Security Police.
> The Security Police office in Berlin has received instructions on this matter from the SD Main Office as well as from the Gestapo. The most important argument against this program is that a totally Jewish ghetto would no longer be under the full control of the Security Police.[20]

---

die Geheime Staatspolizei," BAB, R 58/239; published in full in Michael Wildt, ed., *Die Judenpolitik des SD 1935 bis 1938: Eine Dokumentation*, pp. 118–20.

[20] "SD II 112 an den SD-Führer des SS-O.A. Ost, II 112, Berlin, Betr.: Ghettoisierung der Juden," 1.11.1938, United States Holocaust Memorial Museum Archives, Washington, Sonderarchiv Moskau 500–1–343, p. 243. I would like to thank Dr. Jürgen Matthäus, who was kind enough to send me this document.

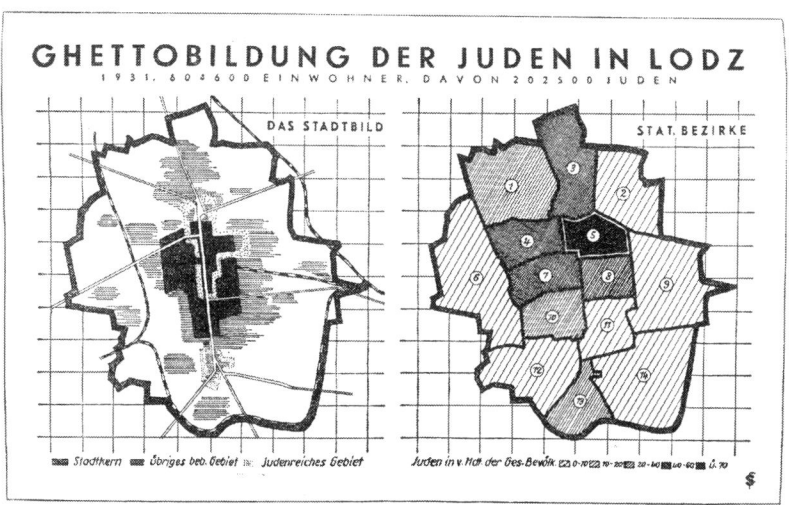

FIGURE 11. Illustration 30 from Peter-Heinz Seraphim's 1938 book, *Das Judentum im osteuropäischen Raum*, showing the formation of the ghetto of the Jews in Lodz, 1931; Lodz had 604,600 inhabitants, 55,000 of whom were Jews.

Finally, today there is no longer any doubt about the existence of close ties between academics, especially historians and social scientists, and Nazi field agents.[21]

When Heydrich opposed the emergence (or creation) of Jewish ghettos in Germany in November 1938, he was taking a stand that on the surface contradicted his own initiative of February 1937 to enact legal measures that would create a "ghetto." The only explanation for this change is that, under the influence of his experts on Jewish affairs, his notion of "ghetto" had undergone a significant semantic shift from the earlier version, which may have survived until the early summer of 1938, when the Gestapo submitted its memorandum. Nor did Heydrich accept the meaning of the term as the Gestapo and Göring understood it. After the publication of Seraphim's book,[22] "ghetto" no longer meant the mental separation of Jews, nor even a separate Jewish residential quarter, as in the Middle Ages and early Modern Age (as reflected in the Gestapo memorandum), but (according to Heydrich on November 12) "a completely segregated

---

[21] Michael Burleigh and Wolfgang Wippermann, *The Racial State: Germany 1933–1945*, pp. 57–8; Ingo Haar, *Historiker im Nationalsozialismus. Deutsche Geschichtswissenschaft und der "Volkstumskampf" im Osten*, esp. pp. 370–1.

[22] On the reception of Seraphim's book, see Petersen, *Bevölkerungsökonomie – Ostforschung – Politik*, pp. 96–105.

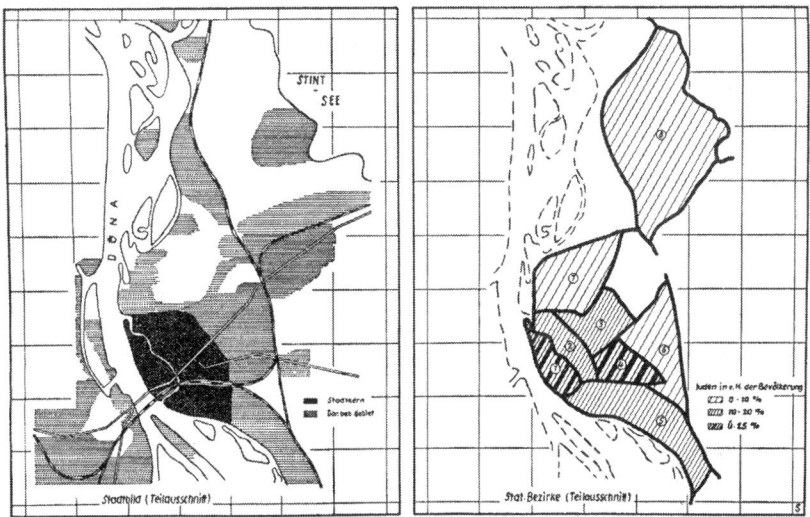

FIGURE 12. Illustration 31 from Peter-Heinz Seraphim's 1938 book, *Das Judentum im osteuropäischen Raum*, showing the concentration of the Jews in Kovno (Kaunas).

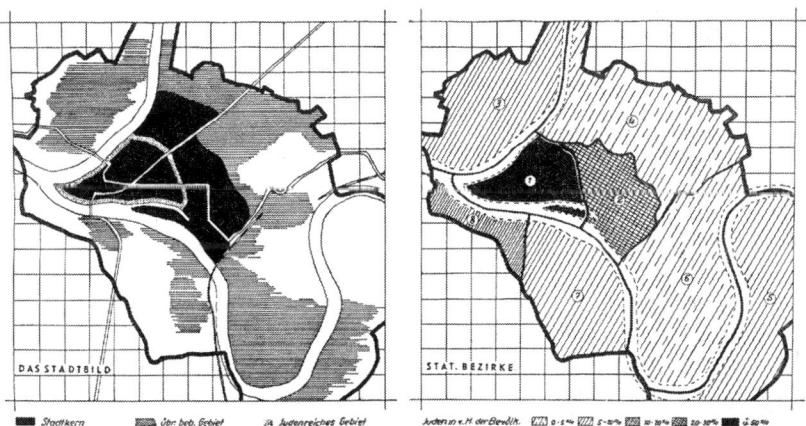

FIGURE 13. Illustration from Peter-Heinz Seraphim's 1938 book, *Das Judentum im osteuropäischen Raum*, showing the distribution of Jews in Riga.

district with only Jews," where "we would have no control" and "the Jew gets together with the whole of his Jewish tribe,... a permanent hideout for criminals and... [a source] of epidemics and the like" – that is, the frightening Polish ghetto of the contemporary discourse, as seen through Seraphim's (pseudo-)scientific lens. This – and remember that at the beginning of his remark about the ghetto Heydrich referred to "the ghetto in [this] form," meaning the Eastern European ghetto and not the "neutral" sense of the term entertained by Göring – is what Heydrich did not want to create or encourage in Germany. When Heydrich added that "control of the Jews by the watchful eyes of the whole population is better than putting thousands upon thousands of Jews together in a single district of a city where uniformed officials will be unable to check on their daily activities," he was repeating almost word for word what Seraphim had written about the dangerous living conditions and lifestyle of the Jews in Eastern Europe. Heydrich considered the German people to be his best partner in keeping an eye on the Jews.[23]

[23] Evidently he was thinking about the practice of informing on one's neighbors and associates, which was on the upswing in Germany at that time. See: Robert Gellately, *The Gestapo and German Society: Enforcing Racial Policy 1933–45*; Eric A. Johnson, *Nazi Terror: The Gestapo, Jews, and Ordinary Germans*.

7

The Invasion of Poland and the Emergence of the "Classic" Ghettos

> The time has come to drive this rabble into ghettos, and then epidemics will erupt and they'll all croak.
>
> Heinrich Himmler, November 1939
>
> A horrid Jewish hole.
>
> From a report by a German military unit that participated in the invasion of Poland, October 8, 1939
>
> The Jew, who crawled out of the dark corners of the ghetto into the surrounding German neighborhoods and gnawed at the body of the nation, like maggots in meat, has been tamed. He has been sent back to the place he came from, before his usury brought him such enormous profits that he could move into a nicer house and even be the landlord of German tenants. The Jewish game is over.... Now the Jews have been tamed in Łódź and the time has come when the yellow Star of David will no longer shine in German neighborhoods.
>
> *Lodscher Zeitung*, February 11, 1940

There is no doubt that after the meeting in Göring's office, and in advance of the invasion of Poland, which would constitute a new stage in Germany's territorial expansion (and, in retrospect, the start of World War II), there was a conscious change in the mindset of the Nazi leaders and their minions. The earlier territorial acquisitions had been defined as steps toward the unification of all German speakers; now the time had come to seize a German *Lebensraum* in the East – a stage in the colonization of Europe, to be followed by expansion into Asia. Occupied Poland was to serve as the proving ground for various concepts of population policy that functionaries of the regime had been entertaining, including the relocation of large masses of people, the planning of new settlements for Germans, and the eradication of potential cores of resistance. The regime encouraged its officials to be creative and left them ample room to maneuver.[1] This phase also included a major escalation of the anti-Jewish policy – both in practice (the brutal treatment of Jews by soldiers and members of the *Einsatzgruppen*, the special units of the Security Police and SD assembled during the fighting in September 1939 to deal with ideological enemies)[2] and in theory (as officials at various levels painstakingly searched for ways to deal with the conquered Jewish population). The existence of extremely large Jewish concentrations made matters worse. Even before the invasion, fairly detailed general information about the Jews of Poland was available in Seraphim's book.[3] There is clear evidence that it was on the desks of German administrators at the start of the occupation.[4] The intelligence work in advance of

---

[1] See, in particular, Michael Wildt, *Generation des Unbedingten: Das Führungskorps des Reichssicherheitshauptamtes*; Michael Wildt, *Generation of the Unbound: The Leadership Corps of the Reich Security Main Office*.

[2] Alexander B. Rossino, *Hitler Strikes Poland: Blitzkrieg, Ideology, and Atrocity*; Jochen Böhler, *Auftakt zum Vernichtungskrieg: Die Wehrmacht in Polen*.

[3] On the extent to which such information, some of it stereotypical, infiltrated the materials distributed to the fighting forces before the invasion, see Rossino, *Hitler Strikes Poland*, chapter 1.

[4] My own copy of Seraphim's book was purchased by my late father, Dr. Jozeph Michman (Melkman), in Amsterdam in the 1980s. The inside cover is stamped "Amt des Generalgouverneurs für die besetzten polischen Gebiete/Bücherei. Buchenverzeichnis Nr. 371." This means that it was one of the first books in the library of the Headquarters of the General-Government, when it was still known as the "Amt... *für die besetzten polnischen Gebiete*" (my emphasis; after several months, in 1940, the title was shortened to General-Government only). Even though Seraphim received little attention until recently, his name and work were very well known in the 1940s and were mentioned by the first scholars to deal with the Holocaust, such as Philip Friedman in his 1954 essay, "The Jewish Ghettos of the Nazi Era." Particularly interesting in this context is Moshe Prager, an Ultraorthodox journalist from Warsaw who reached Palestine with the Hasidic Rebbe of Gur in 1940 and whose *Yeven-metsulah he-hadash* [The new miry pit] (Tel Aviv: Masada, 1941) was one of the first books published in Palestine about the events in Europe. During the first months of the occupation, Prager had taken the initiative to collect documentation on the ongoing persecutions; he took some of this material with him to Palestine, where it served him later in his writings. Prager had already devoted much space to Seraphim and his 1938 book in an article entitled "Hurban ve-nehamah" [Destruction and Consolation], published in the religious-Zionist daily *Hatzofah* on September 1, 1941 (on the second anniversary of the beginning of the war). He wrote that "Seraphim's dream is coming true," and that "recently the role of this oeuvre in the hellish campaign of the Nazis has become clear." In an investigative article, "On the Destruction of European Jewry," published in the review *Keneset* 8 (1944), Prager again devoted ample space to Seraphim, his book, and his standing in the *Generalgouvernement*. I would like to thank my student Mali Eisenberg-Gotdiner for bringing these articles to my attention.

the invasion of Poland, in the late spring of 1939, included the collection of material on Polish Jews by the Jewish Affairs Department of the SD (SD-212).[5] Moreover, popularized versions of the views of Seraphim and his colleagues were disseminated among soldiers, administrators, and others. In the summer of 1939 Hans Hinkel, the *Sonderbeauftragter für die Überwachung der Nichtarier* (Special Officer-in-Charge for the Monitoring of Non-Aryans) in the Ministry of Propaganda who supervised the Jewish *Kulturbund*,[6] put together (as editor) and published a short book entitled *Judenviertel Europas: Die Juden zwischen Ostsee und schwarzem Meer* (The Jewish Quarters in Europe: The Jews between the Baltic and Black Seas). It consisted of Hinkel's introduction on "Germany and the Jews," followed by a series of articles on the Jews in the different Eastern European countries. Seraphim's twenty-page article on Poland was actually a summary of his book; the article was most notable for the photographs that accompanied it (most of them taken from Seraphim's book, too) of "typical" Ostjuden and of "ghettos" and "Jewish streets" in Eastern European cities (as well as Ostjuden in the "Paris Ghetto"!).[7]

Dislodging the Jews played a prominent role in this great colonialist project. One line of action (perhaps not fully crystallized in concept, but certainly implemented on the ground) during the first months of the occupation, until the end of 1939, was to provoke the mass exodus of as

---

On Prager, see Mali Eisenberg (Gotdiner), *Ed, maz'iq, meta'ed u-mantsiah: R. Moshe Prager ve-ha-Sho'ah, 1940–1984* (Witnessing, Protesting, Documenting and Commemorating: Moshe Prager and the Holocaust, 1940–1984). In Germany too Seraphim's pivotal role in the development of the conceptualization of the Nazi ghetto was still known in the beginning of the 1950s: in a 1957 article on the return to public life of Seraphim and cohorts, published in the mouthpiece of the West German Socialist Party (SPD) *Vorwärts*, the author defined Seraphim as "the theoretician of the ghetto policy"; Kurt Hirsch, "Die Restauration erobert unserer Hochschulen," *Vorwärts*, June 12, 1957, quoted in Hans-Christian Petersen, "Ein 'Judenforscher' danach – Zur Karriere Peter-Heinz Seraphims in Westdeutschland," p. 532.

[5] Serious preparations for the war that would break out in 1939 or 1940 began in April, with the focus on Poland; see Geoffrey P. Megargee, *Inside Hitler's High Command*, pp. 67ff.
[6] On Hinkel, see Alan Steinweis, "Hans Hinkel and German Jewry, 1933–1941."
[7] Hans Hinkel, *Judenviertel Europas: Die Juden zwischen Ostsee und schwarzem Meer*. The same ideas were reiterated by another author, Hermann Erich Seifert, in a popular book entitled *Der Jude an der Ostgrenze* [The Jew on the Eastern Border], published by the Central Publication Office of the Nazi Party in 1941. At least 50,000 copies of this book were printed and distributed (for this fact, see the copy in the Württembergische Landesbibliothek/Bibliothek für Zeitgeschichte; I thank my friend and colleague Prof. Dr. Gerhard Hirschfeld, director of the library, for sending me a copy of the book). The last pages of this book were devoted to the ghettos.

FIGURE 14. Pictures of an Eastern European Jewish "ghetto," published in Hans Hinkel, *Judenviertel Europas: Die Juden zwischen Ostsee und schwarzem Meer*, in 1939.

many Jews as possible from occupied Poland, chiefly to the Soviet Union. (Before the Soviets closed the border in late December, some 300,000 Jews escaped or fled across the River Bug, with the active encouragement of the German forces.) Still, it was clear from the outset that many Jews would remain in German-occupied territory. For this reason, from the very start of the occupation the SS and police (merged on September 27, 1939) hatched the idea of taking control of the Jewish communities and organizing them. With this in mind, beginning on September 6, while the fighting in Poland was still in progress, SS and police representatives set up Jewish "headships"[8] all over Poland to reorganize the Jewish communities. This policy was formulated in writing in the *Schnellbrief* that Heydrich sent to the Einsatzgruppen commanders on September 21, ostensibly to summarize the discussions among the heads of the SS departments and Einsatzgruppen commanders who met that day in Berlin.[9]

An entire section of this long note, with its minute details, was devoted to the "Jewish councils of elders" (*Jüdische Ältestenräte*) or "Jewish councils" (*Judenräte*). The word "ghetto," by contrast, came up only in passing, in the section on the Ältestenräte:

(5) The Councils of Elders in the concentration cities [*Konzentrierungsstädten*] are to be made responsible for the appropriate housing of Jews arriving from the countryside.

For reasons of general police security, the concentration of the Jews in the cities will probably call for regulations in these cities which will forbid their entry to certain quarters completely and that – but with due regard for economic requirements – they may, for instance, not *leave the ghetto*, nor leave their homes after a certain hour in the evening, etc.[10] [emphasis added]

The term "ghetto" (written in the original document without an "h"), therefore, was used here only incidentally, with no clear definition, as a cross between the old conservative connotation of the Middle Ages and Seraphim's notion. For clearly the sense is one of negation: the ghetto is the place where Jews will still be allowed to live after they have been forbidden to enter other neighborhoods. And, as the text continues, they will not be allowed to "leave the ghetto...after a certain hour in the

---

[8] The sociological term "headship" is used to distinguish administrative bodies that are appointed by a power outside a group and are committed as a matter of principle to the outside authority, as opposed to "leadership," which derives its standing and legitimacy from within the group and is consequently committed mainly to it. See Dan Michman, *Holocaust Historiography: A Jewish Perspective*, pp. 159–76.

[9] Dan Michman, "Why Did Heydrich Write the *Schnellbrief*? A Remark on the Reason and on Its Significance," *Yad Vashem Studies* 32 (2004), pp. 433–47.

[10] Documents of the International Tribunal at Nuremberg, PS-3363, in Arad et al., eds., *Documents on the Holocaust*, p. 175; my emphasis. The original German runs as follows: "Die Ältestenräte in den Konzentrierungsstädten sind verantwortlich zu machen für die geeignete Unterbringung der aus dem Lande zuziehenden Juden. Die Konzentrierung der Juden in den Städten wird wahrscheinlich aus allgemein sicherheitspolizeilichen Gründen Anordnungen in diesen Städten bedingen, daß den Juden bestimmte Stadtviertel überhaupt verboten werden, daß sie stets jedoch unter Berücksichtigung der wirtschaftlichen Notwendigkeiten – z.B. das Ghetto nicht verlassen, zu einer bestimmten Abendstunde nicht mehr ausgehen dürfen usw."

evening" – a revival of the pre-Emancipation practice of locking the Jewish Quarter at night.[11] But there is no mention of the physical enclosure of this ghetto and it is not presented as a tool or mechanism for achieving a certain purpose.

To supplement the careful phrasing of the order, we also have a note (*Vermerk*) of the meeting of September 21. This yields a different picture, especially with regard to the ghetto, underscoring the fact that the *Schnellbrief* was in fact drafted and written before the meeting. According to this note, Heydrich said:

> Jewry in the cities should be contained in the ghetto, to permit better control and, subsequently, their better removal. Along with this, it is urgent that the Jew as smallholder disappear from rural regions. This operation must be accomplished within the next three to four weeks.... The following comprehensive instructions were issued:
>
> 1. [Moving the] Jews into the cities as quickly as possible
> 2. Jews of the Reich to Poland
> 3. The remaining 30,000 gypsies also to Poland
> 4. Systematic removal of the Jews from the German territories on freight cars.[12]

As pointed out in Chapter 1, most scholars have seen this document, along with the *Schnellbrief*, as evidence that a clear plan to concentrate the Jews in ghettos of the type familiar to us from later years already

---

[11] Benjamin Ravid, "Curfew Time in the Ghetto of Venice."

[12] "Das Judentum ist in den Städten im Getto zusammenzufassen, um eine bessere Kontrollmöglichkeit und später Abschubmöglichkeit zu haben. Hierbei vordringlich ist, daß der Jude als Kleinsiedler vom Land verschwindet. Diese Aktion muß innerhalb der nächsten 3 bis 4 Wochen durchgeführt sein. Sofern der Jude auf dem Land Händler ist, ist mit der Wehrmacht zu klären, wie weit diese jüdischen Händler zur Bedarfsdeckung der Truppe noch an Ort und Stelle verbleiben müssen. Folgende zusammenfassende Anordnung wurde erteilt:

"1. Juden so schnell wie möglich in die Städte,
"2. Juden aus dem Reich nach Polen,
"3. Die restlichen 30.000 Zigeuner auch nach Polen,
"4. Systematische Ausschickung der Juden aus dem deutschen Gebieten mit Güterzügen."

Minutes of the meeting of the heads of SS departments and Einsatzgruppen commanders, September 21, 1939, Yad Vashem Archives TR 3/983. For a facsimile of the document see Michman, "Why Did Heydrich Write the *Schnellbrief*?" facing p. 441.

Christopher Browning, in a recent article, "Before the 'Final Solution': Nazi Ghettoization Policy in Poland (1940–1941)," p. 4, erroneously attributes the first sentence quoted here to the *Schnellbrief*. I have modified the standard English translation of the first phrase for reasons of linguistic accuracy.

existed at this time; that is, they read into the document a situation that did not develop until later. As already noted, we do not have any documents that attest to preparations for the establishment of ghettos, as opposed to the installation of Judenräte, an idea that had already emerged. What is more, an objective reading of the minutes of the meeting reveals that it refers to the Jews of Poland under two headings: the Jews in the cities and the Jews in the rural districts. Concentrating the Jews in "the ghetto" (note the definite article – the ghetto that already exists) was the measure recommended for the Jews in the cities. We cannot fail to see that the minutes depend on the older sense of "ghetto," as employed by Seraphim. An explanation of what was meant by the term "ghetto" and how it should be implemented would otherwise have been required (paralleling the details that the *Schnellbrief* does provide concerning the establishment of the Ältestenräte/Judenräte), and there is none of that here. The instruction was, accordingly, to concentrate all the Jews in the medium-size towns and large cities in "the ghettos" (i.e., largely Jewish neighborhoods) that already existed there, as a temporary measure.

This operation was to be completed within a month, but in fact the instruction remained a dead letter, except for a few harbingers in Warsaw and Piotrków-Trybunalski (as we shall see). The question – a crucial question indeed, if we assign to the meeting of September 21 foundational importance in the history of Nazi anti-Jewish policy in general and of that adopted in Poland in particular – is why the instruction to concentrate Jews in three to four weeks was not carried out. There is no clear answer to this (though part of the answer may lie in the competition among the various German organs of government, which could not coordinate fully among themselves, but this requires deeper study). We may take a hint from the very different degrees of importance assigned to concentrating Jews in "the ghetto" in the policy proposals that can be extracted from the two documents discussed here.[13] In the *Schnellbrief*, an official document that was printed and circulated and therefore carries more weight,[14] concentrating the Jews in ghettos is a marginal issue. It is given much more

---

[13] It is important to remember that we are not dealing with two documents about the establishment of new ghettos, but about the concentration and isolation of the Jews in existing ghettos.

[14] This is clear not only because the *Schnellbrief* is carefully written, but also because the topic of the Judenräte occupies a central place in it, whereas Judenräte are not even mentioned in the minutes of the meeting, even though they were established in many places.

importance in the note of the meeting, which summarizes the main points of the oral discussion, but the objective of concentrating the Jews in ghettos is formulated as a method for the cities, where ghettos already existed, and is assigned a specific time frame (which soon proved to be unrealistic). All of this indicates that the idea of restricting the Jews to "their" ghettos was indeed raised and discussed at the meeting, and perhaps in vigorous terms; but the idea was fairly fluid and may have been a response to the reactions of the units in the field to their encounter with the Polish Jews. This is supported also by a short reference to the "ghetto idea" (*Ghetto-Gedanke*) by *Generaloberst* Walther von Brauchitsch, the army commander-in-chief (*Oberbefehlshaber des Heeres*) who met with Hitler on September 20, one day before Heydrich's meeting with the Einsatzgruppen commanders, and discussed several issues regarding the future of Poland. According to a note in the diary of Franz Halder (the army chief of staff), who was present, the Jewish question was touched upon, in the context of possible population movements: "Ghetto idea [*Ghetto-Gedanke*] exists in broad outline; details are not yet ready; economic needs are prime considerations."[15] What exactly was meant by "Ghetto-Gedanke"? We may assume that the discussion of this issue by Heydrich and the Einsatzgruppen commanders on the following day reflected the contents of the Hitler-Brauchitsch exchange of ideas; namely, that "something" had to be done about the problem of the existing ghettos. The wording of the *Schnellbrief*, "but always with due regard for economic requirements" (*stets jedoch unter Berücksichtigung der wirtschaftlichen Notwendigkeiten*), is almost identical to the second half of the clause in the report of the Hitler-Brauchitsch conversation.[16] Thus initially the thinking about ghettos was not clear. Their establishment was not a calculated administrative measure, as many scholars have thought; economic needs predominated. In any case, an unbiased reading both of the *Schnellbrief* and of the note, against the background of the earlier uses of the word "ghetto" already described, does not support interpreting

---

[15] "Ghetto-Gedanke besteht im großen; im einzelnen noch nicht klarliegend. Berücksichtigung der Wirtschaftsbelange vorweg": in Hans-Adolf Jacobsen, ed., *Generaloberst Halder. Kriegstagebuch*, vol. 1, p. 81; the translation of *Ghetto-Gedanke* as "Ghetto plan" in the English edition is incorrect: see Charles Burdick and Hans-Adolph Jacobsen, eds., *The Halder War Diary 1939–1942*, p. 59. This is also quoted by Klaus-Michael Mallmann, Jochen Böhler, and Jürgen Matthäus, *Einsatzgruppen in Polen. Darstellung und Dokumentation*, p. 61.

[16] An extensive discussion of why this formulation should not be interpreted as a directive by Hitler to plan the establishment of ghettos is in Chapter 12.

The Invasion of Poland and the "Classic" Ghettos

these documents as directives to establish ghettos – as Hilberg, Bauer, and many other scholars have done.[17]

Nevertheless, the September 21 meeting does seem to have allowed a new sense to be added to the term "ghetto" during these weeks. For at least some SS officials, a ghetto was henceforth a place for the forced concentration of the Jews that was initiated by the Germans themselves. This can be found in the operation to deport the Jews from Vienna and from Ostrawa (in the Protectorate of Bohemia and Moravia) to the Nisko district in Poland, known as the Nisko or Lublin Reserve (*Reservat Lublin*) Operation. The person who was to implement this campaign was Adolf Eichmann.[18] On various occasions the future Jewish colony in this region was referred to as the *Reichsghetto* (by Heydrich) and as the Lublin Jewish Ghetto (*Lubliner Juden-Ghetto*) (by Albrecht Haushofer, an official of the Information Department of the Foreign Ministry), even though it was not a densely populated neighborhood inside a city.[19] For the time being, however, this meaning of "ghetto" would be employed only on the margins.

Goebbels, dominated by his welter of anti-Semitic stereotypes, had not yet internalized this minor change. At that time he employed "ghetto" in Seraphim's sense, without serious action to force Jews into one. In October 1939 Goebbels was busy promoting the idea of the anti-Semitic "documentary" film *Der ewige Jude* [The Eternal Jew]. On October 4, the day the Warsaw Judenrat was instituted, he wrote in his diary: "Discussed a ghetto film with Hippler and Taubert; the material for it is now being shot in Poland. It should become a first-rate propaganda film."[20] Goebbels again referred to a *Ghettofilm* in his diary on October 17.[21]

---

[17] This was discussed in Chapter 1.
[18] Christopher R. Browning, with contributions by Jürgen Matthäus, *The Origins of the Final Solution: The Evolution of Nazi Jewish Policy, September 1939–March 1942*, pp. 36–43.
[19] Dieter Pohl, *Von der "Judenpolitik" zum Judenmord: Der Distrikt Lublin des Generalgouvernements 1939–1944*, p. 27 and n78; Götz Aly, *"Final Solution": Nazi Population Policy and the Murder of the European Jews*, p. 23 (for the original German version, see Götz Aly, *"Endlösung": Völkerverschiebung und der Mord an den europäischen Juden*, p. 44); Peter Longerich, *Politik der Vernichtung: Eine Gesamtdarstellung der nationalsozialistischen Judenverfolgung*, p. 261.
[20] Joseph Goebbels, *Die Tagebücher von Joseph Goebbels: Sämtliche Fragmenten*, p. 140; the English translation here is from Saul Friedländer, *Nazi Germany and the Jews 1939–1945*, p. 21.
[21] Goebbels, *Tagebücher*, I-7, p. 157; Friedländer, *Nazi Germany and the Jews 1939–1945*, p. 21.

And on November 2 Goebbels visited Łódź and noted in his diary that he drove "through the Ghetto"; he added:

We get out and inspect everything thoroughly. It is indescribable. These are no longer human beings, they are animals. For this reason, our task is no longer humanitarian but surgical. Steps must be taken here, and they must be radical ones, make no mistake.[22]

In a similar vein, the word "ghetto" is used incidentally, in an internal document of the Wehrmacht unit that occupied Przemyśl, to refer to the Jewish quarter on the left bank of the San: "*in dem das eigentliche Ghetto liegt*" (in which the real ghetto is situated).[23] Thus, although Germans were attaching different senses to the term in this period, these were all very close to one another; not one of them had the meaning of an enclosed Jewish district established as part of a comprehensive and systematic plan.

In his studies of the path that led to the Final Solution, Christopher Browning emphasized that initiatives in the field were behind the creation of the ghettos in Poland. He interpreted the policy of ghettoization as the result of two processes: on the one hand, the success of the measures to concentrate the Jews in the large cities as a temporary expedient until the Final Aim (*Endziel*, which was referred to in the *Schnellbrief*) could be achieved, after which it would be possible to transfer the Jews to their ultimate destination; on the other hand, the failure to implement that Final Aim, which led to a prolongation of the provisional measures and forced commanders in the field to find some way to deal with the unanticipated situation. To explain the emergence of the ghettos, Browning alleged constraints on the ground and inferred the policy on this matter from

---

[22] Goebbels, *Tagebücher*, p. 167.
[23] The text runs as follows:

"24.9.1939

"Przemysl

"Entwurf zu einer Dienstanweisung zur Handhabung des Sperrdienstes am San.

"1.) Die Trennung der Stadt durch den San in einen rechten Stadtteil, der die gesamten lebenswichtigen Betriebe enthält und einem [sic] linken Teil, der vom Geschäftsverkehr stark entblößt in Wasser und Licht vom rechten Stadtteil abhängig ist, in dem das eigentliche Ghetto liegt, macht es unmöglich, den Verkehr in der Übergangszeit bis zur Grenzziehung vollständig zu unterbinden."

BA-MA, RH24-18/5 XVIII. Armeekorps, Abt. Ia, Anlagen zum KTB Nr. 2, 14.09.–22.10.1939, Bd.3: Operationsbefehle 14.09.– 06.10.1939 [S.199]. I would like to thank Dr. Jochen Böhler of the German Historical Institute in Warsaw for bringing this document to my attention.

The Invasion of Poland and the "Classic" Ghettos

a number of large ghettos, mainly those in Łódź (he maintains that the policy of ghettoization actually began in the Warthegau in the spring of 1940) and Warsaw, as well as the later ghettos in the Krakow, Radom, and Lublin districts.[24] He accepts the use of the term "ghetto" in the *Schnellbrief* as something new, without raising the linguistic problem of its use with a later meaning that did not emerge until 1940 and 1941, and ignores the prior history of the term. Nor does he attribute any weight to the fact, commonly accepted by scholars, that the first ghetto to be established was in Piotrków-Trybunalski, a place that does not satisfy the explanation he proposes.

To be precise, however, the question of concentrating the Jews in the *existing* urban ghettos – in the densely populated Jewish neighborhoods that existed before the Nazi invasion of Poland – is mentioned in Heydrich's September 21 orders to the Einsatzgruppen commanders; and this measure was *not* implemented in the field, certainly not in the critical period he specified (within three to four weeks). What is more, the daily reports submitted by the Einsatzgruppen after September 21 do not disclose any special efforts on their part to establish ghettos. For example, a report for September 27, concerning *Einsatzgruppe III*, headed by Dr. Hans Fischer and with headquarters in Łódź, states that "the action against the Jews is being carried out according to plan" (*Die Aktion gegen die Juden wird planmäßig durchgeführt*) – but the steps taken do not include forcing Jews into a ghetto.[25] Later, when the grandiose plan of the "Final Aim" – and it makes no difference what was meant by this term[26] – evaporated and many Jews remained in the small towns, contrary to Heydrich's orders, did the anti-Jewish policy itself require the establishment of ghettos? According to Browning – and here I fully agree with him – a ghetto was not necessarily the best answer to the newly created problem of homeless and uprooted Jews, nor to the problem of the Jews in the cities. The object could have been achieved just as well by controlling the Jewish communities through Judenräte. Indeed, from the very

---

[24] Christopher R. Browning, *The Path to Genocide: Essays on Launching the Final Solution*, pp. 28–56; Browning, *The Origins of the Final Solution*, pp. 111–37.
[25] "Betrifft: Unternehmen Tannenberg. Hier: Tagesbericht für die Zeit vom 26.9.39 1200 Uhr, bis 27.9.39 1200 Uhr," BAB R58 7002, p. 49. On Fischer and Einsatzgruppe III, see: Mallmann, Böhler, and Matthäus, *Einsatzgruppen in Polen*, pp. 28–30, 50–1.
[26] A protracted debate was waged in the literature as to the meaning of the expression "Final Aim." Today it is clear that it was not identical with the later "Final Solution" nor was the latter implicit in it. But scholars still do not agree as to the precise meaning intended by the authors of the document.

first days after the conquest of Poland the SS promoted their establishment. According to the *Schnellbrief*, this measure was more important than ghettos.[27] Such a model – without the establishment of ghettos – was adopted elsewhere in Europe: in Germany itself, in Austria, and in the Protectorate, before 1939; and in the Netherlands, Belgium, and other countries in subsequent years. In fact, forcing the Jews into ghettos, as was done later, created a host of new problems (interference with economic structures and the urban fabric, the need to establish new surveillance and control mechanisms, the threat of epidemics, etc.). In simple and rational terms of utility – Browning emphasizes (and rightly so) the debate among German administrators that pitted the "productionist" group, who wanted to exploit the ghetto for various productive ends, against those who wished to liquidate the Jews by starvation (he calls them the "attritionists")[28] – setting up ghettos was clearly pointless. Given that we can find no traces of a directive to establish them issued by higher authority, we must agree with Browning and others that the emergence of the ghettos was a "grassroots" phenomenon. But the causes are not those he cites. The true causes must explain (1) the protracted period over which ghettos were established in Poland, (2) the fact – which Browning and others hardly touch on (though Friedman noted it long ago) – that even in Poland ghettos were not set up everywhere, and (3) the manner in which ghettos were set up and where they were located in the cities.[29]

The sources available to us indicate, I believe, that we should associate the regime's encouragement of initiatives in the field, as long as those initiatives served the basic goals, with the psychological aspect of the physical, face-to-face encounter with the *Ostjudentum* or "Jews of the East," namely, the Eastern European Jews. We must emphasize that "anti-Semitism" was not a bare fact but a set of dynamic images that shaped the thoughts of policymakers at all levels and that influenced their feelings and behavior. Gutman discussed this point at length in his book, *The Jews of Warsaw*, quoting Jewish sources about the experiences of Jews in general and especially of the "typical Jews" who corresponded to the anti-Semitic stereotype.[30] One point to which we must pay special attention is that the German occupation forces were directly exposed, for the first time, to the

---

[27] On this, see at length Michman, "Why Did Heydrich Write the *Schnellbrief*?"
[28] Browning, *The Origins of the Final Solution*, pp. 138–68.
[29] Friedman, "The Jewish Ghettos of the Nazi Era," p. 71; David Silberklang, "Ha-Sho'ah bimhoz Lublin" (The Holocaust in the Lublin District of Poland), p. 93.
[30] Israel Gutman, *The Jews of Warsaw*, pp. 8–9, 11–12.

The Invasion of Poland and the "Classic" Ghettos 73

"Jewish ghetto" as described by Seraphim and as subsequently discussed in various circles, particularly the SS, during the year before the invasion. The "ghetto Jews" with their "typical appearance" (that is, the one coinciding with the Nazi caricature) disgusted and repelled them.[31] An article in the SS paper *Das Schwarze Korps* refers to them, for example, as the "scum of the ghetto";[32] and there were many similar expressions,[33] frequently employed by soldiers in the field. Jochen Böhler, in his recent study of the Wehrmacht and its conduct during the Polish campaign, offers a long string of disparaging terms from the first weeks of the occupation, after the soldiers' initial encounter with the Jews of Poland: "Jewish peril" (*Judengefahr* – a battalion commander's expression about the Jews of Bilgoraj); "a nest of Jews in the full sense of the word... a colony of filth" (*ausgesprochener Judennest... Dreckbudenkolonie* – referring to Raciąż); "we visited... the Jewish quarter [of Krakow], where we truly became aware of the extent to which the racial law instituted by our Führer is important and essential" (*Besichtigt wurde... das Judenviertel, wo uns so richtig zu Bewusstsein kam, wie überaus wichtig und notwendig das von unserem Führer geschaffene Rassengesetz ist*); "what arouses attention is the large number of repulsive characters of Ostjuden; their appearance is the best visual education that our people could receive on the Jewish question" (*auffallend ist die große Zahl widerlichster Typen von Ostjuden; ihre Erscheinungen sind der beste Anschauungsunterricht, den unsere Leute in der Judenfrage haben können*); "a horrid Jewish hole" (*ein fürchterliches Judenkaff*); "Polish Jews, greasy and filthy" (*polnische Juden, schmierig und dreckig*); and so on.[34] The *Wochenschau* (one of

---

[31] This has also been emphasized by Dieter Pohl and Jürgen Matthäus: Pohl, *Von der "Judenpolitik" zum Judenmord*, pp. 17–20; Jürgen Matthäus, "Die 'Judenfrage' als Schulungsthema von SS und Polizei: 'Inneres Erlebnis' und Handlungslegitimation," p. 59.

[32] "Auswurf der Ghettos," *Das Schwarze Korps*, May 2, 1940.

[33] For other examples see, for instance, Friedman, "The Jewish Ghettos of the Nazi Era," pp. 67–8.

[34] Böhler, *Auftakt zum Vernichtungskrieg*, pp. 46–8, and nn178, 181, 182, 190, and 194. Similar expressions are cited by Markus Roth, *Herrenmenschen. Die deutschen Kreishauptleute im besetzten Polen – Karrierewege, Herrschaftspraxis und Nachgeschichte*; Roth, "The County Chiefs (Kreishauptleute) in the General Government Before and After 1945." For more on the contact between German security forces and Polish Jews, see Bogdan Musial, *Deutsche Zivilverwaltung und Judenverfolgung im Generalgouvernement: Eine Fallstudie zum Distrikt Lublin 1939–1944*, pp. 183–8. On Jews as depicted in the photographs taken by German military personnel in the East, see Judith Levin and Daniel Uziel, "Ordinary Men, Extraordinary Photos," *Yad Vashem Studies* 26 (1998), pp. 265–93.

the weekly newsreels screened throughout Germany) of September 14, that is, a week before the meeting of the Einsatzgruppen commanders and the issuing of the *Schnellbrief*, depicted "Jewish types in the Polish Ghetto."[35] In the *Wochenschau* of the following week the pictures showing "typical" Jews were accompanied by the comment that "in the ghettos of the occupied cities the Ostjuden feel themselves at their best" (*In den Ghettos der besetzten Städte sind die Ostjuden bei bester Laune*).[36] And at the beginning of October German soldiers in Poland were ordered by the Propaganda Ministry to take pictures of all types of Jews, because "this material will serve our [purpose of] internal and external political antisemitic enlightening."[37]

It is no wonder that Goebbels and his propaganda teams raced to photograph the "phenomenon" for a movie. But unlike the propaganda people, who wanted to view the phenomenon and record it for posterity, the administrators in the field were dealing with it on a practical level, and they had to come up with "solutions" appropriate to the ideological context in which they were working. In Poland, the danger to which Heydrich had registered his opposition a year earlier in Germany – the *emergence* of a ghetto – did not exist. There *were* ghettos in Poland already. And if Seraphim had demonstrated that the Eastern European Jewish ghetto in the large cities and mid-size towns was the source of the Jews' power and hence posed a threat to the Germans, and that it was the nucleus from which the cancerous metastases spread to the rest of those cities, then one logical answer might be to return the Jews who lived in those cancerous metastases to the ghetto and to draw its boundaries. In the largest places, in particular, this boundary should be implemented physically, by means of a wall or fence. It is important to emphasize here that, conceptually speaking, the ghettos were not *established* as some new ex nihilo creation, because – as said – ghettos, as the Germans understood them, already existed and were the hallmark of Eastern European Jewry. The Germans merely *demarcated their boundaries* and forced those Jews who

---

[35] *Wochenschau* of September 14, 1939, Ufa Tonwoche 471, Tobis-WS 38, 1939, BA-FA, Koblenz.

[36] *Wochenschau* of September 21, 1939, Ufa Tonwoche 472, Tobis-WS 39, 1939, BA-FA.

[37] "Aus Warschau und aus dem ganzen besetzten Gebiet nach Möglichkeit in grösserem Umfange als bisher Filmaufnahmen von Judentypen aller Art, und zwar sowohl Charakterstudien als auch Juden beim Arbeitseinsatz. Dieses Material soll zur Verstärkung unserer inner- und außenpolitischen antisemitischen Aufklärung dienen" ("Propagandaanweisung des Reichspropaganda-Ministers für den 2. Oktober 1939," BA-MA, RW4/V24, Teil 1).

The Invasion of Poland and the "Classic" Ghettos

had moved elsewhere in the city to return "home." This idea is clearly expressed in a remark made in November 1939 by Heinrich Himmler, who had been appointed Reichskommissar for the Strengthening of the German People (*Reichskommissar für die Festigung deutschen Volkstums*) in October: "The time has come to drive this rabble into ghettos, and then epidemics will erupt and they'll all croak" (*Es wird höchste Zeit, daß dieses Gesindel zusammengetrieben wird, in Ghettos, und dann schleppt Seuchen hinein und laßt sie krepieren*).[38] In theory, of course, precisely the opposite course could have been taken in order to deal with this "peril": the expulsion of the Jews *from* their ghettos. This is indeed what Hans Frank, the governor-general of occupied Poland, proposed in April 1940, when the preparations to establish the Łódź ghetto in the Warthegau were in high gear. At a meeting of the senior echelons of the *Generalgouvernement* (General-Government), Frank proposed removing 50,000 Jews from Krakow and dispersing them throughout the *Generalgouvernement*; "Then the ghetto [i.e., in the old sense – the Jewish quarter of Krakow] will be cleansed and it will be possible to establish pure German neighborhoods in which one can breathe German air."[39]

This internal logic helps us to understand the emergence, during the last three months of 1939, of the first initiatives to set up ghettos. The harbinger of such a different and proactive approach seems to have been Warsaw, which had the largest concentration of Jews in Poland and occupied pride of place in Seraphim's book.[40] In a report that Lothar Beutel, the commander of *Einsatzgruppe IV*, dispatched to Berlin on October 6, 1939, concerning the measures he had taken to organize the Jews of Warsaw after the capture of the city, he noted that in accordance with the directives of the Reichsführer SS and head of the German Police – that is, he credited the directive to Himmler, rather than Heydrich, who was

---

[38] Himmler's remarks, as recorded by an army officer and quoted in his memoirs, cited by Pohl, *"Judenpolitik" zum Judenmord*, p. 49. In the Third Reich, the title *Reichskommissar* was given to administrative positions with special tasks, mostly ideological.

[39] "Er [Frank] beabsichtige deshalb, die Stadt Krakau bis zum 1. November 1940, soweit irgend möglich, judenfrei zu machen und eine große Aussiedlungsaktion der Juden in Angriff zu nehmen, und zwar mit der Begründung, daß es absolut unerträglich sei, wenn in einer Stadt, der der Führer die hohe Ehre zuteil werden lasse, der Sitz einer hohen Reichsbehörde zu sein, Tausende und Abertausende von Juden herumschlichen und Wohnungen inne hätte.... Das Ghetto werde dann gesäubert werden, und es werde möglich sein, saubere deutsche Wohnsiedlungen zu errichten, in denen man eine deutsche Luft atmen könne": Werner Präg and Wolfgang Jacobmeyer, *Das Diensttagebuch des deutschen Generalgouverneurs in Polen 1939–1945*, p. 165 (entry of April 12, 1940).

[40] Seraphim, *Das Judentum*, p. 357.

in fact the signatory of the *Schnellbrief* – a 24-member Jewish Ältestenrat had been set up and made responsible for implementing all orders issued by the Einsatzgruppe, including, he emphasized, the submission of "its own proposals for collecting the Jews in ghettos" (*eigene Vorschläge für die Judenerfassung in Ghettos*: note the plural).[41] Although nothing in his report provides any clear idea of what these ghettos are, the general impression is that they were the traditionally Jewish neighborhoods in Warsaw to which all other Warsaw Jews would be relocated. At a meeting in Krakow on October 7 the governor of the Warsaw district, Dr. Ludwig Fischer, floated the idea of extending this concept to other places as well.[42] At the Warsaw Judenrat meeting on Saturday, November 4, SS officer Dr. Rudolf Batz read out an order in the name of the military commandant of the city, Karl Ulrich von Neumann-Neurode, instructing the Jews to move to certain streets in the old Jewish quarter (the ghetto, according to Seraphim's concept) within three days.[43] In any case, and perhaps because of lobbying by the Jews, though there is no proof of this, implementation of this order in Warsaw was deferred but not canceled.[44] Work on various plans for the location and size of the ghetto in Warsaw continued from January 1940 until it was actually sealed off in November of that year. All the justifications for establishing the ghetto that were advanced on various occasions during these months by Hans Frank, Ludwig Fischer, and the local expert on settlement affairs, Waldemar Schön – the danger posed by the Jews as carriers of disease germs, the political and moral importance (for the racial ideology) of isolating them, and the needs of economic self-defense – are post-factum excuses and not authentic reasons anchored in the actual situation. However, they reflect an internalization of Seraphim's arguments about the baneful influence – on politics, health, and sanitation – that Jews exerted on their surroundings when they were dispersed and could move about freely outside their center.[45] All these arguments come together in Frank's statement that the

---

[41] H. von Krannhals, ed., *Die Berichte der Einsatzgruppen der Sicherheitspolizei in Polenfeldzug 1939 (1.9.1939–31.10.1939)*, pp. 212–13 (typewritten manuscript, copy in the Institut für Zeitgeschichte, Munich). On Beutel, see Wildt, *Generation des Unbedingten*, pp. 931–2.

[42] Friedman, "The Jewish Ghettos of the Nazi Era," p. 70; he quotes from Hans Frank's diary (p. 83n68).

[43] Gutman, *The Jews of Warsaw*, p. 48.

[44] Gutman, *The Jews of Warsaw*, pp. 49–50.

[45] Gutman, *The Jews of Warsaw*, pp. 53–4; Klaus-Peter Friedrich, "Rassistische Seuchenprävention als Voraussetzung nationalsozialistischer Vernichtungspolitik: Vom Warschauer 'Seuchensperrengebiet' zu den 'Getto'-Mauern (1939/40)," pp. 609–36; for

The Invasion of Poland and the "Classic" Ghettos 77

Warsaw ghetto "will be sealed, above all because it has been determined that the danger posed by 500,000 Jews is so great that one must prevent the possibility of their moving about [freely]."[46] Rank-and-file Germans seem to have clearly understood that the ghetto was "a reaction" to some "danger." In a letter written by a German soldier to his family, sent on November 1, 1940, we read: "Now they are shoving all of the Jews into a district and sealing them in with a wall. From now on they can muddle along as much as they want."[47]

To the best of our knowledge, the first true ghetto was established in Piotrków-Trybunalski (Kielce Province) in central Poland.[48] This town, whose 15,000 Jews were 27 percent of its population, was also on

Schön's remarks, see Arad et al., eds., *Documents on the Holocaust*, p. 225. Browning (*The Origins of the Final Solution*, p. 123) quotes the commissar for the Warsaw ghetto, Heinz Auerswald: "Decisive for it [ghettoization] was first of all the desire to segregate the Jews from the Aryan environment for general political and ideological reasons" (Massgebend dafür war in erster Linie der Wunsch, die Juden aus allgemeinen politischen und weltanschaulichen Gründen von der arischen Umwelt abzusondern). On Dr. Fischer's post-factum explanations for the establishment of the Warsaw ghetto, see Präg and Jacobmeyer, *Das Diensttagebuch*, p. 343 (April 3, 1941). It seems, however, that the health reason/pretext for containing the Jews in ghettos was the prevalent one. In the widely disseminated booklet *Der Jude an der Ostgrenze*, its author Seifert summarized the measures taken during the first period of the occupation in Poland, with special attention to the ghettoization process. He explained (p. 84) that "the reason was simply to purify the worst epidemical flock in the ghettos of the Polish cities. It can be clearly proved that in almost all cases of widespread epidemics in Poland, the Jew was the most dangerous spreader. This explains why, still in early 1940 in ghettos everywhere, there were blocked areas, to which the entrance of Germans and Poles was strictly forbidden because of the danger of epidemics" (es ging einfach darum, die schlimmsten Seuchenherde in den Ghettos der polnischen Städte zu säubern. Nachweisbar ist bei fast allen großen Volksseuchen in Polen der Jude der gefährlichste Verbreiter gewesen. So ist es zu verstehen, daß noch im Frühjahr 1940 in den Ghettos überall Absperrgebiete bestanden, daß das Betreten ganzer Häuserblocks Deutschen und Polen wegen Seuchengefahr strengstens verboten war) (*Der Jude an der Ostgrenze*, p. 84).

46 "... daß in Warschau das Ghetto geschlossen wird, vor allem weil festgestellt ist, daß die Gefahr von den 500,000 Juden so groß ist, daß die Möglichkeit des Herumtreibens unterbunden werden muß": Präg and Jacobmeyer, *Das Diensttagebuch*, p. 281 (September 12, 1940); quoted in Leon Poliakov and Josef Wulf, *Das Dritte Reich und die Juden: Dokumente und Aufsätze*, p. 179.
47 "Die Juden wurden jetzt alle in einem Viertel zusammengesprecht und mit einer Mauer eingeschlossen. Da können sie dann wurschteln wie sie wollen": Walter Manoschek, ed., *"Es gibt nur eines für Das Judentum: Vernichtung" – Das Judenbild in deutschen Soldatenbriefen 1939–1944*, p. 18.
48 Friedman, "The Jewish Ghettos of the Nazi Era," p. 72 (he calls it "an experimental ghetto"). See also Alina Skibińska and Jakub Petelewicz, "The Participation of Poles in Crimes Against Jews in the Świetokrzyskie Region," p. 10n13. This contradicts Browning's assertion that the first ghetto was established in the Wartheland.

FIGURE 15. A street sign from the Jewish quarter in Warsaw (before the establishment of the ghetto), in the summer of 1940, indicates that the area beyond is a "Plague-restricted Area" and that entrance (for non-Jews) to the area was forbidden.

Seraphim's list of the "mid-sized cities" with a large concentration of Jews.[49] Nevertheless, with regard to the size of this Jewish community and the number of refugees who had poured into it, its situation was very different from Warsaw's; and it was not near the metropolis. This initiative to establish a ghetto paralleling the initiative in Warsaw means that we cannot accept a historical explanation based exclusively on the situation in the capital. On October 8, 1939, the German-appointed mayor (*Oberbürgermeister*) of Piotrków-Trybunalski, Hans Drexel, issued an order to Rabbi Moshe Chaim Lau, the first elder of the Jews (appointed

[49] Seraphim, *Das Judentum*, p. 717.

The Invasion of Poland and the "Classic" Ghettos

already on September 11), requiring the local Jews to concentrate in a ghetto; Drexel referred to a "Jewish residential quarter" (*Jüdisches Wohnviertel*) – a term often to be used as a synonym for "ghetto." Three weeks later, on October 28, signs bearing the German word "*Getto*" were posted around the designated neighborhood.[50] Although some 28,000 Jews were crowded into this area (meaning that along with local Jews and refugees, Jews from the surrounding countryside were also brought to Piotrków), enforcement of the order was incomplete. Many Poles continued to live in the "ghetto" or to run businesses there until the spring of 1942. It was also several months after the posting of the signs before most of the Jews had been resettled there, and a few Jews continued to live outside the ghetto until its liquidation.[51] This shows that the originators of this project did not have a clear-cut plan. No comprehensive study of this first test case has been conducted to date, however, an omission that indicates the extent to which the study of Holocaust-era ghettos has been based on erroneous generalizations rather than on an empirical approach to history. Following Piotrków-Trybunalski, another ghetto was established in Kielce Province on December 20, 1939, in Radomsko.[52] Ghettos were also established in seven other medium-size towns during the first few months of 1940.[53]

In the Wartheland, talk about the establishment of a ghetto in Łódź had begun some weeks earlier, in December 1939. The most detailed treatment of the concept and practice of ghettos from the early days of this phenomenon seems to be a confidential note, dated December 10, 1939, from Friedrich Uebelhör, the official in charge of the Kalisz district, in which Łódź is located, to Arthur Greiser, the governor (*Reichsstatthalter*) of the Wartheland; to the NSDAP of the Łódź district; to the municipal administration of Łódź; to the local police authorities; as well as to

---

[50] Naphtali Lau-Lavie, *Balaam's Prophecy*, pp. 54–5.
[51] "Piotrków-Trybunalski," in Danuta Dąmbrowska and Abraham Wein, eds., *Pinkas ha-Kehillot: Poland*, vol. 1, *The Communities of Łódź and Its Region*, pp. 194–5. For a description of the ghetto, which contains many inaccuracies but also much useful information, see William Samelson, "Piotrków-Trybunalski: My Ancestral Home."
[52] "Radomsko," in Dąmbrowska and Wein, *Pinkas ha-Kehillot: Poland*, vol. 1, *The Communities of Łódź and Its Region*, p. 251.
[53] Most of the ghettos in this district (22) were established in 1941; another six were established in 1942, though these were already a different type of ghetto (see the discussion in Chapter 11). It is important to note that "in many areas, especially in the countryside and in small towns where the Jewish population was scattered throughout the area, no ghettos were established": Skibińska and Petelewicz, "The Świetokrzyskie Region," p. 10n13.

several economic institutions. It is entitled "Construction of a Ghetto in Łódź" (*Bildung eines Gettos in der Stadt Lodsch*). The use of the active term "construction" indicates that some action was contemplated. Uebelhör reported that because the immediate expulsion of the city's Jews, whom he estimated to number around 320,000, was impossible, the possibility of "collect[ing] all the Jews in a closed ghetto" had been investigated. "Thorough investigations by all offices concerned" had led to the conclusion that "it is impossible."[54] Consequently, it had been decided to concentrate all of the Jews living north of a particular line (that of Listopada/Pommerschestrasse) into a closed ghetto: "Firstly, an area around the Freiheitsplatz, required for the establishment of a German power center, will be cleansed of Jews; and, secondly, the northern part of the city, which is inhabited almost exclusively by Jews, will be included in the ghetto." Jews who were fit for work and who lived outside this area would be employed in labor battalions and housed in barracks under guard. Certain preliminary steps were required to make it possible to seal off the ghetto in a single move, by means of guards and physical barriers. "A Jewish autonomous administration will be set up immediately in the ghetto, consisting of the Jewish Elder [*Judenältester*] and a much enlarged Community Council." In conclusion, Uebelhör noted that

creation of the ghetto is, of course, only a temporary measure. I reserve to myself the decision concerning the times and the means by which the ghetto and with it the city of Łódź will be cleansed of Jews. The final aim [*Endziel*] must in any case be the total cauterization of this plague spot.[55]

Despite Uebelhör's vigorous boast ("I reserve the decision to myself"), a future decision was not his alone to make; but, as far as can be determined, the decision to establish a ghetto in Łódź at that time was indeed

---

[54] "Eingehende Untersuchungen aller in Frage kommenden Dienststellen haben ergeben, dass eine Zusammenfassung sämtlicher Juden in einem geschlossenen Ghetto *nicht moeglich ist*." Note that the translation in Arad et al., eds., *Documents on the Holocaust*, p. 192, erroneously reads the opposite: "it is possible ... "!

[55] "Die Erstellung des Ghettos ist selbstverstaendlich nur eine Uebergangsmassnahme. Zu welchen Zeitpunkten und mit welchen Mitteln das Ghetto und damit die Stadt Lodsch von Juden gesaeubert wird, behalte ich mir vor. Endziel muss jedenfalls sein, dass wir diese Pestbeule restlos ausbrennen." For an English version (abridged) of the document, see Arad et al., eds., *Documents on the Holocaust*, pp. 192–4 (but see my remark in the previous note). The original German text (also abridged) is cited in Isaiah Trunk, *Lodzsher geto: a historishe un sotsyologishe shtudie mit dokumentn, tabeles un mape*, pp. 11–14; a (different) English translation of the full document is in Trunk, *Łódź Ghetto: A History*, pp. 19–21.

his.[56] The actual restriction of the Jews of Łódź to a ghetto took a number of months and was delayed by the construction of the wall, which took some time. In the meantime, other ghettos were established in the Wartheland in Tulisków, in January 1940; in Pabianice, in February; and in Brzeziny, on April 28, 1940. The Kutno ghetto was inaugurated several weeks after the one in Łódź, on June 16, 1940 (the eve of Shavuot 5700).[57] In Łódź itself the Jews were concentrated in a ghetto between February and May. The ghetto was sealed off officially on April 30, though in practice not until early May.[58] Its initiators saw it as an interim measure (as all those who have studied the Łódź ghetto emphasize) until implementation of the "Final Aim," which, as they understood it, was the removal of the Jews. But Uebelhör, in his report to Greiser, offered a justification in principle for concentrating the Jews in a ghetto, based mainly on a pseudo-hygienic argument lifted from the racist ideology: the Jews were a "plague spot." The author of the "Chronicle of the Litzmannstadt District and Administrative Court" explained, in 1942, that before coming to Łódź all he and his colleagues had known about the city was that it was "the most notorious breeding site of the most notorious *Ostjudentum*" (*die berüchtigste Brutstätte des berüchtigsten Ostjudentums*).[59] When the police ordered the Jews to move into the ghetto, the official German newspaper's explanation of the measure was a clear expression of the common feeling about the significance of this step:

The Jew, who crawled out of the dark corners of the ghetto into the surrounding German neighborhoods and gnawed at the body of the nation, like maggots in meat, has been tamed. He has been sent back to the place he came from, before his usury brought him such enormous profits that he could move into a nicer house and even be the landlord of German tenants. The Jewish game is over.... Now the Jews have been tamed in Łódź and the time has come when the yellow Star of David will no longer shine in German neighborhoods.[60]

---

[56] This is quite clear from the most recent study on the Łódź Ghetto administration: Peter Klein, *Die "Gettoverwaltung Litzmannstadt" 1940–1944. Eine Dienststelle im Spannungsfeld von Kommunalbürokratie und staatlicher Verfolgungspolitik*, pp. 40–3.
[57] Friedman, "The Jewish Ghettos of the Nazi Era," p. 72; Dąbrowska and Wein, *Pinkas ha-Kehillot: Poland*, vol. 1, *The Communities of Łódź and Its Region*, pp. 123, 176, 64, 227.
[58] Michal Unger, *Lodz: Aharon ha-getta'ot be-Polin*, pp. 99–111.
[59] Chronicle of the Litzmannstadt District and Administrative Court [Chronik des Land- und Amtsgerichts Litzmanstadt], officially undated (but actually from February 10, 1942, as stated on p. 2 of the document), BAB, Reichsjustizministerium R3001/9722, p. 2.
[60] *Lodscher Zeitung*, February 11, 1940. I would like to thank Dr. Havi Dreyfus-Ben-Sasson for bringing this source to my attention. On the history of the changing names of this newspaper, see Klein, *"Gettoverwaltung Litzmannstadt,"* p. 26n16.

Thus the notion of a closed ghetto, which had begun to emerge after October 1939 with a different motivation – the fear of the "Ostjuden peril" – was now yoked to something else: the need of the administrators of the Łódź District to deal with the problem caused by the suspension of the Jews' expulsion from their zone of jurisdiction, a delay that intensified the original fear of "the Jews." It must be emphasized that this was not, as Browning proposes, the initial reason for the establishment of a ghetto. The suspension of the deportations did not require, in and of itself, the establishment of ghettos; it would have been entirely possible to leave the Jews where they were. Rather, it was the deep fear of "the Jews," especially the Ostjuden, expressed in such expressions as "this plague spot," that "mandated" the taking of defensive measures – their sequestration in a ghetto – against those who remained. I believe that Browning has been led to accept Uebelhör's "explanation" for the establishment of the ghetto as the authentic reason, when it was in fact only a justification framed in terms derived from Nazi ideology. I should also emphasize an important aspect of the Łódź ghetto, beyond its local significance. Once it was established and in operation, the Łódź ghetto and its logistical organization became a symbol and model that was applied, in some fashion or other, in other places as well.[61] Over time it became "a 'tourist attraction' that never failed to excite the most lively interest of visitors from the Old Reich."[62] The first ghetto in the Warsaw district was established in Łowicz in May 1940; the Łódź ghetto, sealed shortly before, served as an example for officials in Warsaw.[63]

What was the situation in the Lublin and Krakow districts? David Silberklang has written that "preparations for some form of ghettoization

---

[61] For example, a delegation of 15 senior German officials from the Warsaw district, headed by Governor Fischer, visited Łódź on September 13, 1940, "to get information from responsible *Referenten* about their experiences" in administering the ghetto, all of this as part of the last preparations for the establishment of the Warsaw ghetto: quoted by Trunk, *Judenrat*, p. 285 (and p. 619IIn52). I would like to thank Dr. Margalit Shlain, who brought this matter to my attention.

[62] "Als Ende April 1940 diese Umsiedlung' beendet war wurde das ganze Wohngebiet der Juden mit einem von Polizeibeamten bewachten Stacheldrahtzaun umschlossen, und damit hatte Litzmannstadt als erste deutsche Stadt ein abgeschlossenes Getto und eine 'Sehenswürdigkeit', die dann immer wieder das lebhafte Interesse der Besucher aus dem Altreich hervorrief": quoted from p. 11 of the Chronicle of the Litzmannstadt District and Administrative Court (Chronik des Land- und Amtsgerichts Litzmanstadt), BAB, Reichsjustizministerium, R3001/9722, p. 11; partially published in *Documente Occupationis Teutonica*, Poznań, 1949, vol. VIII, pp. 57–8; and in English in Browning, *The Origins of the Final Solution*, p. 115.

[63] Roth, "The County Chiefs."

The Invasion of Poland and the "Classic" Ghettos

were made in various parts of Lublin Province starting in January 1941," and

In the Lublin District, at the end of 1941, neither most of the Jews nor most of the communities lived in ghettos in the full sense of the term "ghetto"; the conditions in most communities in no way resembled those that prevailed in Warsaw and Łódź and caused so many deaths. The truth is that the concept of "ghetto" seems to be appropriate to only four communities in the Lublin District in 1941: Lublin itself, Opole-Lubelski, Piaski, and Zamość. Only the ghetto in Piaski was surrounded by a fence, and these four places taken together accounted for scarcely 20 percent of the Jews in the district. A few ghettos were established in 1942, as part of the process of murdering the Jews, but before then ghettoization was generally not part of the anti-Jewish policy here.[64]

The situation was similar in the Krakow District. In the city of Krakow itself – the capital of the *Generalgouvernement* – the ghetto, referred to as "the Jewish residential district" (*der Jüdische Wohnbezirk*), was not established until March 20, 1941.[65] The other ghettos in the district were not established until the second half of 1941 and during 1942.[66] In Radom District, on March 29, 1941, Governor Karl Lasch issued an order regulating residential and economic issues, which included an instruction to establish Jewish neighborhoods in all cities in the district.[67] This was the result of a directive by Governor-General Frank, which Lasch received on February 20, to set up ghettos for Jews all over the district by April 5.[68] In Eastern Upper Silesia (Ost-Oberschlesien), the southern part of the annexed territories, the establishment of ghettos did not begin until the second half of 1941.[69]

---

[64] Silberklang, "Ha-Sho'ah bimhoz Lublin," quotes from pp. 105 and 94. A good example of such a place in the Lublin district is Krasnik, which had about 4,000 Jews. A Judenrat was set up in October 1939, but no ghetto was ever established. See Abraham Wein, ed., *Pinkas ha-Kehillot: Poland*, vol. 7, *Lublin and Kielce*, pp. 520–2. On the hesitations, complications, and slow progress in establishing ghettos in the Lublin district in 1941, see also Pohl, *"Judenpolitik" zum Judenmord*, pp. 66–8.

[65] Yael Peled (Margolin), *Krakow ha-yehudit 1939–1943: Amidah, mahteret, ma'avaq* (Jewish Cracow 1939–1943: Resistance, Underground, Struggle) (Lohamei Hagetta'ot and Tel Aviv: Hakibbutz Hameuchad, 1992), p. 93.

[66] Abraham Wein and Aharon Weiss, eds., *Pinkas ha-Kehillot: Poland*, vol. 3, *Western Galicia and Silesia*, p. xxi.

[67] Jacek Młynarczyk, "Der Holocaust in Kielce/Distrikt Radom," master's thesis, Universität Essen, n.d. (c. 2000), p. 53.

[68] Sara Bender, "Koder Be'eretz Oyev: Yehudei Kielce ve-Hasseviva Bemilhemet ha-Olam ha-Sheniya, 1939–1945" (Darkness in the Enemy's Territory: The Jews of Kielce and the Surroundings during the Second World War, 1939–1945), p. 111.

[69] Alexandra Namysło, "The Situation of the Jewish Population in Eastern Upper Silesia Contrasted with the Situation of the Jews in the Other Polish Territories Incorporated into the Reich," p. 6.

We have seen that the first steps to force the Jews into ghettos began in theory (in Warsaw) and in practice (in Piotrków-Trybunalski) in early October 1939, three weeks before the establishment of the *Generalgouvernement*. The phenomenon began to spread in early December 1939 and gained momentum in the first months of 1940, originally in the Wartheland and afterwards in the Warsaw district. A semantic analysis of what was written about ghettos and why they were necessary indicates that Seraphim's notion about the special danger posed by large urban concentrations of Eastern European Jews (including arguments related to health and sanitation, which were sometimes used to justify the establishment of a ghetto) influenced the adoption of this measure.[70] But there was no central directive that mandated ghettoization of the Jews, even though the question engaged many in the SS and there were some (such as Eichmann) who apparently did want to introduce it systematically.[71] Consequently the initiative, planning, and execution remained exclusively in the purview of the intermediate echelons that were responsible for matters in the field. Most illuminating here is the fact that although the subject of ghettos crops up frequently in Hans Frank's diary, it was always an initiative of his advisers. He never gave the matter any thorough consideration, unlike the question of the Judenräte, which features from the very first pages of the diary as a systematic administrative measure.[72] Similarly, it is most striking that when the "Jewish Department" (*Referat Judenwesen*) of the General-Government summarized the official anti-Jewish activities for the period October 26, 1939, to July 1, 1940, it made no mention whatsoever of the establishment of ghettos![73]

[70] Friedrich, "Rassistische Seuchenprävention"; Unger, *Lodz: Aharon ha-getta'ot be-Polin*.
[71] Adolf Eichmann, a key figure who took an interest in the issue, was also the leading proponent of the Nisko plan. According to the post-war testimony of his aide, Dieter Wisliceny, who was generally reliable in many matters (although we must treat his words with due caution), "Eichmann had relatively little interest in the Jews of Poland until the beginning of summer 1941. He limited himself, so far as I know, to giving general instructions about the establishment of ghettos, institution of Judenräte, etc." See Dieter Wisliceny, "Bericht," November 18, 1946, YVA, M-5/162 [18.11.1946], p. 8; the document is also in the Institut für Zeitgeschichte, Munich, and the Centre de Documentation Juive Contemporaine, Paris [Doc. LXXXVIII-67]. We see that the special department for Jewish affairs in the Reich Main Security Office (RSHA) was interested in the general idea of ghettos and perhaps even in making the phenomenon uniform – but with no success. On Wisliceny's testimony, see Dan Michman, "Täteraussagen und Geschichtswissenschaft: Der Fall Dieter Wisliceny und der Entscheidungsprozess zur 'Endlösung.'"
[72] Präg and Jacobmeyer, *Das Diensttagebuch*, passim.
[73] The section on the activities of the Department for Jewish Affairs *(Referat Judenwesen)* in the overall report on the "Construction of the Administration of the General-Government" (*Aufbau der Verwaltung im Generalgouvernement*), July 1, 1949, BAB,

The Invasion of Poland and the "Classic" Ghettos

Hence we should understand the concentration of Jews in ghettos as a practical initiative taken in the field and promoted by local administrators, based on anti-Semitic stereotypes and in response to their superiors' encouragement to find solutions to the Jewish problem, at a time when the senior political echelons had not yet formulated a comprehensive and explicit solution.[74] This is why the phrase "temporary solution" kept recurring in various statements about ghettos:[75] the expectation was that the higher echelons would take a broader decision and define a solution that would be part of the final aim (*Endziel*); but the ghetto was not a stage on the road toward that as yet unknown solution. Accordingly, it was associated with various lines of policy. The very fact that so many different justifications were given for the establishment of ghettos in different places – hygiene, economics, and others – demonstrates that none of these reasons was the true cause for the spread of the phenomenon.[76]

On the contrary, if we examine the *process* of the establishment of ghettos in Poland along the time axis we see ever-widening circles of application and that an initiative in one place served as a model and inspiration for others: from a handful of ghettos introduced in late 1939 and early 1940, through the large cities that consolidated the model in 1940, to significant expansion in 1941, and the "afterthoughts" of 1942 (more than 300 in that last period). But if we consider the months from October 1939 until the spring of 1941 as a single unit of time, the bottom

---

R 52 II/247, Bl. 190–2, published in Tatiana Berenstein, Artur Eisenbach, and Adam Rutkowski, *Faschismus – Getto – Massenmord. Dokumentation über die Ausrottung der Juden in Polen während des zweiten Weltkrieges*, Doc. 45, pp. 86–8.

[74] For this management style in the Third Reich, see Kershaw's idea of "working towards the Führer": Ian Kershaw, *Hitler (I): 1889–1936: Hubris*, pp. 527–91.

[75] For example, in Uebelhör's 1939 remarks about the Łódź ghetto quoted earlier, and again in an article in the *Litzmanstädter Zeitung*, June 9, 1940; Friedman, "The Jewish Ghettos of the Nazi Era," p. 68.

[76] Of special interest in this context – although from a later period – is a passage in the diary of Herman Kruk of Vilna/Vilnius (January 19, 1943): "WHY ARE THE JEWS ISOLATED IN THE GENERAL GOUVERNEMENT? A document that just arrived gives an answer to that rhetorical question: *Sonderdruck Nr. 1*, published by: Ostland, Halbmonatsschrift für Ostpolitik, Berlin. The publication is titled: *Die Jüdische Wohnbezirke in General Gouvernement*. What is the publication? It says that the Jews have been gathered in specific districts: the most important in Warsaw, Krakow, Radom, Kielce, etc. This was done for the following reasons: (a) sanitary reasons: Jews are dirty and very resistant to dirty diseases; (b) political reasons: Jews and Poles are united [in their opposition to the Germans]. And the Jews still have big influence." See Herman Kruk, *The Last Days of the Jerusalem of Lithuania: Chronicles from the Vilna Ghetto and the Camps 1939–1944*, p. 451; original Yiddish version: *Togbukh fun Vilner Ghetto*, p. 448. I would like to thank Dr. Leah Prais for bringing this text to my attention.

line is that in Poland Jews were isolated in dozens of ghettos, especially in the largest cities (notably Warsaw and Łódź) and mid-size towns. The situation in these places – and especially in the small group of the most populous ghettos, which were surrounded by a fence or wall – left its mark on what might be called the "new Nazi concept of the ghetto" (as opposed to the pre-Nazi ghetto). In this context, the external and internal organization of the Łódź ghetto, the first large ghetto that functioned smoothly, played a large role. The quantum leap of Łódź was that a vague concept, toward which Nazi officials were still groping elsewhere, took on tangible form. Its success – with regard to the various spheres of life in the ghetto – had major long-term repercussions in many places;[77] for example, in one of the discussions (*Arbeitssitzung*) of Hans Frank and his aids dealing with the Warsaw ghetto, which took place on April 19, 1941 (i.e., a year after the establishment of the Łódź ghetto and six months after the establishment of the Warsaw ghetto), Frank said that if the administrators in Warsaw had followed the example of Łódź, the development would have been more successful.[78] This is also why the German authorities in places far away from Łódź – such as Amsterdam[79] and Białystok[80] in 1941 – came to see it as a model to be emulated and sometimes permitted the heads of other ghettos and Judenräte to go see it for themselves.[81]

The vision entertained by the Germans who dealt with ghettos can perhaps be summarized by these two examples. First, in March 1940, the official German newspapers of both Warsaw and Krakow, the *Warschauer*

[77] This suggests that Mordechai Chaim Rumkowsky's organizational abilities exerted broad influence beyond the Łódź ghetto itself. For an assessment of his activity in Łódź, see Michal Unger, *Reassessment of the Image of Mordechai Chaim Rumkowski*; Andrea Löwe, *Juden im Getto Litzmannstadt, Lebensbedingungen, Selbstwahrnehmung, Verhalten*.
[78] "*Wenn ein geschlossener Wohnbezirk mit stufenweiser Anpassung an das Vorbild in Lodsch geschaffen worden wäre, dann hätte man die Wirtschaftsbeziehungen der Juden mit den anderen Bewohnern nich zerrissen.*" Präg and Jacobmeyer, *Das Diensttagebuch*, pp. 359–60.
[79] See Friso Roest and Jos Scheren, *Oorlog in de stad: Amsterdam 1939–1941*, pp. 350–2.
[80] Wolfgang Scheffler, "Zur Organisation der Judendeportation unter besonderer Berücksichtigungdes Schicksals der Juden in Biaystok (1941–1943)," historical report, July 8, 1966, delivered to the Bielefeld regional court, unpublished MS, BAB, B 162/153.4063, p. 19.
[81] Unger, *Lodz: Aharon ha-getta'ot be-Polin*, p. 234; Philip Friedman, "The Messianic Complex of a Nazi Collaborator in a Ghetto: Moses Merin of Sosnowiec," pp. 356, 357. This phenomenon deserves thorough study on its own: who initiated the visits, how were they coordinated among the German authorities in various places, what lessons were learned from them, etc.

Zeitung and *Krakauer Zeitung*, ran an article by Dietrich Redeker under the headline, "German Order Enters the Ghetto": that is, the Germans were imposing proper Aryan method on the characteristic chaos of the traditional Jewish ghetto.[82] Second, Seraphim, who at the time was serving as an adviser to the *Generalgouvernement*, included the following observation in a lecture delivered at the inauguration of the Institute for Research into the Jewish Question, in Frankfurt am Main, in March 1941:

> The ghetto of the Middle Ages was largely a Jewish privilege rather than a forced measure.... The ghetto of today must be different from the medieval ghetto; it must be a compulsory ghetto... without contact or possibility of contact with non-Jews.[83]

Was ghettoization in occupied Poland systematic and complete? The answer, as we have seen, is a categorical negative. Most of the ghettos – numerically speaking – were established in 1941 and 1942; in dozens of localities – chiefly towns and villages with small or moderate-size Jewish populations (up to approximately 15,000 Jews) – the Jews continued to live in their homes as before and no ghetto was ever established (although a Judenrat was frequently, if not always, set up).[84] Light is shed on this

---

[82] Dietrich Redeker, "Deutsche Ordnung kehrt ins Ghetto ein," *Warschauer Zeitung*, March 13, 1940, and *Krakauer Zeitung*, March 21, 1940, the second one also quoted in Friedman, "The Jewish Ghettos of the Nazi Era," p. 63.

[83] Remarks by Seraphim at the inaugural conference of the Institute for Research into the Jewish Question (Institut zur Erforschung der Judenfrage) in Frankfurt, March 26–28, 1941, as quoted in "Bevölkerungs- und wirtschaftliche Probleme einer europäischen Gesamtlösung der Judenfrage," pp. 43–4, excerpted in Friedman, "The Jewish Ghettos of the Nazi Era," p. 64. The institute in Frankfurt launched a special project on ghettos in 1942, collecting material on ghettos of the past as well as the new ones; see Dirk Rupnow, "'Heqer ha-yehudim' ba-Reikh ha-shelishi: Ha-ariyazatsiyah shel ha-historiyah ha-yehudit bi-tqufat ha-mishtar ha-Natsi" ('Jewish Studies' in the Third Reich: The Aryanization of Jewish History under the Nazi Regime), drawing on BAB, NS 15/354 (1942).

[84] Examples: Izbica (Krasnystaw county, Lublin district) had 2,862 Jews before the war; during the occupation about 8,000 were deported to Bełżec in two waves, in March and October 1942. Dubienka (Hrubieszów county, Lublin district) had 2,160 Jews before the war; in June 1942, approximately 2,900 were deported to Hrubieszów and from there to Sobibor. Leczna (Lublin district) had 5,618 Jews before the war and some 12,000 under the German occupation; when the community was liquidated in October 1942, some 3,000 persons were sent to Treblinka and the rest to labor camps, where they died. Działoszyce (Kielce district) had 5,618 Jews before the war and about 12,000 under German occupation; when the community was liquidated on September 2, 1942, most of the Jews were murdered on the spot, though some were sent to Bełżec. Proszowice (Miechów county, Kielce district) had about 2,000 Jews before the war and 3,000 during

situation by a letter from Dov Abramczik, an activist in the religious-Zionist Hashomer Hadati organization from Miechov (Kielce Province). Writing to the movement's headquarters in Palestine on January 28, 1944, from Hungary, to which he had escaped, he told of the activities in which he and his comrades had engaged during the war:

> The cities of Warsaw and Łódź were the first to be affected by the ghetto system. Despite these major difficulties we were in constant communication and contact with them [the members of our movement there]. Committees were founded and organized to provide assistance to the ghettos. In Miechov we set up an assistance committee with the following members.... Our mission was to go out into the provinces, establish assistance committees there, and collect essential commodities and money for the ghettos. This was reported to Rabbi Nissenbaum and to Gottesdiener [in Warsaw]. Soon after [in 1941], new ghettos were set up in the provinces as well.[85]

We see from this incidental Jewish testimony (alongside the impact of the Warsaw and Łódź ghettos while the Holocaust was raging) that for a number of months the people of the smaller towns saw the ghettos as a phenomenon applying only to the larger cities and endeavored to assist the people trapped in them; it was only later that the phenomenon expanded.

The acceptance by local administrators, the Security Police, and the SS of the idea of concentrating the Ostjuden in ghettos, which began after the invasion of Poland – even though the precise nature of the ghetto was not totally clear at first and was never actually defined, not even later – reflects the preoccupation of those at the forefront of this activity with finding the most appropriate way of coping with the "Jewish problem." But the ghetto was not the only method for dealing with the Jews. There was

---

the occupation. On August 28, 1942, more than 2,000 Jews were sent to Bełżec; the rest were murdered locally in November 1942. For other places, see Friedman, "The Jewish Ghettos of the Nazi Era," pp. 71-2.

[85] The original Yiddish-influenced German reads as follows: "Mit den System der Ghettos wurden als erste die Städte Warschau und Lodz betroffen. Trotz dieser sehr grossen Schwierigkeit waren wir mit ihnen [unser Kameraden] in ständiger Verbindung und Kontakt. Es wurden gegründet und organisiert Hilfskomitt-éten [sic!] für die Ghettos. Bei uns in Miechov wurde ein Hilfskomitté gegründet der von folgende Chawerim [Kameraden] bestand:... Unsere aufgabe war sofort in die Provinz zu fahren und dort zu organisieren Hilfskomittéten um Sammlungen von Lebensmittel und Geld für die Ghettos durchzuführen. Die Sachen wurden übergeben Rav [Rabbi] Nissenbaum und Gottesdiener [in Warschau]. Nach einen kurzen Zeit [in 1941] wurden auch auf der Provinz neue Ghettos gegründet": Dov Abramczik to Mosche Krone, January 28, 1944, private collection of Mizrachi activist Dov Tsahor. I would like to thank Dr. Hava Eshkoli for bringing this document to my attention.

The Invasion of Poland and the "Classic" Ghettos 89

also the SS strategy of controlling Jewish communities through Judenräte and a policy of segregating the Jews by means of laws and regulations, as had been done as a matter of principle in Germany and Austria during the 1930s – though now with greater violence and rigor because of the encounter with the Ostjuden and also with greater ease, because the occupation authorities were bound by fewer constraints than were those back home in the Reich. All the while, ongoing population transfers (variously *Aussiedlung*, *Umsiedlung*, *Räumung*, and *Abschiebung* in the bureaucratic jargon employed by German institutions at the time), whose goals changed over time, were being conducted in different regions of occupied Poland. Thus the ghetto took form as part of a variety of anti-Jewish measures. There was no organized and regular correlation between ghettoization and the establishment of the Judenräte and other steps to isolate the Jews, as Hilberg proposed. The erratic timing of the establishment of ghettos also rules out any inherent link with the population transfer policy, contrary to the opinions of Götz Aly and Christopher Browning.[86]

[86] Götz Aly has suggested such a link between the failure of the Nisko plan and the establishment of the Łódź ghetto and between the failure of the Madagascar plan and the establishment of the Warsaw ghetto. His only evidence is the proximity in time of the shelving of these projects and the actual establishment of these ghettos; he totally ignores the discourse about the ghettos, the manner in which ghettos were implemented in Poland in general, and the earliest traces of the idea, especially in Łódź and Warsaw. He wrote: "The organizers of the deportations considered the ghettos to be provisional, a sort of mass detention pending deportation that would end immediately as soon as the original resettlement plans could be carried out. Conversely, of course, the ghettoization would put pressure on other participating authorities, who might still be reluctant due to technical concerns or contrary partisan interests, to organize the deportations rapidly and ruthlessly": Aly, *"Final Solution,"* p. 79. For his idea that the failures of the resettlement projects were linked to the establishment of the ghettos, see p. 81: "Just as the failure of the 'Jewish reservation of Lublin' project had led to the ghettoization of the Lodz Jews, the failure of the Madagascar Plan led to the ghettoization of the Warsaw Jews in late autumn 1940." See also the original German version, Aly, *"Endlösung,"* pp. 131, 135.

8

Methodological Interlude: The Term "Ghettoization" and Its Use During the Holocaust Itself and in Later Scholarship

> The Jewish Star: The Start of Ghettoization
> Title of a chapter in Helmut Eschwege, *Kennzeichen J*, on the fate of the Jews in Nazi Germany (1966)

As we have seen, concentrating Jews in ghettos was not part of a methodical process to isolate the Jews from their surroundings in Poland, but a parallel development; hence we should give some attention to the meaning of the term "ghettoization." The research literature refers not only to the establishment of physical ghettos but also to a process that includes the segregation of the Jews from the surrounding society and their concentration in certain locations. Philip Friedman, for example, devoted a section of his important essay, "The Jewish Ghettos of the Nazi Era," to "'Ghettoization' Attempts in Western, Southern, and Central Europe," immediately after a section on the "Crystallization of the Segregation Policy." Here he discussed the concentration of Jews in various cities across Europe. But the examples he cited (such as in Slovakia) are not sufficiently representative: they were either concentrations of Jews as a preliminary step to deportation or ghettos in the old, pre-1938 sense.[1] Hilberg, as we have seen, identified ghettoization, as a concept, with one phase of the emerging anti-Jewish policy, that of residential concentration and segregation, which began in the late 1930s. In the wake of these two scholars, the term "ghettoization" came to refer to all

---

[1] Friedman, "The Jewish Ghettos of the Nazi Era," pp. 65–7, 63, 80 (n39). As for his incorrect data on Slovakia, see Yehoshua Robert Buchler, ed., *Pinkas ha-Kehillot: Slovakia*, pp. 42–4.

Methodological Interlude

processes to isolate the Jews. For example, Helmut Eschwege entitled his chapter on the imposition of the Jewish badge in Germany "The Jewish Star: The Start of Ghettoization."[2] Similarly, Marlis Buchholz's book on the *Judenhäuser* (Jews' houses in Germany) bears the subtitle "On the Jews' Situation During the Period of Ghettoization and Persecution." "In a Ghetto Without Walls" is the title of Avraham Barkai's chapter on the Nazi period in the multi-volume survey of modern German Jewish history.[3] The most conspicuous example of the entrenchment of this generalization is provided by a dictionary on Nazi jargon intended for editors and translators, which offers the following definition: "*Ghettoisierung = Zwangsanweisung (auch von westeuropäischen Juden) ins Ghetto*"; that is, "ghettoization = forced transfer to a ghetto (also of Western European Jews)."[4]

But the process of isolating the Jews began in Germany at the very start of the Nazi regime in 1933 and became a fundamental element of German policy and legislation in all occupied countries. In and of itself it did not require that the Jews actually be concentrated in certain locations. The process of "encouraging" Jews to live in specific districts, too, began in Germany in the 1930s, and was an important part of the measures that preceded the deportation of Jews to the East from all over Europe. For example, starting on August 29, 1941, the Jews of Belgium were required to relocate to four large cities (Brussels, Antwerp, Liège, and Charleroi);[5] similarly, the freedom of movement of the Jews of the Netherlands was gradually restricted, starting in the summer of 1941, until most of them were required to live in Amsterdam.[6] But these actions never led to the establishment of ghettos or even to a residential pattern

---

[2] See Helmut Eschwege, ed., *Kennzeichen J. Bilder, Dokumente, Berichte zur Geschichte der Verbrechen des Hitlerfaschismus an den deutschen Juden 1933–1945*, p. 153.

[3] Marlis Buchholz, *Die hannoverschen Judenhäuser: Zur Situation der Juden in der Zeit der Ghettoisierung und Verfolgung 1941 bis 1945*; Avraham Barkai, "In a Ghetto Without Walls."

[4] Heinz Brackmann and Renate Birkenhauer, *NS-Deutsch: Selbstverständliche Begriffe und Schlagwörter aus der Zeit des Nationalsozialismus*, pp. 86–7.

[5] Lieven Saerens, *Vreemdelingen in een wereldstad: Een geschiedenis van Antwerpen en zijn joodse bevolking (1880–1944)*, p. 502.

[6] Jacques Presser, *Ashes in the Wind: The Destruction of Dutch Jewry*, pp. 214–18; Jozeph Michman, Hartog Beem, and Dan Michman, *Pinkas. Geschiedenis van de joodse gemeenschap in Nederland*, pp. 172–3, 182, 198; L. de Jong, *Het Koninkrijk der Nederlanden in de Tweede Wereldoorlog*, vol. 5, pp. 547–8, 567, 1074–8, 1101; Bob Moore, *Victims and Survivors: The Nazi Persecution of the Jews in the Netherlands 1940–1945*, pp. 80–1, 88.

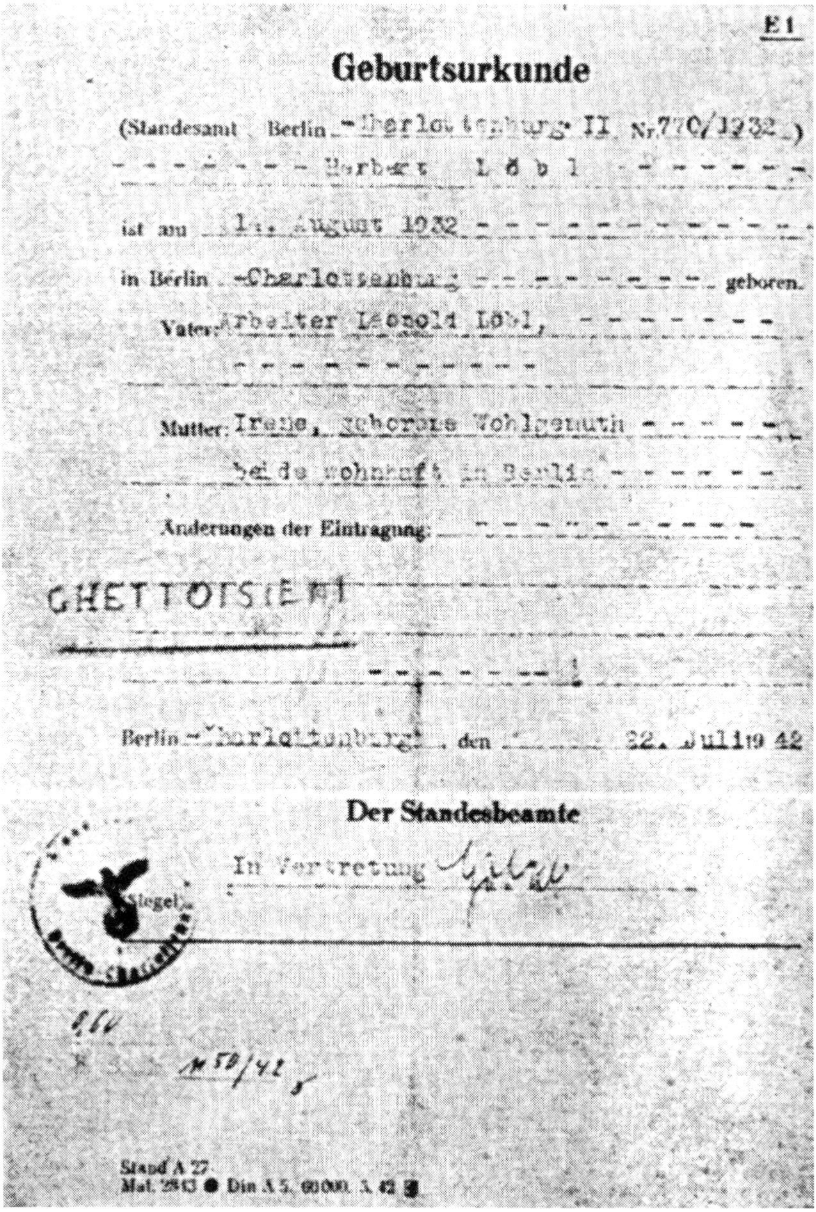

E 1

Geburtsurkunde

(Standesamt Berlin-Charlottenburg II Nr. 770/1932)

Herbert Löbl

ist am 11. August 1932

in Berlin-Charlottenburg geboren.

Vater: Arbeiter Leopold Löbl,

Mutter: Irene, geborene Wohlgemuth

beide wohnhaft in Berlin

Änderungen der Eintragung:

GHETTOISIERT

Berlin-Charlottenburg, den 22. Juli 1942

Der Standesbeamte

In Vertretung

(Siegel)

Stand A 27
Mat. 2813 ● Din A 5. 60000. 3. 42

FIGURE 16. Deportation document from Berlin, July 22, 1942, indicating that the person was "ghettoized," that is, deported to a ghetto in Eastern Europe.

Methodological Interlude

resembling ghettos. Nor did the German administrators ever refer to these moves as "ghettoization."[7]

In most instances, when German contemporary authors used the word *Ghettoisierung* they meant the forcing of the Jews into physical ghettos or establishing such ghettos. The few exceptions do not necessarily indicate that the term was applied to a policy of segregation. Curiously, the Gestapo stamped the documents of some Jewish deportees from Germany with the word *Ghettoisiert*, that is, "ghettoized."[8] Given that at least some of these deportees were transported to ghettos in Eastern Europe (such as Riga), it evidently refers to the fact that they were being sent to physical ghettos and was not meant to describe them en route.

---

[7] In early February 1942, the editor of a non-Jewish underground newspaper in the Netherlands responded to the decree that the Jews – who were being forced to leave other cities and resettle in Amsterdam – concentrate in three neighborhoods that were already heavily Jewish by noting that "three ghettos will evidently be created in Amsterdam" (*In Amsterdan zullen naar alle waarschijnlijkheid drie ghetto's worden gevormd*); see de Jong, *Koninkrijk*, vol. 5, p. 1074. This comment found its way into later scholarship as "a fact," as if there were three ghettos in Amsterdam; see Raul Hilberg, *The Destruction of the European Jews*, p. 374. On the question of a ghetto in the Netherlands, see Chapter 9.

[8] "Stempel auf den Ausweispapieren der zur Deportation bestimmten Juden," in Brackmann and Birkenhauer, *NS-Deutsch*, p. 87; Eschwege, *Kennzeichen J.*, p. 173.

9

Would the Idea Spread to Other Places? Amsterdam 1941, the Only Attempt to Establish a Ghetto West of Poland

> Marking the Jewish quarters and Jewish streets and blocking off the Jewish neighborhoods furthers the lowering of the Jews' status [*Deklassierung*].
> Reichskommissar Arthur Seyss-Inquart, the Nazi administrator of the occupied Netherlands, March 25, 1941

If the idea of concentrating the Jews in a physical ghetto evolved from the notion that the Ostjuden posed a special danger, the question naturally arises as to whether the model, once created in Poland, was exported to other places under Nazi control. On the one hand, information about the ghettos in Poland was disseminated in newspaper articles, movies,[1] and rumors, making it possible to copy the idea. On the other hand, as Seraphim had noted, "in most of the cities of central, western, and southern Europe, and in the towns of Eastern Europe where there are only a few Jews, it is impossible to ghettoize the Jews; there aren't enough of them."[2] It is true that Seraphim was not of high enough rank to dictate the extent to which the idea of concentrating Jews in ghettos would be implemented; nor was he ever actively involved in these efforts at ghettoization. I believe, nevertheless, that his logic, as well as his understanding of the concept of ghettoization – the concentration of Jews in physical ghettos and not simply a process of isolation from their surroundings – lay at

---

[1] See Baruch Gitlis, "'Redemption' of Ahasuerus: The 'Eternal Jew'" in *Nazi Film*, pp. 116–17; Joseph Wulf, *Theater und Film im Dritten Reich: Eine Dokumentation*, pp. 456–9.
[2] See the remarks by Seraphim at the opening conference of the Institute for Research on the Jewish Question in Frankfurt am Main, March 27, 1941: "Bevölkerungs- und wirtschaftspolitische Probleme einer europäischen Gesamtlösung der Judenfrage," *Der Weltkampf*, 1941 Heft 1/2 (April–September), p. 49.

the basis of the actions taken on the ground.³ The conspicuous fact is that ghettos were not established in Western Europe or in the Greater Reich. The only place in Western Europe for which we have explicit evidence of discussions about the possibility of establishing a real physical ghetto, in the classic sense (as in the ghettos of Poland in 1940–1941), is Amsterdam. As such, this case requires attention.

The German occupation regime imposed on the Netherlands in May 1940 was a civilian authority (*Zivilverwaltung*), unlike the German administrations in Belgium and France. Its senior officials, most of them of Austrian origin, including Reichskommissar Arthur Seyss-Inquart himself, were strongly committed to the Nazi ideology. Another unique feature of the situation in the Netherlands is that during the early months of the occupation the Jewish Department of the SD had no resident representative in the country. The key figure overseeing implementation of anti-Jewish policy was the Generalkommissar for Special Tasks, Fritz Schmidt, the only German in the administration, who represented the Nazi Party and was a confidant of Martin Bormann. Schmidt was a committed party man who had served in various propaganda-related roles, including, from 1939, as the party representative in the Reich Ministry for Popular Information and Propaganda, which was headed by Goebbels.⁴ He worked in cooperation with Dr. Hans Böhmcker, the former mayor of Lübeck,⁵ who was the commissioner for the city of Amsterdam (*Beauftragter für Amsterdam*). According to testimony by a member of the SIPO/SD, Böhmcker also served as Reichskommissar Seyss-Inquart's Special Commissioner for Jewish Affairs.⁶

In mid-January 1941, the German administration in the Netherlands began to give thought to the establishment of a ghetto in Amsterdam. Although Schmidt may well have been the originator of the idea, Reichskommissar Seyss-Inquart took part in the discussions from the outset; on January 13 he instructed Böhmcker to take measures with regard to "the question of the Jews' presence in Amsterdam."⁷ On January 16,

---

3 See Chapter 7, n4.
4 L. de Jong, *Het Koninkrijk der Nederlanden in de Tweede Wereldoorlog*, vol. 4a, pp. 95–7; Konrad Kwiet, *Reichskommissariat Niederlande. Versuch und Scheitern nationalsozialistischer Neuordnung*, pp. 86–91.
5 Friso Roest and Jos Scheren, *Oorlog in de stad: Amsterdam 1939–1941*, pp. 55–6.
6 "Gesamtbetrachtung über den 'Februarstreik 1941' in Amsterdam," p. 26, NIOD, Doc. I-998, 2–5. See also Bob Moore, *Victims and Survivors: The Nazi Persecution of the Jews in the Netherlands 1940–1945*, p. 66.
7 "Böhmcker aan de Regeeringscommissaris en Burgermeester van Amsterdam, Betr. Judenviertel- und Strassen in Amsterdam," 7 April 1941, NIOD, Doc II-361, map T, J 56; Ben A. Sijes, *De Februaristaking: 25–26 Februari 1941*, p. 92.

Böhmcker sent a letter to the Amsterdam Municipality, ordering its officials to provide him expeditiously with answers to his questions and data on a series of topics related to the Jews' residence in the city, and, first and foremost,

> those neighborhoods in which Jewish residents are in the majority. In addition I ask you to attach a map, in four copies, with the precise boundaries of the Jewish neighborhoods marked on it.[8]

In a report to Berlin he stated that the intention was "to arrive at some form of ghetto" (*um zu einer Form Ghetto zu kommen*).[9] The municipality assigned employees to collect the requested information. When it was ready, on February 15, it was sent to the German authorities.[10] This does not mean that, before this time, Böhmcker and other senior Nazis were ignorant about the Jewish population of Amsterdam. They had been walking through the city for several months and could form their own impressions of the Jews' presence and living conditions. The expression "to arrive at some form of ghetto" returns us to the semantic issue: "some form of ghetto" in what sense (given that Schmidt referred to the existing Jewish neighborhood as the "old ghetto")? Note that on February 8, 1941, the Dutch Nazi newspaper *De Misthoorn*, which enjoyed a subvention from Schmidt's office, published an article that, evidently under the influence of reports on developments in Poland, called for all Jews in the Netherlands to be confined to ghettos.[11] The very publication of such information, during a period of tight censorship, may indicate (as some scholars believe) that the article was a deliberate leak by the authorities. Since this newspaper did not have a large readership, however, it is more likely that the article simply reflects information that had come to its author's attention. Even more puzzling is the fact that the idea of a ghetto

---

[8] "In welchen Stadtteilen überwiegend Juden wohnen. Dazu bitte ich, eine Karte in vierfacher Ausfertigung beizufügen, aus der sich die Grenzen der Judenviertel genau ergeben" ("Van den Beauftragte aan de Gemeente Amsterdam, 16 Januar 1941," NIOD, Doc II-361, J17; de Jong, *Koninkrijk*, vol. 4b, pp. 881–2; Roest and Scheren, *Oorlog in de stad*, p. 335. Browning's picture of the Amsterdam ghetto episode, in his *The Origins of the Final Solution*, p. 203, relies on an article by Guus Meershoek, "The Amsterdam Police and the Persecution of the Jews," in Michael Berenbaum and Abraham J. Peck, eds., *The Holocaust and History: The Known, the Unknown, the Disputed, and the Reexamined*, Bloomington: Indiana University Press, 2002, pp. 284–300, and is distorted.

[9] Stimmungsbericht Nr. 29 (Januar 1941), NIOD, 61–76 (ZbV), 40394 ff.; quoted in Roest and Scheren, *Oorlog in de stad*, p. 335.

[10] Roest and Scheren, *Oorlog in de stad*, p. 340.

[11] Roest and Scheren, *Oorlog in de stad*, pp. 233, 352.

appeared at this time, in mid-January 1941, rather than earlier, immediately after the occupation of the Netherlands in May 1940, among the initial anti-Jewish measures, or later, in preparation for the deportations that were part of the Final Solution, as in Poland and Salonika. We have no answer to this, aside from noting that some of the senior Nazis in the Netherlands had served previously in occupied Poland (Seyss-Inquart had been Hans Frank's deputy until he was sent to the Netherlands in May 1940;[12] Wilhelm Harster, the commander of the Security Police in the Netherlands [*Befehlshaber der Sicherheitspolizei*], had been the commander of the SIPO/SD in Krakow)[13] and as such were aware of events in Poland and of the discussions there concerning ghettos. As we have seen, 1940 was a significant year for this development; information about the two largest ghettos, in Łódź and Warsaw, circulated in newspaper articles and films (including *The Eternal Jew*, which was screened all over Europe and included footage from Warsaw and Łódź). It is quite possible that it was in this atmosphere, reinforced by the Polish service of some of those involved, that the idea of an Amsterdam ghetto was placed on the table.

How could the German administrators in the Netherlands perceive the Jews of Amsterdam as if they were Ostjuden? More than 80,000 Jews, many of them working-class, lived in Amsterdam.[14] There was a crowded Jewish neighborhood in the center of town (home to 28,000 Jews, but also

---

[12] From the end of September 1939 Seyss-Inquart headed the Civilian Section of the Military Administration in Krakow (see the earlier discussion about Poland for an evaluation of the importance of this position for his familiarity with our topic). When the *Generalgouvernement* was established at the end of October 1939 he was appointed deputy to Hans Frank, while retaining his position as Reichsminister, which he had held since the summer of 1939. See de Jong, *Koninkrijk*, vol. 4a, pp. 51–7. See also Nachman Blumenthal, *To'udot mi-geto Lublin: Judenrat lelo Derech*, p. 24.

[13] In 1938, after the Anschluss, Harster set up the Gestapo office (*Staatspolizeileitstelle*) in Innsbruck. In October 1939 he was appointed commander of the Security Police and SD (BdS) in Krakow, when the position was instituted there. He served in that capacity in October and November 1939. See Alwin Ramme, *Der Sicherheitsdienst der SS. Zu seiner Funktion im faschistischen Machtapparat und im Besatzungsregime des sogenannten Generalgouvernements Polen*, p. 142.

[14] The local population registry listed 85,897 Jews in May 1941: see Archief stadsingenieur Van Heemskerck van Beest (no file number), SAA; cited in Roest and Scheren, *Oorlog in de stad*, p. 350. According to the official Jewish census conducted by the Germans in 1941, there were 79,497 "full" Jews in the city, 5,359 first-degree Mischlings (at least two Jewish grandparents), and 1,435 second-degree Mischlings (one Jewish grandparent); see *Statistiek der Bevolking van Joodschen Bloede in Nederland*, p. 6. See also Michman, Beem, and Michman, *Pinkas*, p. 269; Dan Michman, "Amsterdam, 1870–1940: Rapid Growth and the Creation of an Amsterdam Dutch-Jewish Sub-culture."

to 24,000 non-Jews).[15] In mid-February Schmidt referred to this district as the "ghetto" and as "the old ghetto."[16] The Jews of Amsterdam, too, had a long tradition of applying this term to the neighborhood.[17] Even though most of its Jewish residents were long settled in the Netherlands – the percentage of recent immigrants (from Eastern Europe since the start of the twentieth century and from Germany after 1933) did not exceed 10 percent or so – they constituted a distinct subculture, with an extremely low rate of intermarriage (only 16.9 percent in 1931–1934).[18] From the perspective of the Nazis' anti-Semitic stereotypes and Seraphim's analysis, the Jews of Amsterdam had a strong resemblance to the large Jewish concentrations in Eastern Europe. Schmidt's references to the local Jewish neighborhood as a "ghetto" are an indication of this.

Let us return to the sequence of events in Amsterdam. In the interim, just a few days before the municipality provided Böhmcker's office with the information about Jewish residential patterns in Amsterdam, there had been a significant development. Starting on February 7 there were a number of confrontations between Dutch Nazis and Jews in the center of town, in what Amsterdammers referred to as the Jewish Quarter (*Joodenbuurt*) and sometimes as the "ghetto." These clashes peaked on February 11, when a Dutch Nazi was seriously wounded (he died several days later). Subsequent to and evidently on account of this unrest, Böhmcker phoned Schmidt and proposed sealing off that Jewish neighborhood (ostensibly to search for weapons). Part of the Jewish Quarter was indeed sealed the next morning.[19] But the closure lasted only a few days and was never enforced stringently. To judge by remarks made by Böhmcker later, his intention at the time may well have been to make the closure permanent, but in the event it was soon canceled. Various plans

---

[15] De Jong, *Koninkrijk*, vol. 4b, p. 880.

[16] "Aufgrund des Fernschreibens teile ich mit, dass sich einzelne Männer der Wehrabteilung unerlaubt ins Ghetto begeben haben. Aus dem Verhalten dieser Männer heraus ergab sich im Ghetto eine Schlägerei. Hierbei ist leider ein WA-Mann schwer verletzt worden, der heute Morgen gestorben ist. Obiger Grund wurde vor uns sofort zum Anlass genommen, das alte Ghetto abzuriegeln, ein Judenrat wurde gebildet, Ausweispflicht wurde eingeführt, Arier wurden ausgesiedelt, dafür Juden aus dem Stadtrand ins Ghetto gebracht. Eine Durchkämmung des ganzen Gebietes ist vorgesehen": telex, Schmidt to Gutterer, Berlin, 15.2.1941, NIOD, 15; quoted in Roest and Scheren, *Oorlog in de stad*, pp. 41, 244.

[17] See the reference to Herman Heijermans's play *Ghetto* from 1898 in Chapter 3, n9.

[18] Michman, Beem, and Michman, *Pinkas*, p. 127.

[19] Roest and Scheren, *Oorlog in de stad*, p. 231, 240–1; de Jong, *Koninkrijk*, vol. 4b, p. 882.

and directives of those days referred to requiring non-Jews (especially Dutch Nazis) to leave the area, but nothing was actually enforced.[20] Nor were Jews from other parts of the city relocated there. The only change, several days later, was that signs bearing the German designation "Jewish Quarter" (*Judenviertel*),[21] a term that was used alongside the more common "ghetto" in internal discussions, were posted on a number of streets that led into the Jewish neighborhood. After the Holocaust, Hanns Albin Rauter, who had been the Generalkommissar for Security Affairs, referred to this as an "optical ghetto" ("optische Ghetto," as the Dutch version reads);[22] Eichmann, during his interrogation in Jerusalem in 1960, called it a "loose" or "porous" ghetto ("ein lockeres Ghetto").[23] But a ghetto of the new Polish model it certainly was not.

The idea was not shelved at once. There were debates, hesitations, and changes of positions among the highest German echelons in the Netherlands for another four months or so, until the idea was finally quashed in early June, perhaps because of Rauter's opposition.[24] It is hard to know exactly what it was that finally carried the day: it is true that both the Amsterdam municipality and the permanent undersecretaries (*Secretarissen-generaal*) of the Dutch government ministries (who constituted the senior legitimate representatives of the occupied Dutch nation after the queen and elected government fled to London in May 1940) expressed their opposition to the step,[25] chiefly on the grounds of the intolerable dislocation of urban life that the closure of a district in the center of the city would cause to transport and commerce. One German

---

[20] Böhmcker to Franken, "Betr. Einrichtung des Amsterdamer Ghettos," SAA, 100/64 A.Z. 1941; Roest and Scheren, *Oorlog in de stad*, pp. 235, 244–5, 341–2.

[21] De Jong, *Koninkrijk*, vol. 4b, p. 882.

[22] N. W. Posthumus and L. de Jong, "Verslag vierde gesprek met H. A. Rauter, 13 febr. 1947," p. 7, NIOD, Doc I-1380, h-5; quoted by de Jong, *Koninkrijk*, vol. 4b, p. 883.

[23] Israel Police, Bureau 06, Interrogation of Adolf Eichmann, vol. 1, p. 259; mimeograph, Yad Vashem Library, Y 61-760 I; also in NIOD, coll. nr. 270c (Proces Adolf Eichmann, 1937–45, 1960–61).

[24] J. Presser, *Ondergang. De vervolging en verdelging van het nederlandse jodendom 1940–1945*, vol. I, p. 395 (in the English version, *Ashes in the Wind*, p. 216, the description of this issue is abridged). On the problems of the establishment of a ghetto there is also a report of March 1, 1941, by the person in charge of collecting information for Generalkommissar Schmidt, F. W. Wickel of *Referat Sonderfragen*; NIOD, HSSPF 25A–27b.

[25] See the correspondence among Böhmcker, Seyss-Inquart, and the Amsterdam municipality during April and May: NIOD, Archief HA Inneres 124t; see also Roest and Scheren, *Oorlog in de stad*, pp. 348–50.

report, at least, mentioned the intolerable "total upside-down [situation]" (*volle Umkrempelung*) that would be the result from such a measure.[26] It is possible that it was these technical problems that led Seyss-Inquart to briefly float the idea of "several Jewish quarters," supplemented by a number of streets "for the Jews";[27] there is photographic evidence that signs reading "Jew Street" (*Judenstrasse/Joodschestraat*) were hung in several locations outside the "old ghetto."[28] Another argument was the absence of ghettos in Germany itself: clearly it was possible to do without them. In any case, as we have seen, all the decisions to set up ghettos in Poland were local and there was no "mandate" or obligation to do so. Consequently the idea was rejected, despite its undoubted attractions.[29] With regard to the hesitations and obstacles, as well as the vacillation between one large ghetto and several smaller ones, the debate in Amsterdam closely resembled that in Warsaw less than a year earlier.[30] From our perspective, it is important to note the comment of Seyss-Inquart on March 25, 1941, that "marking the Jewish quarters and Jewish streets and blocking off the Jewish neighborhoods furthers the lowering of the Jews' status [*Deklassierung*]."[31] That is, for him a "ghetto" was part of the process of trumpeting the Jews' inferiority – both to the Jews themselves and to the Dutch. It is far from clear that this was also the intention when the idea of a ghetto was first raised in January: perhaps we should see this definition, at this time, as a continuation of what Seyss-Inquart

---

[26] Wickel, report of March 1, 1941, quoted by Margot Lifmann, "The Policy of the German Occupation in Holland during 1940–1945: The Impact of this Policy on Dutch Attitudes Towards this Policy as Reflected in German Reports (*Stimmungs- und Lageberichte*) and Dutch Newspapers," p. 163.

[27] "*Die Juden in Amsterdam sollen in bestimmten Wohnvierteln und Wohnstrassen zusammengezogen werden. Diese Viertel und Strassen sollen besonders gekennzeichnet werden. Die Viertel sollen grundsätzlich nur an bestimmten Stellen passierbar sein. Die Viertel sollen in übrigen abgeschlossen sein*"; quoted in Böhmcker to the Reichskommissar and the Generalkommissar, April 17, 1941, NIOD, HA Immeres, 124t.

[28] See a photograph of the corner of Amstel and Nieuwe Kerkstraat, near the Magere bridge, taken by Fritz Rotgans, in SAA, and published in Veronica Hekking and Flip Bool, *De Illegale Camera 1940–1945. Nederlandse fotografie tijdens de Duitse bezetting*.

[29] After the Holocaust, various persons claimed credit for the fact that no ghetto was established in Amsterdam: see Roest and Scheren, *Oorlog in de stad*, pp. 357–60.

[30] See the lecture by Waldemar Schön, on January 20, 1941, reviewing the establishment of the ghetto in Warsaw: in Arad et al., eds., *Documents on the Holocaust*, pp. 222–8. For a description of the problems involved in managing the Warsaw ghetto, from the German point of view, see Christopher R. Browning, with contributions by Jürgen Matthäus, *The Origins of the Final Solution*, pp. 158–68.

[31] Seyss-Inquart's statement was quoted by Böhmcker in his letter to the Reichskommissar and the Generalkommissar, April 17, 1941, NIOD, HA Immeres, 124t.

had said in his programmatic speech of March 12, 1941, in reaction to the popular strike on behalf of the Jews, which took place in Amsterdam and its environs on February 25–26 (the February strike):

We do not consider the Jews to be Dutch. They are an enemy with whom it is impossible to reach an armistice or peace.... We will smite the Jews wherever we find them, and anyone who goes with them will bear the consequences. The Führer has declared that the role of the Jews in Europe is finished, and consequently their role is finished.

The only thing that can be discussed is the institution of a tolerable transition stage that maintains the fundamental attitude that the Jews are enemies, in other words, that takes the caution appropriate for enemies.[32]

In sum, the discussion about the possibility of setting up a ghetto was confused and moved in various directions; in some senses it resembled the vacillation and hesitation that had caused the process of segregating the Jews of Warsaw in a ghetto to drag out for an entire year. In Warsaw, though, the idea was implemented in the end, whereas in Amsterdam it was not. It was raised again, briefly, in November 1941 (only to be rejected again), but at that date it must be seen in the context of the decline toward the implementation of the Final Solution.

---

[32] Reichsminister [Arthur] Seyss-Inquart, *Vier Jahre in den Niederlanden: Gesammelte Reden*, pp. 57–8. Emphasis is in the original printed version of the speech. A Dutch version was produced and published right after the speech was delivered: *Rede van den Rijkscommissaris Rijksminister Dr. Seyss-Inquart gehouden op Woensdag 12 Maart 1941 in het Concertgebouw te Amsterdam voor het Arbeitsbereich der N.S.D.A.P. in de Nederlanden*.

10

Ghettos During the Final Solution, 1941–1943: The Territories Occupied in Operation Barbarossa

> The establishment of ghettos should be undertaken in places where Jews constitute a large share of the population, especially in cities, when their establishment is essential or at least serves the goals.
> Gen. Franz von Roques, military directive, August 28, 1941
>
> In no circumstances should the establishment of ghettos be viewed as urgent.
> Gen. Franz von Roques, military directive, September 3, 1941
>
> [It is inconceivable that in Lemberg] the Jews will be handled differently than in Krakow and Warsaw. Consequently, in the days to come, the Jews will be concentrated in Jewish neighborhoods in Lemberg, too, as in the other cities of Galicia, and disappear from the streets.
> Dr. Karl Lasch, governor of Lemberg province, October 21, 1941

Operation Barbarossa, the invasion of the Soviet Union in June 1941, was intended to be the start of Nazi Germany's apocalyptic war against Judeo-Bolshevism. In the wake of the Wehrmacht's rapid advance through Lithuania, Latvia and Estonia, Belorussia, prewar eastern Poland, and the Ukraine, the first stage of the organized mass murder of the Jews took shape in the space of a few weeks. For many years after 1945 the Final Solution was considered to be the implementation of an idea that had crystallized in advance; only later was this so-called intentionalist view replaced by the perception that the emergence of the genocidal campaign was more complex. In fact, the intentionalist interpretation was not constructed only by scholars after the Holocaust; it took root at an early stage of World War II among individuals who were not at the center of the decision-making process – both Jews, such as the members of the underground group headed by Abba Kovner in the Vilna ghetto, during the last weeks of 1941,[1] and Germans in the field. Consider the post-war testimony of Andreas von Amburger, an interpreter who served with Arthur Nebe, the commander of *Einsatzgruppe B*, concerning the assignment to liquidate the Jews and its implementation:

> This is how the Jews were killed: The *Sonderkommandos* would arrive in a place immediately behind the frontlines. All the Jews were concentrated in one section, which was declared to be a ghetto. They were forced to wear a round yellow patch on their clothes as a mark of identification. After that they set up a *Judenrat*, which had to see to order and implementation of the *Kommando*'s orders in the ghetto. Some of the Jewish men, mainly the intelligentsia, were immediately subjected to "special processing" [*sonderbehandelt*]; that is, they were shot.[2]

This seems to indicate that in this time and place ghettos were a deliberate and systematic stage in the Einsatzgruppen's implementation of the Final Solution. But a close reading of Einsatzgruppe reports, on the one hand, and of testimonies by Jews and local gentiles, on the other, shows unequivocally that this description, supposed to be the classic example of what took place, is totally off the mark. In truth, the introduction of the ghetto "system" in the occupied territories of the Soviet Union, even if strongly influenced by the experience acquired in Poland during the previous year and a half and implemented on a broader scale, was never absolute, full, and consistent, nor a formal part of the execution of the Final Solution of the Jewish Problem.[3] Even Yitzhak Arad, who believes that "the ghettos established in the regions of the *Generalgouvernement* in Poland in 1939–1940 were a stage in the policy of the Final Solution of the Jewish Problem and preceded the stage of extermination," is aware that the picture in the occupied Soviet Union is more complicated and perplexing:

> In the occupied territories of the Soviet Union... the ghettos were established... in tandem with the implementation of the killing; in some localities [this happened only] after most of the local Jews had already been murdered. In

---

[1] See Dina Porat, *Me'ever lagashmi. Parashat hayav shel Abba Kovner* (Beyond the Reaches of Our Souls: The Life and Times of Abba Kovner), pp. 89–94. An English version of this book was just published: *The Fall of a Sparrow: The Life and Times of Abba Kovner*.

[2] Andreas von Amburger, Camp-Nr. 6/5507, Mossburg, den 27. Dezember 1945 (transcript), in Berlin Document Center (now in BAB), 457, RSHA, Sipo-SD (41-4).

[3] In a recent publication on Białystok, which is otherwise an excellent analysis of the local situation, the author still pushes the old view that "in the territories captured after the German invasion of the Soviet Union in 1941... the ghettos were set up immediately": Sara Bender, *The Jews of Białystok during World War II and the Holocaust*, p. 278.

places where it was possible to kill the Jews immediately, during the initial weeks and months of the occupation, ghettos were usually not established. Nevertheless,... because of all of these [impediments, which he enumerated], it sometimes took many months to implement the extermination. Sealing off the Jews in ghettos, as a temporary solution, did not run counter to the intention to exterminate them; it simply made it easier for the murderers to catch them.

The instructions to establish ghettos left broad freedom of action to the executive echelons in the field.... And in fact there was no uniformity on this matter.[4]

Leni Yahil, in her comprehensive work on the Holocaust, also attempts to cope with the questions raised by the actual situation in the occupied Soviet Union:

By the beginning of winter [in 1941], the Einsatzgruppen had managed to exterminate only about two-thirds of the remaining Jews [meaning the 1 million to 1.5 million who had not managed to escape to the Soviet hinterland when the Germans invaded]. This was partly because of economic constraints, that is, the need for skilled laborers, and that the number of people who were engaged in these murderous activities was insufficient to cover the entire area. It also became necessary to deal with the Jewish population by concentrating the Jews in central ghettos and organizing them into forced labor units. The Germans now applied the lessons learned in occupied Poland. In many places, particularly the Baltic states, the Jews were rapidly herded into ghettos, but the intention now was not to keep them there, but to transport them directly to their deaths.... Some of these ghettos existed for very brief periods: sometimes months, sometimes only a few weeks.[5]

Both Arad and Yahil, like many other scholars, are aware that it is difficult to understand why ghettos were established during the extermination phase, but their problem stems first and foremost from their implicit assumption that all ghettos were essentially alike and that they were part and parcel of the Final Solution or a step leading to it.

What is important for us here is that hundreds of ghettos – constituting the largest single group – were established in the occupied Soviet Union (including what, until September 1939, had been eastern Poland).[6] Some

---

[4] Yitzhak Arad, *Toledot ha-Sho'ah: Berit ha-mo'atsot ve-ha-shetahim ha-mesuppahim* (History of the Holocaust: The Soviet Union and Annexed Territories), p. 255.
[5] Leni Yahil, *The Holocaust: The Fate of European Jewry, 1932–1945*, p. 258. Note that the Hebrew original refers to *one-third* of the 1.5 million Jews who had remained in the German-occupied areas. It is not clear whether "two-thirds" is a mistake by the translators or a revision of the text by Yahil herself.
[6] The *Yad Vashem Encyclopedia of the Ghettos During the Holocaust* and the *Encyclopedia of Ghettos and Camps* being produced by the Holocaust Museum in Washington list more than 500 ghettos in this territory. I would like to thank Dr. Martin Dean of the United States Holocaust Museum for providing me with this information.

of them were created long after the massacres began; what is more, many ghettos in Poland (the majority, in fact) were established at the same time as those in the Soviet Union and thus belong to the same later stage of the process. Hence for the purpose of historical analysis we must deal both with the complexity and broad scale of the introduction of ghettos in this region as well as with the parallels in Poland. Scholars have studied only a few of the ghettos in the Soviet Union in depth; in general, the farther east the ghetto was, the less we know about it. Although this lacuna makes analysis and generalization difficult, we do have sufficient information to rule out several hypotheses and to define certain general characteristics of these ghettos. It is important to look at events in the occupied Soviet Union in the broader context of the consolidation and implementation of the Final Solution, on the one hand, and of the change in the meaning of "ghetto," which reflects the Germans' evolving view of the concept, on the other.

On the eve of the invasion of the Soviet Union there was a marked increase in references to ghettos and their importance. A conference was held in Frankfurt am Main March 26–28, 1941, to mark the opening of the Institute for Research into the Jewish Question, a branch of the Higher School for National Socialism that was to be set up under Alfred Rosenberg. After Rosenberg opened the gathering,[7] Peter-Heinz Seraphim delivered a lecture on "Population and Economic Problems in an Overall European Solution of the Jewish Question," in which he mentioned three possible ways to solve the Jewish problem: dissimilation, ghettoization, and the removal of the Jews from Europe through a planned program of population transfer (*Dissimilierung, Ghettoisierung, Entfernung aus Europa*). Although each of these had its difficulties and advantages, he believed that ghettoization was appropriate only for Eastern Europe (an idea he had expressed in earlier years, as we have seen). By "ghettoization" he meant the involuntary concentration of Jews in geographically defined neighborhoods. He noted that for the Germans to recover the costs incurred by controlling these neighborhoods, with all their ills, the ghettos would have to yield economic benefit. Alternatively, he suggested that, instead of an "urban ghetto" (*Stadtghetto*) the Jews could be concentrated in a particular district, creating a "mass" or "wholesale" ghetto (*Massenghetto*) that would be a "gigantic ghetto" (*Riesenghetto*).

---

[7] "Nationalsozialismus und Wissenschaft," Ansprache von Reichsleiter Alfred Rosenberg anlässlich der Eröffnung der 'Aussenstelle der Hohen Schule Frankfurt am Main, Institut zur Erforschung der Judenfrage', am 26. März 1941, *Der Weltkampf* 1 (1941), pp. 3–6.

However, because this would exacerbate the problems found in urban ghettos, his ideal solution was the total removal of the Jews from Europe, if possible.[8] It should be emphasized that the other option referred to by Seraphim – dissimilation – means precisely what many Holocaust scholars have meant by "ghettoization" (see Chapters 1 and 8). In any case, Rosenberg seems to have internalized what Seraphim said. About a month later, on April 29, in a memorandum (*Denkschreiben*) he drew up on the basis of the work his office was performing in preparation for administering the Soviet territories soon to be occupied ("the East"), he noted that ghettoization would be one means of dealing with the Jews.[9] He returned to this more explicitly a week later, in an order defining the tasks of the future Reichskommissar in the Ukraine.[10] Several days earlier, on April 21, Hans Frank had issued an order to "contain" (*Zusammenfassung*) the urban Jews of the *Generalgouvernement* in ghettos.[11] As previously discussed, in two provinces adjacent to the border with the Soviet Union – Krakow and (to a much lesser extent) Lublin – brisk activity to establish ghettos indeed began in March to May 1941.

Thus, by the time Barbarossa was launched, ghettos, in the version introduced in a number of Polish cities and towns, were a well-known phenomenon and part of the available stock of ideas – even if no order had been issued to institute them in the newly occupied areas of the Soviet Union (Rosenberg had not yet received his official appointment as Reichskommissar for Ostland). The practice of leaving the initiative for their establishment to middle- and low-level administrators was also widespread. Against this background it bears noting that along with the earliest massacres (chiefly though not exclusively of men) during the first weeks of the fighting, ghettos were established in several places at the initiative of the Einsatzgruppen and military commanders. Kovno (Kaunas) is a good example: on July 7, Colonel Jurgis Bobelis, the local Lithuanian provisional military commander, reported in a meeting that Einsatzgruppe commander Franz Stahlecker had ordered the establishment of a ghetto. The next day, Stahlecker and SS Standartenführer (colonel) Karl

---

[8] Peter-Heinz Seraphim, "Bevölkerungs- und wirtschaftspolitische Probleme einer europäischen Gesamtlösung der Judenfrage," pp. 43–51. He was alluding, of course, to the Madagascar Plan.
[9] "Allgemeiner Aufbau und Aufgaben einer Dienststelle für die zentrale Bearbeitung der Fragen des osteuropäischen Raumes," April 29, 1941; Doc. 1024–PS, *Trial of the Major War Criminals*, vol. XXVI, p. 561.
[10] "Instruktion für einen Reichskommissar in der Ukraine," May 7, 1941, Doc. 1028–PS, *Trial of the Major War Criminals*, vol. XXVI, p. 571.
[11] Werner Präg and Wolfgang Jacobmeyer, *Das Diensttagebuch*, p. 437 (Zusammenfassung der Juden in den Städten in Ghettos).

Jäger, commander of Einsatzkommando 3, "suggested" to five Jewish leaders who had been summoned to a meeting that, for their own good and to escape the prevailing anarchy in which Lithuanians were attacking Jews, they "leave the city and move into a ghetto" by August 15. The suburb of Slobodka (Viljampole) was "proposed" as the site for the ghetto. It was not in the center of town, but it had a large concentration of poor religious and lower-middle-class Jews.[12] On Seraphim's map of Kovno it was marked as having the highest concentration of Jews in the entire city.[13] At the same meeting the Jewish leaders present were co-opted to serve as a Jewish council that would be responsible for the Jews' relocation to Slobodka. The process of moving into and organizing the ghetto – more precisely, two ghettos – lasted for about a month.[14] Similarly, on July 9 in Slavnoye, in the Tolochin district of Vitebsk oblast in Belorussia, the 143 local Jews were moved into a single street, which was fenced off and referred to as a "ghetto."[15]

The possibility of establishing separate Jewish neighborhoods was included in the second official order, issued on July 13, 1941, by General Max von Schenckendorff, the rear echelon commander of Army Group Center. The formal recognition of ghettos in this document went beyond anything that had ever existed in Poland. Nevertheless, Schenckendorff's explanation of the motives for ghettoization is interesting:

IV. Prohibition on Evicting Jews
1. In many communities the Jews have been evicted. Diverse factors led to the eviction. It was argued inter alia that the Jews' homes had been damaged in the war, that Jews are forbidden to continue living together with Poles, etc. Because of their eviction, many Jews, with no regard to age or sex, are wandering in the countryside from village to village and from town to town. Because of the enormous danger caused by the eviction of such Jews, due to the lack of supervision, I hereby order as follows:

   a. The Jews are to be concentrated [zusammenzufassen] in a closed community in buildings occupied exclusively by Jews.
   b. In principle, Jews who live in a place are not to be evicted any more.

---

[12] Avraham Tory, *Surviving the Holocaust: The Kovno Ghetto Diary*, pp. 9–10; Christoph Dieckmann and Saulius Sužiedėlis, *Lietuvos žydų persekiojimas ir masinės žudynės 1941 m. vasarą ir rudenį* (The Persecution and Mass Murder of Lithuanian Jews during Summer and Fall of 1941), 59–60.
[13] Compare the maps in Seraphim, *Das Judentum*, p. 367, and Tory, *Surviving the Holocaust*, p. 533.
[14] Christoph Dieckmann, "Das Ghetto und das Konzentrationslager in Kaunas 1941–1944," pp. 442–3.
[15] See the entry on Vitebsk in the *Yad Vashem Encyclopedia of the Ghettos During the Holocaust*, pp. 890–1.

Der Befehlshaber H.-Qu., den 13. Juli 1941
des rueckw. Heeres-Gebietes Mitte
Abt. VII/Mil.-Verw.

Verwaltungs - Anordnungen Nr. 2.

I. Verwendung deutscher Hoheitszeichen und Anwendung des deutschen Grusses.

1. Die Fahnen des Deutschen Reiches und die Symbole der nationalsozialistischen Bewegung duerfen im besetzten russischen Gebiet bis auf weiteres nur von Reichsdeutschen verwendet werden.
2. Die Anwendung des Deutschen Grusses ist alleiniges Vorrecht der Reichsdeutschen.

II. Behandlung der Volksdeutschen.

Ein Teil der Volksdeutschen im besetzten Gebiet ist politisch im hoechsten Grade unzuverlaessig. Aufgrund eines nach Beendigung des Polenfeldzuges zwischen dem Reich und der UdSSR. abgeschlossenen Abkommens, hatten die Volksdeutschen in dem von Russland besetzten Gebiet die Moeglichkeit, fuer Deutschland zu optieren. Da viele der hier zurueckgebliebenen Volksdeutschen die Heimkehr in das Grossdeutsche Reich abgelehnt haben, verdienen sie keine bevorzugte Behandlung. — Bei der Durchfuehrung der Verwaltungs-Anordnungen Nr. 1 vom 7. Juli 1941 — zu VII: Erfassung der Volksdeutschen — ist auf diesen Gesichtspunkt besonders zu achten.

III. Einsetzung von Juden-Raeten.

1. In jeder Gemeinde wird eine Vertretung der Juden gebildet, die die Bezeichnung Juden-Rat fuehrt.
2. Der Juden-Rat besteht in Gemeinden bis zu 10.000 Einwohnern aus 12, in Gemeinden ueber 10.000 Einwohnern aus 24 Juden, die der ortsansaessigen Bevoelkerung entstammen. Der Juden-Rat wird durch die Juden der Gemeinden gewaehlt. Scheidet ein Mitglied des Juden-Rates aus, so ist sofort ein neues zu waehlen.
3. Der Juden-Rat waehlt sofort aus seiner Mitte einen Obmann und einen Stellvertreter.
4. Spaetestens bis 31. Juli 1941 ist der Obmann des Juden-Rates der zustaendigen Ortskommandantur die Besetzung des Juden-Rates zu melden. Der Ortskommandant entscheidet im Einvernehmen mit der zustaendigen Dienststelle der Sicherheitspolizei darueber, ob die mitgeteilte Besetzung des Juden-Rates anzuerkennen ist. Er kann eine andere Besetzung verfuegen.
5. Der Juden-Rat ist verpflichtet, durch seinen Obmann oder seinen Stellvertreter die Befehle von Dienststellen der deutschen Wehrmacht und Polizei entgegen zu nehmen. Er haftet fuer ihre gewissenhafte und rechtzeitige Durchfuehrung in vollem Umfange. Den Weisungen, die er zum Vollzuge dieser deutschen Anordnungen erlaesst, haben saemtliche Juden und Juedinnen zu gehorchen. — Grundsaetzliche Weisungen sind schriftlich zu erteilen, nachdem sie der zustaendigen deutschen Dienststelle vorgelegt worden sind.
6. Der Obmann, sein Stellvertreter und alle sonstigen Angehoerigen des Juden-Rates haften mit ihrer Person fuer alle Vorkommnisse innerhalb der juedischen Gemeinde, soweit diese sich gegen die deutsche Wehrmacht, die deutsche Polizei und deren Anordnungen richten.

Die Feld- und Ortskommandanten haben in solchen Faellen, je nach der Schwere der Zuwiderhandlungen, nicht nur gegen die Taeter, sondern auch gegen die Mitglieder des Juden-Rates die schaerfsten Massnahmen, bis zur Todesstrafe, zu ergreifen.

FIGURE 17. General von Schenckendorff's decree regarding the establishment of ghettos in the occupied Soviet Union, July 1941.

c. An attempt should be made to apprehend Jews who left their communities and to return them to their original communities.[16]

---

[16] Der Befehlshaber des rueckw. Heeres-Gebietes Mitte [von Schenckendorff], H.-Qu., den 13 Juli 1941, *Verwaltungs-Anordnungen Nr. 2*, YVA, DN-7-2. Also cited in Wolfgang Benz, Konrad Kwiet, and Jürgen Matthäus, eds., *Einsatz im "Reichskommissariat*

IV. Verbot der Evakuierung von Juden.

1. In zahlreichen Gemeinden sind Juden evakuiert worden. Die Gruende, die zur Evakuierung fuehrten, waren verschiedenartig. Unter anderem wurde angefuehrt, dass die Wohnhaeuser der Juden infolge des Krieges zerstoert waren, dass Juden mit Polen nicht mehr zusammen leben duerfen und dergleichen mehr. Die Judenevakuierung hat zur Folge, dass zahlreiche Juden ohne Ruecksicht auf Alter und Geschlecht von Dorf zu Dorf und von Stadt zu Stadt ueber Land wandern. Da die Gefahren derartiger Judenevakuierungen wegen des Fehlens jeglicher Kontrollen ausserordentlich gross sind, ordne ich an:
  a) die Juden sind innerhalb einer geschlossenen Gemeinde in nur von Juden bewohnten Unterkuenften zusammen zu fassen.
  b) Ortsansaessige Juden duerfen grundsaetzlich nicht mehr aus der Gemeinde evakuiert werden.
  c) Es ist anzustreben, Juden, die ihre Gemeinden verlassen haben, unverzueglich aufzugreifen und ihrer Heimatgemeinde wieder zuzufuehren.

Ausnahmen von dieser Regelung sind nur aus dringenden militaerischen oder polizeilichen Gruenden zulaessig. Die Entscheidung trifft, soweit es sich um militaerische Belange handelt, der Ortskommandant, soweit polizeiliche Belange infrage kommen, die zustaendige Dienststelle der Sicherheitspolizei im Einvernehmen mit dem Ortskommandanten.

2. Die Buergermeister sind anzuweisen, die Anordnung zu 1. unverzueglich durchzufuehren.

Die Ortskommandanten koennen zu dieser Arbeiten Juden heranziehen.

XIX. Berichtigung der Verwaltungs-Anordnungen Nr. 1 v. 7. Juli 1941.

Abtlg. VII Kr.—Verw.

Die Verwaltungs-Anordnungen werden zu II Ziffer 1 dahin abgeaendert:
Die Bevoelkerung hat sich in ihren Wohnungen aufzuhalten:
a) in den Staedten in der Zeit von 21.00 Uhr bis 5.00 Uhr.
b) auf dem Lande in der Zeit von 21.00 Uhr bis 4.00 Uhr.

XX. Lageberichte

Die Divisionen bezw. unmittelbar unterstellten F. K. haben alle 2 Wochen, erstmalig zum 20. Juli 1941 Lageberichte nach folgenden Gesichtspunkten zu erstatten.
  a. Politische Lage,
  b. Verwaltung (allgemeine Verwaltung, Verwaltung der Gemeinden, Sicherheit und Ordnung, Gesundheits—und Vaeterinaerwesen usw.)
  c. Stimmung und Verhalten der Bevoelkerung,
  d. Wirtschaft,
  e. Ernaehrung und Landwirtschaft,
  f. Besondere Vorkommnisse,
  g. Dringende Wuensche.

Um eine Doppelarbeit zu vermeiden, koennen zu d. und e. Durchschlaege von Berichten an die Wirtschaftsinspektion verwendet werden.

Der Befelshaber des rueckw.
Heeresgebietes Mitte
von SCHENCKENDORFF

FIGURE 17 (continued)

We see that the instruction to concentrate the Jews together in a "closed community" – the word "ghetto" was not used – came as an ostensible reaction to the Jews' flight and vagabondage (so it seems, although there are indications that the main points of the order had been outlined before

Ostland": Dokumente zum Völkermord im Baltikum und in Weißrußland 1941–1944, pp. 120–1.

the invasion);[17] this recalls what had taken place 22 months earlier, during and immediately after the conquest of Poland. Now, as in Poland, the orders to make Jews wear a badge and to establish Judenräte were independent of the establishment of ghettos. The decree that Jews wear an identifying badge was issued about a week before the decree on the establishment of ghettos.[18] The order to set up Judenräte appears in the same document of July 13, before the section on ghettos, but is clearly unrelated: unlike the ghettos, no justification based on the situation is mentioned with regard to the Judenräte. In this, Schenckendorff's order differed from Heydrich's *Schnellbrief*, which did mention ghettos in its discussion of a "Council of Elders." Here we must not combine these three measures – ghetto, badge, and Judenrat – in a single package, as scholars have frequently done, even if they were often implemented within days or weeks of one another.[19]

Ghettos were established in the wake of Schenckendorff's directive. On July 19, for example, an order was issued to establish a ghetto (actually a "Jewish quarter"), surrounded by stone walls, in Minsk,[20] and several days later in Bialystok[21] and then in other places, including some that lay outside Schenckendorff's jurisdiction. We have already seen that the ghetto in Kovno was established very early. Similar initiatives were taken later, in the Baltic states, although there was no parallel to Schenckendorff's order. On July 21, officers of the military administration met in Riga with Dr. Rudolph Batz, the commander of the local Einsatzkommando (in 1939 he had been in Warsaw, ordering its Judenrat to establish a ghetto), and his deputy SS-Hauptsturmführer Arnold Kirste. According to their report, "our proposal to mark the Jews, concentrate them in a ghetto, and then appoint a Judenrat, through which the broad-scale mobilization of Jews for labor could be managed, was accepted.... Marking the Jews and containing them in a ghetto [sie in

---

[17] Dan Zhits, *Geto Minsk ve-Toledotav le'Or ha-Te'ud he-Hadash* (The History of the Minsk Ghetto [in light of the new documentation]), p. 13; Hannes Heer, "Killing Fields: The Wehrmacht and the Holocaust in Belorussia 1941–1942," p. 81.

[18] "Auszug aus der Verwaltungs-Anordnung Nr. 1 des Befehlshabers des rueckw. Heeres-Gebietes Mitte, 7. Juli 1941," in Benz, Kwiet, and Matthäus, *Einsatz im "Reichskommissariat Ostland,"* pp. 118–19.

[19] Benz, Kwiet, and Matthäus are among those who follow Hilberg's lead, including all of these measures in their chapter on the ghetto system: *Einsatz im "Reichskommissariat Ostland,"* pp. 115–220.

[20] Zhits, *Geto Minsk ve-toledotav*, p. 15.

[21] Bender, *The Jews of Białystok*, p. 103.

einem Ghetto zusammenzufassen] will be implemented."[22] The ghetto (here, again, there were actually two ghettos) was established in August. It is worth noting here that Seraphim's book had a detailed map of Riga, along with a reference to the city in the body of the text.[23] On the same day as the meeting in Riga in the north, July 21, a similar directive was issued by General Karl von Roques, Schenckendorff's counterpart for Army Group South.[24] His jurisdiction included Eastern Galicia, where many ghettos were established during the summer and autumn of 1941.

The ghetto concept became standard and was taken for granted to the point that it was incorporated into plans for the future of the occupied territories when the relevant bureaucrats began to formulate the operative regulations in late July 1941. They seem to have been influenced not only by the orders issued by military commanders but also by Rosenberg's pre-Barbarossa directive. According to the "administrative directives" (*Richtlinien für die Verwaltung*) for Lettland (Latvia), issued on July 27, "the Latvian authorities should be incited" (*lettischen Behörden anzuregen*) to establish ghettos (*Bildung von Ghettos*).[25] Another administrative directive, issued by Security Division 281 on July 30, states that "the Jews' behavior requires separating the Jews from the rest of the population and housing them in ghettos."[26]

All these ideas are stated systematically in the "Directives for Dealing with the Jewish Question" (*Richtlinien für die Behandlung der Judenfrage*), issued by the office of Reichskommissar Rosenberg (*RMfdbO – Reichsministerium für die besetzten Ostgebiete*, the Reich Ministry for the Occupied Eastern Territories) in early August. According to this document, "one of the first main aims of the German measures must be the strict isolation of the Jews from the rest of the population" ("*Ein erstes Hauptziel der deutschen Maßnahmen muß sein, das Judentum streng von der übrigen Bevölkerung abzusondern*"). Ever since the Bolshevik

---

[22] Quoted in Andrej Angrick and Peter Klein, *Die "Endlösung" in Riga: Ausbeutung und Vernichtung 1941–1944*, p. 94.
[23] Seraphim, *Das Judentum*, p. 369.
[24] Thomas Sandkühler, *"Endlösung" in Galizien: Der Judenmord in Ostpolen und die Rettungsinitiativen von Berthold Beitz 1941–1944*, p. 126; Jürgen Förster, "Die Sicherung des 'Lebensraumes,'" p. 1034n28; English edition, *The Attack on the Soviet Union*, p. 1194n28.
[25] Angrick and Klein, *Die "Endlösung" in Riga*, p. 98.
[26] Benz et al., *Einsatz im "Reichskommissariat Ostland*," p. 122: "Das Verhalten der Juden zwingt, die Juden allgemein von der übrigen Bevölkerung zu trennen und in Ghettos unterzubringen" (Verwaltungsanweisungen der Sicherungs-Division 281).

Revolution, the document explained, Soviet Jews had been striving to attain positions of power, employing various methods to camouflage their goals and to avoid attracting attention: they had abandoned their religion and adopted Russian names. It was necessary to fight against this and to bat down the Jewish mask (*Zerschlagung der jüdischen Tarnung*), employing all means, including records from the archives, to roll back this phenomenon and identify cases in which it took place. The Jews' ability to climb higher in society and disguise themselves had been made possible, particularly in the Soviet Union, by the freedom of movement allowed them. Consequently,

Freedom of movement must be abolished for all Jews. Transfer to ghettos [*Überführung in Ghettos*] should be striven for, which will be easier in Belorussia [*Weißruthenien*] and the Ukraine, because there are many more or less exclusively Jewish settlements there. These ghettos can be placed under a Jewish autonomous administration with a Jewish police force. The *Kommissariat* police will be responsible for guarding the boundaries between the ghetto and the outside world.[27]

Note the fundamental axiom of these instructions, namely, that there are still large and dense concentration of Jews – of the sort described by Seraphim – in these occupied territories, and that the other Jews should be forced into the ghettos in and around which this nucleus lives.

But then something unexpected happened. In early August, when Reichskommissar Hinrich Lohse transmitted the first comprehensive general directives for Ostland to the field echelons to elicit their reactions, the commander of Einsatzgruppe A, Franz Stahlecker, saw them as incompatible (*Nicht im Einklang*) with the measures he was implementing – which "cannot be discussed in writing," according to the instructions issued by a higher authority in the Reich Main Security Office (RSHA) – and as liable to interfere with them. Later, on August 29, Stahlecker advised the members of his Einsatzkommandos to carry out their assignment "using totally different means than those proposed by the Reichskommissar."[28] In plain terms, Jews could be murdered without ghettos.

[27] Benz et al., *Einsatz im "Reichskommissariat Ostland,"* pp. 33–5. A slightly different version, though essentially identical, is in *Trial of the Major War Criminals*, 25, p. 302 (PS-1212), as well as in United Restitution Organization, *Dokumentensammlung*, vol. 1, p. 136.

[28] "Wenn auch jede Unterstützung der Dienststellen des Reichskommissars gerade in der Judenfrage für uns selbstverständlich ist, müssen wir doch unser Hauptaugenmerk z. Zt. auf die endgültige Lösung der Judenfrage mit ganz anderen als den vom Reichskommissar vorgesehenen Mitteln richten": quoted in Christopher R. Browning, "Before the 'Final Solution': Nazi Ghettoization Policy in Poland (1940–1941)," p. 1; Benz et al., *Einsatz im "Reichskommissariat Ostland,"* pp. 42–6, 47–8 (Dok. 12, 13, 15).

Ghettos During the Final Solution, 1941–1943

What did Lohse's directives say that is relevant to our topic? According to section 5d:

To the extent possible Jews should be concentrated in cities or in neighborhoods in large cities where the population is already predominantly Jewish. That is where ghettos should be established. The Jews must be forbidden to leave the ghettos.

In the ghettos they should be allowed only just enough food as can be spared by the rest of the population, but in any case no more than is essential for the survival of the ghetto residents. This applies equally to the supply of other essential goods.

The residents of the ghetto will administer their internal affairs themselves, under the supervision of the district or city commissioner [*Gebiets-(Stadt) Kommissar*] or his representative. Jews can be enrolled in a police force to maintain internal order. They are to be equipped at most with rubber truncheons or batons, and will wear white armbands with a yellow Jewish star on their right upper arms.

An auxiliary police force of local inhabitants should be used to maintain a hermetic guard on the ghetto from the outside.

Entering the ghetto will require the approval of the district commissioner.[29]

For our purposes, the most important thing here is the first line: that ghettos be established "to the extent possible" (*tunlichst*). This formula extended freedom of action and absolute discretion to the local echelons, even though the intention was more general.[30] To this we can add two directives issued by General Franz von Roques, the commander of Army Group North Rear Area, in late August and early September 1941. First, on August 28:

The establishment of ghettos should be undertaken [*in Angriff zu nehmen*] in places where Jews constitute a large share of the population, especially in cities, when their establishment is essential or at least serves the goals. It should be avoided when the means of executive and administrative support are inadequate, according to the situation prevailing in the area or when more urgent actions must be taken.[31]

---

[29] Benz et al., *Einsatz im "Reichskommissariat Ostland,"* p. 41.

[30] It was around this time that *Einsatzgruppe B*, whose headquarters were then located in Smolensk, reported that "where advisable and possible, ghettos were instituted, Jewish Councils of Elders were set up, badges were introduced for the Jews, labor battalions were established, and so on, in concert with the local headquarters and relevant field headquarters. To preserve order in the residential areas just set up, Jewish order services were instituted. To prevent the outbreak of plague, it is recommended that Jewish health offices be set up in the Jewish residential quarters" (Ereignismeldung UdSSR Nr. 43, Berlin, 5. August 1941, p. 10, YVA 051/67-2, p. 403).

[31] Anordnung des Befehlshabers des rückwärtigen Heeresgebiets Nord, 28. August 1941, betr. Die Einrichtung von Ghettos, BA-MA, RH 22/6, quoted in Benz et al., *Einsatz im "Reichskommissariat Ostland,"* p. 123 (Dok. 85).

An almost identical order was issued on September 3:

> According to the orders of the Army High Command [OKH], ghettos may be set up in the larger places where there is a substantial Jewish population, if there is enough time and manpower to carry out the work involved. In no circumstances should the establishment of ghettos be viewed as urgent (*Als Vordringlich ist die Bildung von Gettos unter keinen Umständen anzusehen*).
> The Senior SS and Police Leader [*Höhere SS- und Polizeiführer*] should be involved in the implementation [of the establishment of the ghettos].[32]

"The establishment of ghettos should be undertaken in places where Jews constitute a large share of the population, especially in cities, when their establishment is essential or at least serves the goals;" and "[i]n no circumstances should the establishment of ghettos be viewed as urgent." These two statements encapsulate our entire story. That is, in the occupied territories of the Soviet Union, the presence of a large concentration of Jews was a good reason to organize a ghetto, motivated by the notion of the danger posed by the Jews of Eastern Europe (supplemented, in the Soviet Union, by the link between the Jews and Bolshevism). But the decision whether or not they should be set up was left to local discretion and dictated by the needs of a particular place: ghettos were useful, but not urgent or essential.

In light of this, we may ask what carried the day – the directives issued by the civil administration and army commanders or the Einsatzgruppen's murderous mission? In practice, many ghettos were established in the occupied Soviet territories, to a large extent pursuant to the directives issued for Ostland (and later for the Reichskommissariat Ukraine), but also in compliance with military orders. The Einsatzgruppen were involved, too, as their reports indicate. For example, according to "Activity and Situation Report No. 2," issued by the Einsatzgruppen to summarize the period between July 29 and August 14, "in many places Jews who remained behind were concentrated into ghettos."[33] Ghettos were established throughout the occupied Soviet Union,[34] to the very farthest edges

---

[32] Anordnung des Befehlshabers des rückwärtigen Heeresgebiets Nord, 3. September 1941, betr. Die Einrichtung von Ghettos im Befehlsbereich, BA-MA, RH 26–285/45, quoted in Benz et al., *Einsatz im "Reichskommissariat Ostland,"* p. 123 (Dok. 86); also in Norbert Müller, ed., *Deutsche Besatzungspolitik in der UdSSR. Dokumente*, p. 71.

[33] Peter Klein, ed., *Die Einsatzgruppen in der besetzten Sowjetunion 1941/42: Die Tätigkeits- und Lageberichte des Chefs der Sicherheitspolizei und des SD*, p. 136. "An vielen Orten wurden die zurückgebliebenen Juden in Ghettos zusammengefaßt" ("Tätigkeits- und Lagebericht Nr. 2").

[34] See the situation and activity report No. 10 for February 1942, in Klein, ed., *Die Einsatzgruppen in der besetzten Sowjetunion*, p. 295.

of the territory that came under German control, including the Crimea.[35] Many ghettos were established in the second half of 1941 (especially in Eastern Galicia, which had been annexed to the *Generalgouvernement*),[36] but some only later, in 1942.[37] In these territories there were also a few cases (Vilna and Riga, and also Bar in Vinnitsa Province in the Ukraine and elsewhere) where two ghettos were set up in one locality. There was only one precedent for multiple ghettos in Poland – in Radom (spring 1941), though, as we have seen, the idea was floated at the same time in Amsterdam. Ghettos continued to exist throughout the occupied Soviet Union into 1944 (in some cases, local German commanders may have emphasized the essential nature for "their" ghetto as a ploy to avoid reassignment to the frontlines). Despite the divergence in the aims of the Einsatzgruppen and the administrators in early August 1941, in practice there were no conflicts about setting up ghettos when the local commander or administrator decided to do so. But *such a decision was not taken*

[35] Ghettos or Jewish neighborhoods were established in three places in Crimea: in Yalta, in early December 1941; in Dzhankoi, also in early December; and in the village of Voikovstat. In the first two places both the Jews and locals referred to it as a ghetto. No ghettos were established in the seven other large and mid-size towns in the Crimea where Jews lived, nor in dozens of smaller places. In the Caucasus there were ghettos only in Mikoyanshakhar and Elista; the first was established in late August 1942, the second in the middle of that same month. But we do not know of any use of the term "ghetto." No ghettos were established in 19 other large and medium-size cities and villages. I would like to thank Mr. Kiril Fefferman for providing me with this information.

[36] In Lwów (Lemberg) the order to establish a ghetto was not issued until November 8, 1941, even though the Germans had entered the city on June 30 and appointed a Judenrat on July 22; see Danuta Dąbrowska, Avraham Wein, and Aaron Weiss, eds., *Pinkas ha-Kehillot: Poland*, vol. 2, *Eastern Galicia*, pp. 36–7. This came after a meeting of the *Generalgouvernement* on October 21, 1941, at which the governor of Lemberg Province, Dr. Karl Lasch, pushed for the establishment of a ghetto in the town, arguing that it was inconceivable that in Lemberg "they would treat the Jews differently than in Krakow and Warsaw. Consequently in the coming days the Jews will be concentrated in Jewish neighborhoods in Lemberg as well, as in the other cities of Galicia, and will disappear from the streets of the city." (*"Es sei nicht einzusehen, daß in Lemberg die Juden anders behandelt werden sollen, als in Krakau und Warschau. Die Juden sollen deshalb in den nächsten Tagen auch in Lemberg, wie in den übrigen Städten des Distrikts Galizien, in jüdischen Wohnvierteln zusammengefaßt werden und aus dem Straßenbild der Stadt verschwinden"*). Quoted in Sandkühler, *"Endlösung" in Galizien*, p. 155.

[37] For example, in Wolyn (Wolhynien/Volhynia) province, ghettos were established in Sarny on April 15 and Rokytno on May 1, 1942, even though the area had been occupied at the start of July 1941 and Judenräte had been established shortly thereafter. See Yehuda Bauer, "Sarny and Rokitno in the Holocaust: A Case Study of Two Townships in Wolyn (Volhynia)," esp. pp. 266–7. But even in Eastern Galicia, where – as noted – many ghettos were established in 1941, some were not set up until the fall of 1942: see the example of Brzezany in Shimon Redlich, *Together and Apart in Brzezany: Poles, Jews and Ukrainians, 1919–1945*, p. 112.

in every place. It was clear to all parties that these ghettos would have a very limited duration. In Riga, for example, a relatively junior officer, Major Karl August Hermann Ludwig Heise, told Latvian officers and the commanders of the Riga police that the establishment of the small ghetto there was only an interim stage (*Zwischenetappe*) in the "Solution of the Jewish Problem."[38] In places where ghettos were set up, they served to segregate the Jews and at least nominally to exploit their labor for the military and government (Lohse referred to this issue on November 14, 1941: "I have forbidden the unauthorized ['wild'] executions of Jews in Libau.... Of course the cleansing of Ostland of Jews is a most important task; its solution, however, must be in accordance with the requirements of war production"[39]), even if, in principle, Judenräte could have handled this; or they were established because other reasons justified postponing for a while the Jews' extermination.[40]

Once the aspect of exploiting the ghetto for economic ends had been emphasized – alongside and within the frenzy of murder taking place all around it – the practice of allowing the inhabitants to die because of the harsh living conditions, or even killing residents who were not "productive," was taken for granted and seen as a matter of course: if they were not "useful," there was no problem making them "disappear" (*verschwinden* was the German term that recurred frequently in this context).

---

[38] See "Protokoll Nr. 6 der Chefs der Lettischen Hilfspolizei, gez. Veiss, einer Besprechung von hohen Polizeibeamten Riga, am 15.9.1941, Central State Archive Riga, (LVVA), R 0998/1/. It will be published in a volume on the Soviet Union, edited by Dr. Bert Hoppe, as one of 16 volumes of Holocaust documents, in *Judenverfolgung 1933–1945 (VEJ): Die Verfolgung und Ermordung der europäischen Juden durch das nationalsozialistische Deutschland 1933–1945*. This joint project of the University of Freiburg, the Institute of Contemporary History in Munich, and the German Federal Archives will appear over the next decade. I thank Dr. Hoppe for providing me with this document.

[39] Lohse to Rosenberg, November 15, 1941, Nuremberg document PS-3663; quoted in Arad et al., eds., *Documents on the Holocaust*, p. 394. See also Shmuel Spector, *The Holocaust of Volhynian Jews, 1941–1944*, pp. 108–11. According to Situation and Activity Report No. 7, for the entire month of November, "the Jewish question in Ostland should be seen as resolved. Mass executions have decimated the Jews, and those who remain have been ghettoized" ("Die Judenfrage ist im Ostland als gelöst anzusehen. Größere Exekutionen haben Das Judentum stark dezimiert, und die verbliebene Juden wurden ghettoisiert"): Klein, *Die Einsatzgruppen*, p. 248.

[40] Gennadiy Vinnitsa in his study on the Holocaust in Eastern and Central Belarus found that in this area there were 246 cities, towns, and villages in which more than 28 Jews lived; in 147 of these, ghettos were established, in 99 they were not (although in 26 of these the local Jews were sent to some ghetto in the vicinity): Vinnitsa, "The Nazi Policy of Genocide of the Jewish Population in the Eastern and Central Parts of Belarus, 1941–1944," chapter 2.1.

Economic exploitation was not important enough to justify a significant improvement of conditions in the ghetto for those who served as a labor force. Nevertheless, in contrast to the killing on the outside, the ghetto offered Jews a chance to survive and some tenuous hold on life (for the moment, at least), despite the terrible conditions there – and the Jews grasped at this straw. In some cases the Germans exploited this chimera as a deceptive measure to facilitate murder. For example, in Rostov on Don in southern Russia, which the Germans retook on July 27, 1942, the local Einsatzkommando made rapid preparations to liquidate the Jews. As a first step, a Jewish council was appointed and made responsible for the registration of all the Jews (August 4). Then, on August 9, the Germans informed the Jews that they intended to establish a ghetto and ordered them to report to a designated assembly point for transfer there at 8 a.m. on August 11. Once assembled, they were transported to a site outside the city and shot.[41] Another tack was adopted in the city of Yevpatoria, in the Crimea. On November 21, 1941, the Einsatzkommando concentrated hundreds of Jews in several buildings that were referred to as the "ghetto" and held them there for two or three days before murdering them.[42]

Nevertheless, even if the German documents indicate an overall policy that permitted and even encouraged the establishment of ghettos while the Final Solution was taking root, as manifested in the hundreds of ghettos established in the territories occupied during Barbarossa, we must not ignore the other side of the coin. Most of the ghettos were not established immediately after the Germans occupied a town, but several weeks later; in fact, quite a few were not established until after several months of German rule (in the second half of 1941),[43] by which time a Judenrat

---

[41] The commander of Einsatzgruppe 10A published an order in which he justified the measure on the grounds that the German authorities could protect the Jews against attacks by the local population only "if they are concentrated in a separate section of town." See Tatiana Blumenfeld, "Mahoz Rostov tahat ha-kibbush ha-Natsi 1941–1943" (The Rostov district under Nazi occupation, 1941–1943), pp. 78–9; Shmuel Spector, "Rostov-on-Don," *Encyclopedia of the Holocaust*, p. 1306; Arad, *Toledot ha-Sho'ah: Berit Ha-mo'atsot*, pp. 521–2.

[42] Yitzhak Arad, Shmuel Krakowski, and Shmuel Spector, eds., *The Einsatzgruppen Reports: Selections from the Dispatches of the Nazi Death Squads' Campaign Against the Jews, July 1941–January 1943*, p. 265.

[43] For example, Lwów was occupied on June 30, 1941, and the order to set up a Judenrat was issued on July 22. But the order to establish a ghetto was not issued until November 8, at which time the Jews were given five weeks to relocate. See Dąbrowska et al., *Pinkas ha-Kehillot: Poland*, vol. 2, *Eastern Galicia*, pp. 36–7. Grodno, too, was occupied in late June; but the two ghettos there (which were some distance apart), as well as other small ghettos in the vicinity, were not set up until October to December. See

was usually already in operation. Some ghettos were not established until late 1942 (for example, in Volhynia, in the second half of that year).[44] What is more, not only were there Judenräte with no ghetto, there were also ghettos without a Judenrat, not to mention places where no ghetto was ever established but Jews continued to live for a short time.

The way ghettos were administrated also differed immensely from place to place. This bothered the Reichskommissariat für das Ostland after more than a year of occupation; consequently a secret circular regarding "the administration of the Jewish ghettos" (*Verwaltung der jüdischen Ghettos*) was sent by the financial department of the Reichskommissariat to the General Commissars (*Generalkommissare*) in Riga, Kovno, and Minsk on August 27, 1942. It stated that

> In Riga, Kauen [Kovno], Wilna and Minsk greater Jewish ghettos were established, [while] in some other places (residences of District Commissars [*Gebietskommissaren*]) – more tiny [ones]. The administration of the ghettos is not regulated in a uniform manner. Especially unclarified is the financial responsibility.
>
> The General Commissars should act according to the following directives. [However] it is not said that all details of these directives are binding, as local situations often differ from place to place.

In spite of this effort – the document is quite lengthy (four pages) and tries to cover the different facets of ghetto life from the point of view of the German authorities (financial responsibility for the ghetto, the direct supervision, security issues, forced labor, housing, etc.) – the actual situation did not change much after this document was released.[45]

Here we should note that a relatively large number of ghettos were established in the districts closer to the Polish border (those that had been part of Poland before the war), although some of them were not established until months after the start of the occupation.[46] Evidently,

---

Tikva Fatal-Knaani, *Zo Lo Otah Grodna. Kehillat Grodna u-Sevivatah be-Milhama uve-Shoah 1939–1945*, pp. 134–7.

[44] Spector, *The Holocaust of Volhynian Jews*, pp. 117–18; Spector, "Getta'ot ve-yudenrattim be-shithei ha-kibbush ha-Natsi bi-vrit ha-mo'atsot (bi-gvulot september 1939)" (Ghettos and Judenräte in the Nazi-occupied Soviet Union [September 1939 Borders]."

[45] Der Reichskommissar für das Ostland, Abt. Finanzen H 1356–29-, Riga, an die Herren Generalkommissare in Riga/Kauen/Minsk, 27. August 1942, YVA O-53/1; BKA, R 90/145.

[46] Christian Gerlach, *Kalkulierte Morde: Die deutsche Wirtschafts- und Vernichtungspolitik in Weißrußland 1941 bis 1944*, p. 532. But the Bialystok ghetto was set up in late

Ghettos During the Final Solution, 1941–1943

these regions were home to large and conspicuous concentrations of Jews who matched the old notion, propagated by Seraphim, of the Ostjuden peril. But as the Germans penetrated further east into the Soviet Union they had increasingly to deal with Jews who had spent two decades under Soviet rule. It was more difficult for the Germans to identify these Jews on the basis of their place of residence, occupation, and so on. Wendy Lower, who conducted comprehensive research on Zhytomyr Province, wrote:

For example, in the Jewish centers of Zhytomyr and Berdychiv, the Germans established ghettos but did not bother with a Jewish self-administration, for the ghetto served mainly as a temporary staging area while Nazi killing units were mustered for the killing *Aktion*. In the smaller communities, army village commanders and SS police personnel "ghettoized" Jews by herding them into bombed-out buildings, freight cars, and barns. Other regional chiefs avoided ghettoization altogether because they considered ghettos to be unnecessary or not useful in their local campaigns of persecution and annihilation.[47]

Lower adds that during the establishment of the Berdychiv ghetto – initiated by the Senior SS and Police Leader (*Höhere SS- und Polizeiführer*) in the southern zone, SS General Friedrich Jeckeln, soon after his arrival in the city on August 26, 1941, after some *Aktionen* had already taken place – the German commanders did not use the term "ghetto" in their correspondence.[48]

As stated, some of the ghettos continued to exist almost until the end of the German occupation. The protracted existence of ghettos such as those in Kovno, Vilna, and Bialystok, made possible the development of a community life that resembled the situation in the Polish ghettos established in 1940, with regard to institutions and procedures, even though the general awareness of their role was different because of the ongoing killing. In their later stages, these ghettos increasingly took on the character of forced-labor camps. But very few ghettos survived that long; in fact, there were extreme differences in the life spans of the various ghettos and many were used explicitly by local commanders as a brief

---

July on the orders of the military commanders, before control was transferred to civilian authorities in mid-August. See Nachman Blumenthal, *Darko shel yudenrat: te'udot mi-geto Bialystok* (Conduct and Actions of a Judenrat: Documents from the Bialystok Ghetto), p. 278.
[47] Wendy Lower, "Facilitating Genocide: Nazi Ghettoization Practices in Occupied Ukraine 1941–1942," p. 121.
[48] E-mail from Wendy Lower to Dan Michman, April 28, 2007.

prelude to murder and for nothing else.⁴⁹ But ghettos were not *necessary* for the genocide. There were quite a few places – including some with large Jewish populations, such as Kiev, Vinnitsa, Zaporozhe, Simferopol, and Dniepropetrovsk – where no ghetto was ever established.

As a general rule, the essential nature of the ghettos in the occupied Soviet Union differed from that of the earlier ghettos in Poland, even if they resembled them superficially in certain spatial and organizational parameters. Whereas the ghettos established in Poland before the summer of 1941 were seen as a *temporary expedient* until the regime worked out the contours of the solution to the Jewish Problem, after that their ephemeral nature was *part* of the solution that had been defined and was being implemented – and that solution had no need for a ghetto. But like other anti-Jewish measures that had emerged in previous years, here too habit and inertia helped preserve the now-outmoded phenomenon, at least from an external perspective. The old justifications for setting up ghettos, such as the threat of epidemics, were now supplemented by new arguments about the need to evict the Jews from their homes in order to provide housing for the general population, because of the damage to or destruction of buildings during the fighting; or by the shortage of food, which made it necessary to decide who should be fed and who should not. All of these arguments should be seen as no more than excuses and rationalizations; even the needs of forced labor and the Final Solution could be satisfied by other means (such as Judenräte only), but this is not what was said.⁵⁰ Basically, the entrenchment of the ghetto phenomenon in the period before Barbarossa seems to have led some officials to the idea that confining the Jews to ghettos was a good idea per se (even if only because there were still Jews around), because these were East European Jews. In such cases a ghetto could also be, as a by-product, an appropriate tool for achieving new goals. But ghetto conditions were harsher than in the years before the Final Solution, because it was clear that the ghetto was not only a temporary but a very short-term expedient. With regard to semantics, however, the term "ghetto" changed and branched out in this period, taking on in part the sense of "camp." Hence it is not surprising that Rosenberg's aforementioned directives for dealing with the Jewish question, dated August 2, 1941, refer more than once to "ghettos or

---

⁴⁹ Wendy Lower, *Nazi Empire-Building and the Holocaust in Ukraine*, p. 87; Vinnitsa, "The Nazi Policy of Genocide of the Jewish Population in the Eastern and Central Parts of Belarus, 1941–1944," chapter 2.1.

⁵⁰ Gerlach, *Kalkulierte Morde*, pp. 521–33.

camps" (*Ghettos oder Lager*) in tandem: in many cases they were actually the same thing, and only their location (the former being in an urban area) distinguished them.[51]

[51] Benz et al., *Einsatz im "Reichskommissariat Ostland,"* p. 3. In 1943, the Kovno ghetto became, officially, a "concentration camp" (Konzentrationslager Kauen). See Dov Levin, ed., *Pinkas Hakehillot: Lithuania*, p. 550; Tory, *Surviving the Holocaust*, p. 481. Similarly, after the liquidation of the Bialystok ghetto in August–September 1943, about 700 Jews were housed in a new compound that, so far as the Germans were concerned, was a labor camp, but which the Jews referred to as the "small ghetto"; see Bender, *Mul Mavet Orev* (Facing Death), p. 289.

11

Ghettos During the Final Solution Outside the Occupied Soviet Union: Poland, Theresienstadt, Amsterdam, Transnistria, Salonika, and Hungary

Par. 13. The Jews will live only in ghettos, colonies and labor camps which are designated by the authorities.

All Jews found in the territory of Transnistria who do not report to the authorities to be assigned a place to live within ten days of the posting of this order will be executed.

Jews may not leave the ghettos, colonies and camps without permission from the authorities. Violators of this order will be punished by death.

>> Romanian Military Order, posted throughout Transnistria in August 1941

For the possible establishment of a ghetto [in the Protectorate Bohemia and Moravia] only a poor and remote suburb is feasible (a section of the center of a city is not possible, it is not appropriate), or a small village or small town with perhaps some industry.

The concentration [of the Jews living in the Protectorate] will begin in the three large cities [Prague, Brünn and Mährisch-Ostrau]. Jews who are dispersed outside the cities will be forced to move there.

>> From the protocol of a meeting about the establishment of ghettos in the Protectorate Bohemia and Moravia, chaired by Reinhard Heydrich, October 10, 1941

The ghettization [sic] was implemented in such a way, that the Jews were forced to take up apartments in two large quarters of the city, which until now had been inhabited almost exclusively by Jews. One of these areas is situated in the western part of the city, the other in the eastern part. While the Jewish stores that are located outside the two ghettos may be maintained, they must be marked with a placard bearing the inscription "Jüdisches Geschäft – Εβραϊκόν κατάστημα" [Jewish business].

>> From a report by the German consul (Schönberg) in Salonika, February 26, 1943

Now we must expand our perspective to include events outside the occupied Soviet Union during the implementation of the Final Solution (1941–1944). Where else were ghettos established or planned? What was their significance in the overall anti-Jewish policy?

In these years, too, the phenomenon expanded in Poland, but it never spread to the territories under Nazi control in Western Europe. In Central Europe there was one exception: Theresienstadt. Something very much like a ghetto existed briefly in Salonika (Thessaloniki). Additionally, the term was adopted by two German allies: Romania, which toyed with the idea at home but discarded it, while applying it in some fashion in the newly acquired territories and the Soviet territories it administered; and Hungary, where ghettos were eventually established by the Hungarians themselves to facilitate the deportation of Hungarian Jews in the Final Solution. Let us examine these cases.

Poland

As mentioned earlier, a series of new ghettos were established in several areas of Poland starting in March 1941, that is, shortly before the invasion of the Soviet Union. In the Radom district this was triggered by the directive issued by Hans Frank on February 20, 1941, which called for the rapid and massive establishment of ghettos throughout the district and set a deadline (not met) of April 5.[1] It cannot be proved that this had any connection with the imminent start of Barbarossa, but a link is possible. Then, in the second half of 1941, with the spread of the first reports of a new Europe-wide solution of the Jewish problem, there was a fresh wave of ghettoization in Poland, even in the regions of Poland that the Germans had controlled since September 1939 and where ghettos already existed. This may have been influenced by the establishment of ghettos just across the border, in the Soviet Union; but again, the connection remains far from clear.[2] In any case, the establishment of ghettos in

---

[1] Sarah Bender, *Koder be'eretz oyev: Yehudei Kielce ve-Hasseviva Bemilchemet ha-Olam ha-Sheniya*, p. 111.
[2] See my remarks in Chapter 7 about Kielce and Lublin provinces, and the literature cited there, as well as Golczewski, "Polen," pp. 435–40. The question is whether the establishment of ghettos during this period should be associated with the establishment of the ghettos in the territories overrun during Barbarossa or as a continuation of the establishment of ghettos in the spring of 1941 in Lublin and Krakow provinces. Because historians, until recently, tended to shape their treatment of many Holocaust-related topics to coincide with political boundaries, discussions of the ghettos in Poland have not investigated the possible broader links of this wave of the establishment of ghettos.

Poland in the autumn of 1941 was an astonishing development, inasmuch as it ran counter to the intentions that had been stated only a short time before. On July 17, 1941, when Eastern Galicia (Polish until 1939 and occupied by the Germans as part of Barbarossa) was annexed to the *Generalgouvernement*, Hans Frank said that "he was not interested in the establishment of additional ghettos, because, according to a clear statement by the Führer on June 19 of this year [1941], the Jews will be eliminated from the Generalgouvernement in the foreseeable future."[3] This is clear evidence that until that time the ghettos in Poland were a containment measure, pending a clear decision on a solution to the Jewish problem, and that the establishment of ghettos was a function of local decisions (note the wording: Frank did not order that no more ghettos be set up, but only observed that he was not interested in their establishment). However, on October 21, 1941 the government of the *Generalgouvernement* decided about a prohibition (*Verbot*) to establish new ghettos, "because of the hope that it will be possible to have the Jews removed from the General Government in the near future."[4]

The change that took place between the date of Frank's declaration in the summer and the decision of October and the further establishment of ghettos later on corresponds to the gradual alteration in the meaning and purpose of the ghetto. Whereas formerly it had been intended to keep the Ostjuden peril in check until a decision had been taken on a comprehensive solution, now it meant in Poland as well what it had become in the Soviet Union: a sort of camp – for labor, transit, and the like, that is, the difference between "ghetto" and "camp" became increasingly blurred. On the official level this was well expressed in 1942, in the wake of Heinrich Himmler's order to the Senior SS and Police Commander (HSSPF) *Ost* Obergruppenführer Friedrich Wilhem Krüger (whose position was secretary of state [*Staatssekretär*] in the government of the *Generalgouvernement*) on July 19, that

until December 31 1942 the resettlement (*Umsiedlung*) of the entire Jewish population of the General-Government should be applied and finished. As of December 31, 1942 no persons of Jewish descent should be present in the

---

[3] "Der Herr Generalgouverneur wünsche keine weitere Ghettobildung mehr, da nach einer ausdrücklichen Erklärung des Führers vom 19. Juni d. J. die Juden in absehbarer Zeit aus dem Generalgouvernement entfernt werden": Werner Präg and Wolfgang Jacobmeyer, *Das Diensttagebuch des deutschen Generalgouverneur in Polen 1939–1945*, p. 386.

[4] "Da die Hoffnung besteht, daß die Juden in naher Zukunft aus dem Generalgouvernement abgeschoben werden könnten"; Werner Präg and Wolfgang Jacobmeyer, *Das Diensttagebuch des deutschen Generalgouverneur in Polen 1939–1945*, p. 436.

Ghettos Outside the Occupied Soviet Union

General-Government. Except for if they will be in the collection camps (*Sammellagern*) Warsaw [Warschau], Krakow [Krakau], Częstochowa [Tschenstochau], Radom, Lublin.[5]

Now some comprehensive directives were decreed: a "Police Order on the Establishment of Jewish Residential Districts in the Warsaw and Lublin Districts" (*Polizeiverordnung über die Bildung von Judenwohnbezirken in den Distrikten Warschau und Lublin*), dated October 28, 1942, and a supplementary directive of November 10 that listed places in Krakow, Radom, and Galicia districts that were assigned as *Judenwohnbezirke*; the order was signed by Kruger.[6] On the practical level the change in meaning and purpose can be demonstrated by the following examples. The Częstochowa ghetto was liquidated on October 7, 1942. Three weeks later, on November 1, it was replaced by what the Jews called the "little ghetto," because it occupied part of the former ghetto and because of some of the regulations that applied to it (the Germans seem to have used the same designation in their daily speech); formally, however, the Germans called it "a Jewish forced labor camp" (*Jüdisches Zwangsarbeitslager*).[7] In Łódź, too, there was a significant change in the nature of the ghetto as early as January 1942, and especially after the September 1942 *Aktion* known as the *Sperre*, when all "nonproductive elements" were deported. After that the Łódź ghetto was in fact a labor camp and the status of the *Judenältester* Rumkowski declined precipitously.[8] This also happened in the Warsaw ghetto, whose character changed significantly after the Great Deportation of July 1942.[9]

The Netherlands

In October and November 1941, the highest echelons of the Nazi administration in the Netherlands were again looking at the possibility of establishing a ghetto – principally in Amsterdam, but also perhaps elsewhere in

---

[5] Himmler to Krüger, [No title], "Geheim" [Secret], July 19, 1942, YVA JM.2094 (TR.2-NMT, 5575), 19.7.1942. For the context of the anti-Jewish policies in Poland at that time, see Peter Longerich, *Politik der Vernichtung*, pp. 504–11.
[6] The order and directive were published in *Verordnungsblatt für das Generalgouvernement* 94/1.11.1942, p. 665f.; 98/14.11.1942, p. 683 ff. (typed copy also in YVA 06/430). See Frank Golczewski, "Polen," p. 471.
[7] Abraham Wein, ed., *Pinkas ha-Kehillot: Poland, vol. 7, Lublin and Kielce*, p. 450.
[8] From that time on, the Jewish slogan of "Survival through Work" became critical. See Michal Unger, *Lodz: Aharon ha-getta'ot be-Polin*, pp. 326–34, 505.
[9] Israel Gutman, *The Jews of Warsaw*, pp. 277–9.

the country.[10] When the discussion took place, Reichskommissar Seyss-Inquart and his closest colleagues were already aware of the impending imposition of the new Jewish policy – the Final Solution – in their jurisdiction. Several weeks earlier, in late August, "Special Office J" (*Sonderreferat J*) had been established in the office of the head of the Security Police, Harster, to conduct "the fight against the Jews as a whole, aiming at the Final Solution of the Jewish Question by the relocation of all the Jews."[11] In early October, Hans Böhmcker (the special commissioner in charge of Amsterdam) drafted a series of proposals for actions to be taken as part of the new stage of the anti-Jewish policy. Noting that Jews were seeking to move to less-Jewish neighborhoods of the city, he suggested that

> even if it cannot be recommended that Jews be required to move to the Jewish neighborhoods [meaning those neighborhoods that already had a high percentage of Jews, as identified in the report of February 15, 1941, by the Amsterdam Municipality], in any case one should prevent their leaving them, and if Jews do move one should make sure that they move into the Jewish neighborhoods.[12]

The general tenor of this idea recalls what the Gestapo had proposed in Berlin in May 1938.[13] But it does not seem to have been enough for some members of the Nazi hierarchy in the Netherlands; the discussions chaired by Seyss-Inquart a week and a half later reached the following conclusions:

> A denser spatial concentration of the Jews living in Amsterdam should be aimed at. The following are accordingly recommended:
>
> a) An absolute and final demarcation of the Jewish neighborhoods, streets, and canals (*Grachten*).

---

[10] Jacques Presser, *Ondergang: De vervolging en verdelging van het nederlandse jodendom 1940–1945*, vol. 1, pp. 396–8. This section is not included in the relevant paragraph (p. 216) in the abridged English translation, *Ashes in the Wind*; Roest and Scheren, *Oorlog in de stad: Amsterdam 1939–1941*, pp. 355–7, 520–1.

[11] "Zur Bekämpfung des Judentums in seiner Gesamtheit, deren Ziel die Endlösung der Judenfrage durch Aussiedlung sämtlicher Juden ist": quoted in L. de Jong, *Het Koninkrijk der Nederlanden in de Tweede Wereldoorlog*, vol. 5b, p. 1024.

[12] "Wenn auch nicht befürwortet werden soll, die Juden zwangsweise in die Judenviertel umzusiedeln, so muß doch das Ausziehen aus diesem verhindert und beim Wohnungswechsel der Juden erreicht werden, daß sie, wenn sie umziehen, in die Judenviertel ziehen": Böhmcker to Seyss-Inquart, October 2, 1941, NIOD, Arch. VuJ, HA Inneres, Mappe 122 ad., 23A.

[13] See the discussion in Chapter 5.

b) Rerouting tramways (*Straßenbahnen*), etc., that pass through the Jewish neighborhood.
c) A more stringent police control of the entry to the Jewish neighborhoods, canals, and streets.
d) Promoting the removal of Aryans from the Jewish neighborhoods, streets, and canals, especially by means of confiscation in favor of the city [= municipality] for the purpose of future sanitation.
e) Marking of the Jewish businesses, where only Jews are permitted to shop.[14]

The Amsterdam branch of Eichmann's office, the *Zentralstelle für jüdische Auswanderung* (Central Office for Jewish Emigration),[15] also tracked Jewish residential movements with reference to three "Jewish neighborhoods" (the *Altes Judenviertel* [i.e., the old Jewish quarter], the *Transvaalviertel*, and the *Rivierenviertel*).[16]

This time, too, as during the first half of 1941, the idea came to nothing. The reasons are not clear, but it seems that the effort required was not considered to be worthwhile. In any case, in late November 1941, that is, seven weeks after the issue had come up for discussion again, Seyss-Inquart ruled unequivocally that "at the moment there is no intention to set up a ghetto. The police will deal with restricting the Jews' residence and domicile options."[17]

Consequently, the traditional, historical meaning of the term "ghetto" – not the new, Nazi one – was preserved in the discourse of some leading personalities in the German bureaucracy in the Netherlands. This becomes clear in the way the term was used in a secret report of the Commander of the Security Police of June 6, 1943, in which the deportation of the Jews from the Netherlands was described, that is, more than a year and a half after the discussion described here:

---

[14] "Niederschrift: Besprechung beim Reichskommissar am 10. Oktober 1941," gez.: Böhmcker, 11. Oktober 1941, NIOD, coll. Nr. 56: Arch. Generalkommissar FuW, Abteilung Siedlung und Bauten, E1.
[15] On the establishment and operation of this office, see Anna Hájková, "The Making of a Zentralstelle: Die Eichmann-Männer in Amsterdam."
[16] "Umzugsanträge (bis zum 24. November 1941)"; Umzugsanträge (bis 13.1.1942.)" NIOD, Arch. HSSPF, Zentralstelle für jüdische Auswanderung, map 249c (film 112 = 165.1). "Transvaalviertel" and "Rivierenviertel" are anacoluthic terms: half in Dutch, half in German.
[17] "Es ist vorerst nicht beabsichtigt, ein Ghetto einzurichten. Beschränkungen der Wohn- und Aufenthaltmöglichkeiten für Juden erfolgen durch die Polizei" ("Zur Behandlung der Judenfrage," 25 November 1941, NIOD, Arch. HSSPF, BdS, IVB4, 185a: "Zuständigkeit in Judenfragen" [film 311, 057.1], 27a, p. 2).

FIGURE 18. Sign with the inscription "Jewish Street" on a corner of a street in the center of Amsterdam, 1942.

Early in the morning on May 26, after thorough preparation, the historical Amsterdam ghetto (Jewish Quarter I) was encircled, barred and emptied of Jews, apartment after apartment with the involvement of the German Order Police.[18]

Romania

No academic study to date tracks the discussions of the ghettos idea by the Romanian Fascist regime. Consequently this will be a limited description based on a number of published documents and developments on the ground, from which we shall try to learn what we need for our discussion.

The idea of concentrating the Jews in a specific neighborhood was first raised on February 7, 1941, with reference to the Jews of Bucharest.

---

[18] "Es wurde deshalb nach genauer Vorbereitung am frühen Morgen des 26. Mai unter Zuziehung der deutschen Ordnungspolizei das historische Amsterdamer Ghetto (Judenviertel I) umstellt, abgeriegelt und Wohnung für Wohnung von Juden geräumt." Otto Bene, "Der Vertreter des Auswärtigen Amtes bei der Reichskommissar für die besetzten niederländischen Gebiete, an das Auswärtige Amt, Berlin," *Inhalt: Geheimbericht der Befehlshabers der Sicherheitspolizei betr. Juden*, June 6, 1943, www.diplomatiedervervolging.nl, Doc. 455.

The country's ruler, Marshal Ion Antonescu, referring to the "Jewish problem" in Romania, stated that

Were times normal... I would deport them all en masse from the country, beyond its borders. I cannot do that today, however.... Where would I send them? I cannot leave them to perish of hunger and die. I see this problem as unique in the current international situation. We must deal with it and solve it, for the Jews of Bucharest and the country. I would like to establish a special Jewish neighborhood in the capital [Bucharest], along Văcărești and Dudești streets, its boundaries to be demarcated, and require all the Jews of the city to move into it, into this Jewish bastion, within two years, while all the Romanian inhabitants left it. After that the kikes [Antonescu used the term "Yids"] could live among themselves, with their own commerce and their own synagogues, until more settled times arrive and we can deport them beyond our borders, to territories to be set aside for them. This is a problem that the Romanian people cannot solve alone, because it is an international question pertaining to the entire European continent.[19]

Ultimately this idea was not implemented, evidently as a result of lobbying by Jewish leaders following the initial steps to implement it in April 1941.[20] But this train of thought is interesting. On the one hand, we see that already in February 1941 Antonescu had adopted Hitler's vision of a Europe-wide solution of the Jewish problem, while continuing to think of the ghetto in its traditional and medieval sense, referring to residential buildings and commerce within it and never hinting that Jews would not be allowed out of the ghetto during the day for any purpose whatsoever. Nor, given that he had a two-year process in mind, did he see the establishment of ghettos as a particularly urgent need, and he spoke of the ghettoization of the Jews of Bucharest only.

Several months later, in June 1941, Romania, in alliance with Germany, declared war on the Soviet Union. Romania's harsh and independent anti-Jewish policy was reinforced when its armed forces came into contact with the German army and SS, especially Einsatzgruppe D, which was active in the districts adjacent to (and in some cases overlapping) those where the Romanian army was fighting in southern Ukraine. Thus the Romanians' general awareness of German activities against the Jews in previous years, mainly in Poland, was now supplemented by direct knowledge of German policy on the ground. On July 10, 1941, the Romanian authorities in Bessarabia and Bukovina (ceded to the Soviet

---

[19] *Evreii din România 1940–1944: Legislatia anti-Evreiasca*, vol. 1, p. 292.
[20] Jacob Geller, *Ha'amidah ha-ruhanit shel yehudei Romania bi-tqufat ha-Sho'ah (1940–1944)* (Spiritual Resistance of Romanian Jewry during the Holocaust [1940–1944]), p. 69.

Union in 1940 and recovered in the first days of Barbarossa) began setting up "ghettos and camps." This was not done in compliance with a directive issued by Ion Antonescu or in accordance with a formal plan. Romanian reports, like those of the Einsatzgruppen, did not have a precise definition of "ghetto"; they employed it, as a term that was apparently perfectly clear to authors and readers, in conjunction with the word "camp," frequently in the same breath. Nevertheless, there was a desire to learn from the German experience: on August 9, 1941, Mihai Antonescu, the deputy prime minister, sent a cable to Prime Minister Ion Antonescu informing him that a councilor in the Prime Minister's Office, Stănescu (whose first name was not mentioned), had left for Warsaw to learn how the Germans had concentrated their Jews in a particular neighborhood (*cartiere*) there.[21] There is no information about the results of this visit, but the fact that it took place indicates an intention to copy the German model, which the Romanians had heard about but did not know in detail.

The crux of the matter is that, at this stage, the establishment of ghettos in Romanian-controlled territories expressed a desire for ethnic cleansing on the one hand and a modicum of coordination with the German forces on the other. These camps and ghettos served as way stations for deportation, mainly to Transnistria. Ghettos were established in Kishinev (Chişinău) on July 31,[22] although the discussions about the need for a ghetto had begun more than a week earlier,[23] in Czernowitz (Cernăuţi) on October 11,[24] and in several other smaller places. The documents about them explicitly use the term "ghetto" (*ghettou*) or "Jewish ghetto" (*ghettoul evreese*).[25] There were no fundamental differences between the perception of these "ghettos" and the camps outside the cities, but there was a practical one – their size and the buildings in which Jews were housed. Most of them were overseen by the Romanian Gendarmerie.[26]

---

[21] Jean Ancel, *Transnistria, 1941–1942: The Romanian Mass Murder Campaigns*, vol. 1, p. 545; vol. 2, p. 26.

[22] See, for example, the report on the Romanian activity in the Einsatzgruppen Activity and Situation Report No. 2, for the first half of August 1941, Peter Klein, ed., *Die Einsatzgruppen in der besetzten Sowjetunion 1941/42: Die Tatigkeits- und Lageberichte des Chefs der Sicherheitspolizei und des SD*, p. 140 (and see also pp. 387–8).

[23] Ancel, *Transnistria 1941–1942*, vol. 1, p. 543; vol. 2, p. 17.

[24] For a detailed description, see, for example, Avigdor Shachan, *Burning Ice: The Ghettos of Transnistria*, pp. 116–20.

[25] See, for example, Ancel, *Transnistria 1941–1942*, vol. 1, p. 543; vol. 2, pp. 28–9 and passim.

[26] Jean Ancel, *Toledot ha-Sho'ah: Romania* (History of the Holocaust: Romania), pp. 571–85, 625–96.

Ghettos Outside the Occupied Soviet Union

In Transnistria – the name applied to the area of southern Ukraine east of the Dniester, which came under Romanian administration – the term "ghetto" was applied to one of the three forms of imposed Jewish domicile. First there was a directive (dated August 12) to concentrate the local (Ukrainian) Jews in ghettos.[27] Later, after the Romanians consolidated their control of the region, measures were taken that recalled what the Germans had done in various places, particularly in the Soviet Union, but also in Poland. According to Order No. 1 of the Romanian army, posted in Romanian, German, and Russian in the streets of occupied cities from August 1941:

> Par. 13. The Jews will live only in ghettos, colonies and labor camps which are designated by the authorities.
>
> All Jews found in the territory of Transnistria who do not report to the authorities to be assigned a place to live within ten days of the posting of this order will be executed.
>
> Jews may not leave the ghettos, colonies and camps without permission from the authorities. Violators of this order will be punished by death.[28]

Here, "ghettos" meant concentrations of Jews in defined residential areas in the major cities, but without walls or fences. Nevertheless, Jews who left the designated area would be shot. On September 3 the prefect of Balta County, whose seat was Balta, from 1924 to 1929 the capital of the Moldavian Autonomous Socialist Republic, and from 1941 to 1944 the capital of Transnistria, ordered all Jews (he used the derogatory terms *Yid* in Romanian and *Zhid* in Russian) in the city and its environs to move to the ghetto in the city, whose boundaries were specified in the decree. A head was nominated for the ghetto, one Sloimu Abramovici; an internal Order Service (i.e., police force) was established; Jews aged from 14 to 60 were subject to forced labor; all Jews were required to register, carry a numbered identity card, and wear a badge with the Jewish star and their

---

[27] Ancel, *Transnistria 1941–1942*, vol. 1, p. 546; vol. 2, p. 27.
[28] Ancel, *Toledot ha-Sho'ah*, p. 786. The German version of the order reads as follows:

> Art. 13. Juden dürfen nur in dem von den Behörden festgesetzten Gettos, Kolonien und Arbeitslagern wohnen.
> Alle im Gebiet Transnistriens befindlichen Juden welche binnen 10 Tagen nach Veröffentlichung vorliegender Verordnung sich nicht den Behörden zwecks Bestimmung ihres Wohnortes melden, werden mit dem Tode bestraft.
> Juden ist das verlassen der Ghettos, Kolonien und Lager ohne Benehmigung der Behörden verboten.
> Zuwiderhandelnde werden bestraft mit dem Tode.

Ancel, *Transnistria 1941–1942*, vol. 2, doc. 28, p. 50.

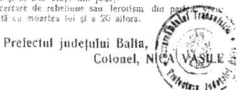

FIGURE 19. Early Romanian order, in Romanian and Russian, to establish ghettos in Transnistria, September 3, 1941.

ID number on it.[29] Later, mainly in October, the local Transnistrian Jews were transferred to similar residential districts. In this way the ghetto model was copied and firmly entrenched in the Romanian system within a few weeks.

The system spread through Transnistria following the mass deportation there of the Jews of Bessarabia and Bukovina. These Jews, too, were placed in "ghettos," but many others were settled in "colonies" and camps, and still others found themselves in villages and towns without a ghetto. These ghettos and camps were no longer way stations until the Jews could be removed from Romanian districts, but places where the surviving exiles (many had been murdered or had died en route) could live, in the absence of any clear decision about their ultimate fate.

The living conditions and arrangements for these places were specified in Order No. 23, issued by the governor of Transnistria, Gheorghe Alexianu, on November 11, 1941; here he repeated the distinction among

[29] Ancel, *Transnistria 1941–1942*, vol. 1, p. 549; vol. 2, pp. 52–3.

ghettos, colonies, and labor camps (some of which were in practice also in concentration camps). Later, in various official reports and internal correspondence, the terms "ghetto" and "colony" were frequently used interchangeably. This alternation was not limited to official correspondence. Even those who saw these places with their own eyes did not discern any real difference between ghetto, camp, and colony. S. Belyavsky of Odessa, who was married to a Jewish woman named Katia, wrote several letters to his brother-in-law. In one of them, dated, July 1, 1944, he wrote: "All our [family] were driven away to the camp 'ghetto,' in the winter time, during bitter cold and frost."[30] For the writer, clearly, it was a camp, but for his correspondent he added the explanation that this camp was referred to as a "ghetto." Many of the places in Transnistria where Jews were concentrated and which were defined as "ghettos" or "colonies" had populations that did not exceed 1,000 persons (and many had fewer than 150 residents).[31] The largest ghettos were in Odessa, Shargorod, Bershad, Golta, Verhovka, Luchinetz, Sadova, Tibulovca;[32] the largest of all was in Moghilev.[33]

The profile of the ghettos established by the Romanians fits into the broader picture. They were instituted in July 1941, at the time of the German campaign in the Soviet Union. The phenomenon expanded and was anchored in official occupation policy (military orders), especially in Transnistria in late 1941 and afterwards. In Romania, too, the terminology was somewhat vague. Jews were domiciled in approximately one hundred places, all told; but the uncertainty about the distinction among colony, ghetto, and camp has produced different counts in the research literature.[34] At first, the living conditions in the ghettos of Transnistria resembled those in the ghettos in the German-occupied territories of the Soviet Union. Over time, however, differences emerged as a result

---

[30] S. Belyavsky, July 1, 1944, YVA 033/2560. I would like to thank Dr. Diana Dumitru of the Department of World History, State Pedagogical University Ion Creanga, Chișinău, Moldova, for bringing this letter to my attention.

[31] Dennis Deletant, "Ghetto Experience in Golta, Transnistria, 1942–1944," pp. 5–6.

[32] Geller refers to Tibulovca as a camp: see *Ha'amidah ha-ruhanit*, p. 92.

[33] I would like to thank Dr. Ronit Fischer for helping me come up with these figures. The sources are: YVA, Jägendorf files, P-9/10 (for 1941–1946); YVA O-11/42; YVA, Shraga collection: JM/3356, JM/2824, JM/2808; USHMM, RG 54001 M, Reel I; Ancel, *Toledot ha-Sho'ah*. On the Moghilev ghetto, see Shraga Yeshurun, "Ha-hit'argenut ha'atsmit shel yehudei Bukovina be-geto Mogilev" (Self-organization by the Jews of Bukovina in the Moghilev Ghetto).

[34] The numbers cited by various scholars are: 120; 51 ghettos and 57 camps; 155. See Geller, *Ha'amidah ha-ruhanit*, p. 80n23.

of the Romanian authorities' looser administration of the ghettos in Transnistria and the lifestyle which crystallized there over time.[35] Here we should emphasize the important change that took place in Romania: after Antonescu decided to modify his Jewish policy for political reasons and put a stop to the widespread killings, at the end of 1942, the ghettos in Transnistria – despite their harsh conditions – became livable places that were far better than anything that existed under Nazi rule. Some Jews in the Ukrainian districts under Nazi control tried to flee to the ghettos of Transnistria, which continued to exist until the end of the war.

Theresienstadt

As the ghetto phenomenon expanded rapidly in the Soviet Union, Poland, and Romania, senior SS officers conceived the idea of ghettoizing the Jews of the Protectorate of Bohemia and Moravia, too. At the important secret meeting convened by Heydrich on October 1, 1941, in Prague, a week after he was named *Reichsprotektor* of Bohemia and Moravia on September 24, and at which Eichmann, too, was present, the "solution of the Jewish questions in the Protectorate and in part in the Old Reich" (*Lösung der Judenfragen im Protektorat und teilweise im Altreich*) was discussed. One of the proposals was deportation to various places in the East; it was clear, however, that it would be impossible to deport all the Jews by the end of the year. Consequently, the conclusions ran along the following lines:

On the Possibility of Ghettoization in the Protectorate
[For the establishment of a ghetto in the Protectorate] only a somewhat remote suburb should be considered (not a section of a city center; that is not appropriate), or a small village or small town with perhaps some industry.
 The concentration [*Zusammenziehung*] [of the Jews living in the Protectorate] will begin in the three large cities [Prague, Brünn (Brno), and Mährisch Ostrau (Moravská Ostrava)]. The Jews who are dispersed outside the cities will be forced to move into them [*zwangsweise hereingezogen*].
 Because it is more practical from the perspective of control and the provision of food and the like, only two ghettos will be established, *one ghetto in Bohemia [and] one in Moravia*, which will be subdivided into a work camp and a supply camp [*ein 'Arbeits-' und ein 'Versorgungslager'*].
 It will be easy *to provide employment opportunities* to the Jews (in the camp, producing small tools without mechanical needs, such as [making] wooden shoes, weaving straw for the Wehrmacht units in the north, etc.). The "Council of

---

[35] On these issues, see Dalia Ofer, "Life in the Ghettos of Transnistria."

Elders" will collect these objects and receive in return the bare minimum of food, with the calculated smallest amount of vitamins, etc. (under the supervision of the Security Police). – Small units [*kleine Kommandos*] may be permitted to work in part outside the ghettos, under guard; this is applicable especially in the case of special manpower [= experts] for whom there is a demand.[36]

The ghettos envisioned here – the model from which Theresienstadt would emerge – were thought of as an interim measure that was part of the new stage of purging the Protectorate of its Jews. The concept is diversified but quite different in its nature and meaning from that of an urban district in which Jews are compelled to live, like the Polish ghettos of 1940 and early 1941. First of all, the two ghettos were to serve as camps, especially labor camps, which indicates that in this discussion – as in the Soviet Union, Poland, and Romania – the distinction between ghetto and camp was not clear cut. Second, although the ghetto is still part of an existing locality – a remote suburb, a small village, or a small town – it is emphatically not in the center of the city; that is, not like in Poland! The idea of setting up ghettos in small villages or towns may have been a reincarnation of a notion that Eichmann had tried to promote two years earlier – the Reichsghetto in Nisko. Similarly, the proposal to

---

[36] The original text reads as follows:

> Über die Möglichkeit der Ghettoisierung im Protektorat.
> In Frage kommt nur ein etwas abgelegener Vorort (nie ein Teil einer Innenstadt, das hat sich nicht bewährt), oder ein kleines Dorf oder eine kleinere Stadt mit möglichst geringer Industrie.
> Die Zusammenziehung [der Juden] beginnt in den drei großen Städten [Prag, Brünn und Mährisch-Ostrau], die verstreut auf dem Lande lebenden Juden werden zwangsweise hereingezogen.
> Da es zweckmässiger ist wegen der Überwachung und Belieferung mit Lebensmitteln usw., sollen nur zwei Ghettos eingerichtet werden: ein Ghetto in Böhmen, eines in Mahren, die zu unterteilen sind in ein 'Arbeits-' und ein 'Versorgungslager'.
> Die Juden können gut mit Arbeitsmöglichkeiten versorgt werden (im Lager durch Anfertigung von kleineren Gegenständen ohne maschinellen Aufwand, z. B. Holzschuhe, Strohgeflechte für die Wehrmachtsteile im Norden, usw.). Der 'Ältestenrat hat diese Gegenstände einzusammeln und bekommt dafür das geringste Mass an Lebensmitteln mit dem errechneten Minimum an Vitaminen usw. (unter Kontrolle der Sicherheitspolizei). – Teilweise können auch kleine Kommandos ausserhalb des Ghettos unter Bewachung arbeiten, dies gilt insbesondere für benötigte Spezialkräfte.

Meeting of SS commanders on the solution of the Jewish question in the Protectorate and, in part, in the Old Reich (Notizen aus der Besprechung am 10.10.41 über die Lösung von Judenfragen), YVA, Eichmann Trial TR3-1193; printed, with several mistakes (evidently transcription errors) in Hans Guenther Adler, *Theresienstadt 1941–1945: Das Antlitz einer Zwangsgemeinschaft*, pp. 720–1.

relocate the Jews to a suburb echoes the idea floated for Berlin in 1938 (see Chapter 5).

Roughly at the same time as this meeting, or somewhat earlier, a new department – Department G, for "ghetto" – had been set up in the Jewish community council of Prague, which was totally subordinate to Eichmann's *Zentralstelle für jüdische Auswanderung*. Its role was to draft plans for camps for the Jews; these camps were also referred to as "ghettos."[37] After that, the idea began to evolve, eventually producing the "Theresienstadt Ghetto."[38] Over the years, scholars – and, even more so, the popular discourse – have conducted a retrospective debate as to whether Theresienstadt was a "real" ghetto or a camp.[39] The basic premise of this discussion, however, is that the Łódź and Warsaw ghettos are the defining case; if that is the standard, Theresienstadt was certainly more like a camp (although it was also different from the camps). The debate thus assumed a particular model of ghetto as the touchstone and ignored the historical reality reflected in the use of the word by those who actually created the ghettos. As we have seen, Theresienstadt was established as a collection point (*Samellager*),[40] but from the very beginning it was also explicitly referred to as a ghetto. Later, when it was assigned additional functions, that designation, too, was modified in various ways: a "ghetto for the elderly" or "old-age ghetto" (*Altersghetto*); a "ghetto for distinguished persons" (*Prominentenghetto*); the "city of the Jews" (*Judenstadt*);[41] and finally, for propaganda purposes, the "model ghetto" (*Musterghetto*) and "state of the Jews" (*Judenstaat*).[42] The changes in the meaning of the term should not astonish us. The ghetto/camp debate is – from the perspective of the present volume – quite superfluous: yes, the Theresienstadt Ghetto had some of the distinctive characteristics of concentration camps, labor camps, and transit camps – but this was also

---

[37] Adler, *Theresienstadt*, p. 21.
[38] Adler, *Theresienstadt*, p. 21; Margalit Shlain, *Ha-hanhaggah ha-yehudit be-ma'avakah le-hissaredut: Terezyenshtat 1941–1945* (Jewish Leadership in Theresienstadt: Struggle for Survival, 1941–1945), pp. 59ff.
[39] In his book, Adler repeatedly uses the term "ghetto" in quotation marks to suggest that it was not really a ghetto (e.g., p. 24). For the debate in Israel, see, briefly, Ruth Bondy, *Shorashim aqurim: peraqim be-toledot Yahadut Chekhyah, 1939–1945* (Uprooted: Essays on the History of the Czech Jews, 1939–1943), pp. 9–12.
[40] Adler, *Theresienstadt*, p. 25.
[41] Adler, *Theresienstadt*, p. 25.
[42] Livia Rothkirchen, *The Jews of Bohemia and Moravia: Facing the Holocaust*, pp. 233–4; Michael L. Miller, "Czech Holocaust or Holocaust in the Czech Lands?"

Ghettos Outside the Occupied Soviet Union

the case with many other ghettos. What gave the Theresienstadt Ghetto the classic parameters of a camp is the fact that it was not established in a city where Jews already lived but was instead a special facility to which the Jews were transferred. Dieter Wisliceny, Eichmann's deputy, noted in his memoirs that the place was both a ghetto and "Camp Theresienstadt" (*Lager Theresienstadt*).[43]

As for *Altersghetto*: this designation was coined at the meeting in the Villa Wannsee on January 20, 1942, where the implementation of the Final Solution throughout Europe was discussed (it is known in the literature as the Wannsee Conference, even though it was not actually a conference of department heads but a working meeting of senior middle-level officials [a *Dienstbesprechung*]). This authoritative consultation provides evidence of another semantic shift in the word "ghetto." In the general overview he gave at that meeting (according to the formal minutes kept by Eichmann), Heydrich noted that "Europe is to be combed through from West to East in the course of the practical implementation of the final solution."

> The evacuated Jews will first be taken, one after the other,[44] to so-called transit ghettos [*sogenannte Durchgangsghettos*], in order to be transported further east from there....
>
> It is intended not to evacuate Jews over 65 years old, but to place them in an old-age ghetto – Theresienstadt is being considered.[45]

That is, for Heydrich there were various types of ghettos: ghettos of the type that already existed (which he did not mention, because they were a familiar phenomenon), and two new types to which he attached adjectives: one for Jews who would be deported to them, that is, ghettos that were not in their original hometowns but elsewhere, en route, serving as way stations, like the Riga Ghetto – the transit ghettos; and the ghetto for the elderly and for German Jews who had performed special services for the Reich – the *Altersghetto*.

---

[43] Dieter Wisliceny (Zelle 106), "Bericht," Bratislava, 18.11.1946, YVA M-5/162, p. 14.

[44] "*Zug um Zug*": this German expression is erroneously translated in several publications in English and Hebrew as "group by group" or "train by train."

[45] English: Arad et al., eds., *Documents on the Holocaust*, p. 256. See also *Trials of the Major War Criminals*, NG-2586-G; quoted in Léon Poliakov and Josef Wulf, *Das Dritte Reich und die Juden: Dokumente und Aufsätze*, p. 123; Adler, *Theresienstadt*, pp. 22–3.

Salonika

The operation to deport the Jews of Salonika in Greece, overseen by Dieter Wisliceny, took place in two stages. First, in February and March 1943, the Jews were concentrated in one part of the city; then, between March and August of that year, they were deported to Auschwitz. A series of decrees were published, starting in early February. The first of them, M.V.1237, issued on February 6, required all Jews, except those of foreign nationality in possession of a valid passport, to move into certain neighborhoods by February 25 (the deadline was met). One of the three sites, the Baron Hirsch camp, was fenced off; eventually it became the largest concentration of Jews in the city.[46]

The February 6 order itself did not use the word "ghetto." Rather, it stated that "all Jews living in Salonika – exceptions have been specified above – must hereafter concentrate in a specific part of the city."[47] But the term "ghetto" keeps recurring in the discussions about these neighborhoods. On February 26, the day after the move into the ghettos was completed, the German consul in Salonika, Schönberg, referred in a memorandum to this transfer as "ghettization" [*Ghettisierung* (sic) – twice], and described the course of events as follows:

As first measures against the Jews here, two orders were published and took effect on the 25th of this month: the marking [of the Jews] by a yellow Star of David and ghettization. The two steps were implemented by the local Jewish community council with astonishing speed, on the orders of a committee that arrived here, headed by Hauptsturmführer Wisliceny, and with the participation of the German Security Service here, both of whom reported to me on a regular basis....

The ghettization was implemented in a manner that required the Jews to move to [live in] apartments in two sections of the city, which until now had been inhabited almost exclusively by Jews. One of them is in the western part of the city, the other in the eastern part. The Jews are permitted to continue to run the Jewish businesses located outside the two ghettos, but they must be marked with a sign that reads *Jüdisches Geschäft* – Εβραϊκόν κατάστημα [Jewish business].[48]

---

[46] Brachah Rivlin, ed., *Pinkas ha-kehillot: Greece*, pp. 277–80. In his memoirs, Wisliceny asserted that even before the deportation campaign, "the military government had planned to set up a ghetto and local forced labor installations for the Jews as part of the Todt Organization" ("Die Militärverwaltung plante eine Ghettobildung und örtlichen Arbeitseinsatz der Juden in Rahmen der OT [Organisation Todt]"): see Wisliceny, "Bericht," 18.11.1946, p. 17.

[47] See a facsimile of the document in Michael Molho and Joseph Nehama, *Sho'at yehudei Yavan 1941–1944* (The Destruction of Greek Jewry, 1941–1944), between pp. 64 and 65.

[48] Schönberg's memorandum, "Maßnahmen gegen die hiesigen Juden," Salonik [sic], 26 February 1943 (attached to a letter from von Hahn of Department D III in the Foreign

In Italian diplomatic reports about Salonika, too, we read that "the Jews are now forbidden to leave the ghetto" (March 6) and that "the Jews of Salonika are facing a total ban on all activities whatsoever and for more than a week have been locked up in the ghetto without being able to leave for any reason" (March 14).[49] The use of the term "ghetto" thus reflects what everyone understood: the newly imposed residential district was explicitly a ghetto. The Italian reports on the Jews of Salonika are curious in another way: they employ the term "ghetto" in the language in which it was first coined, more than four centuries earlier, but with a different sense. The Jews' confinement to these three ghettos was explicitly in preparation for their deportation, so that they were in fact transit camps for Jews (*Judendurchgangslager*), as were Westerbork, Mechelen/Malines, and Drancy in Western Europe. The greatest similarity in all respects was to the camp in Mechelen/Malines, Belgium, which was a three-story Austrian barracks dating from the 18th century, built around a courtyard and inside the city, like the Baron Hirsch camp in Salonika. As for the semantic shift, the ghettoization in Salonika was a prologue to what would happen 14 months later in Hungary.

Why was the term "ghetto" used in Salonika, which is not in Eastern Europe? The documents from 1943 provide no answer to this question. Nevertheless, it is interesting to note a photo from the Institute for Research into the Jewish Question in Frankfurt, with which Seraphim was affiliated; taken by a photographer working for the Institute who was sent to Salonika in September 1941, it bears the caption "the Jewish Quarter in Salonika" (*Das Judenviertel in Salonika*). It was filed with a newspaper article (the newspaper's name and the date of the article have been cut off) about Salonika, under the headline "The Warsaw of the

---

Ministry to Adolf Eichmann, March 3, [19]43, YVA TR.3 1003); for a facsimile of the original, see Irith Dublon-Knebel, comp. and trans., *German Foreign Office Documents on the Holocaust in Greece (1937–1944)*, pp. 115–16, 292–3; the English translation given there has been modified. Joseph Ben erroneously reports that the document was attached to a letter by von Thadden: see his *Yehudei Yavan ba-Sho'ah uva-hitnaggedut 1941–1944* (Greek Jewry in the Holocaust and the Resistance 1941–1944), p. 42.

49 Consul General Zamboni to the Italian Diplomatic Mission to Athens and for the information of the Ministry of Foreign Affairs, Rome, 6.3.1943: "è stato ora proibito agli ebrei di uscire dal ghetto"; Consul General Zamboni to the Italian Diplomatic Mission to Athens and for the information of the Ministry of Foreign Affairs, Rome, 14.3.1943: "Gli ebrei di Salonicco sono stati totalmente esclusi da qualunque attività e si trovano da più di una settimana chiusi nel ghetto, senza poter ascire per nessuna ragione": in Daniel Carpi, ed., *Italian Diplomatic Documents on the History of the Holocaust in Greece (1941–1943)*, pp. 133, 136.

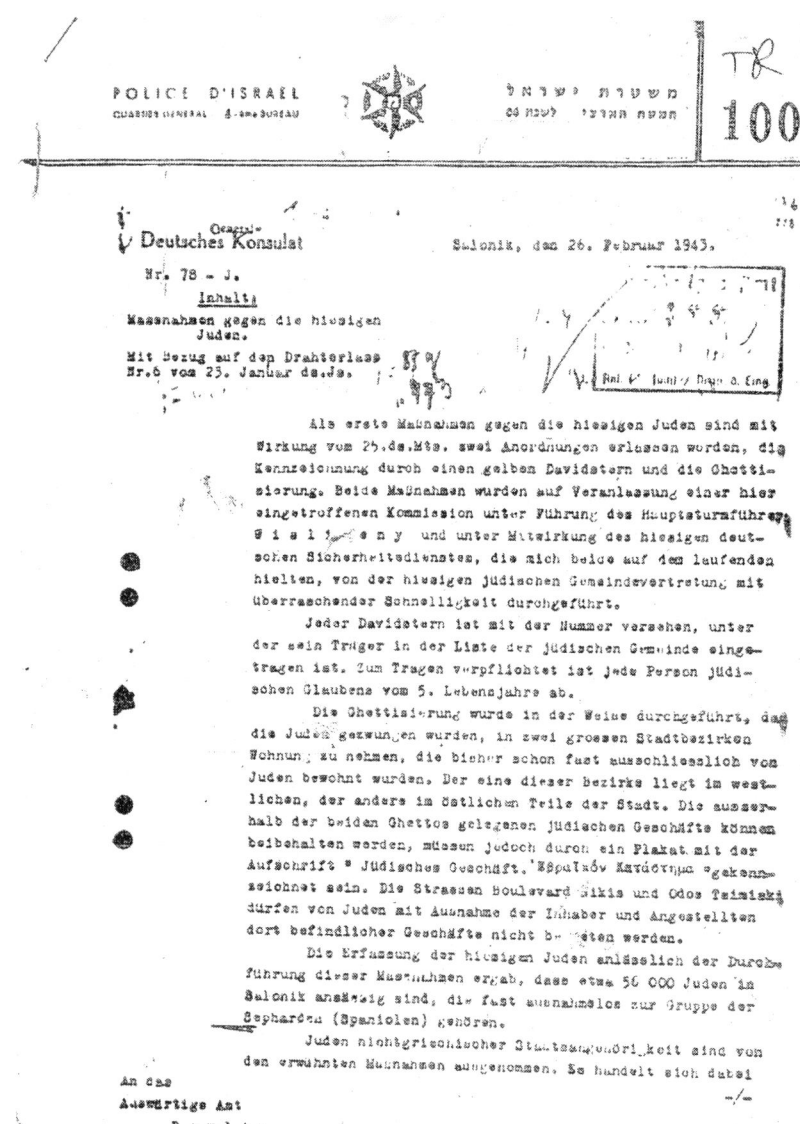

FIGURE 20. Report of the German consul in Salonika on the creation of ghettos in this city, February 26, 1943.

Mediterranean"! This means that at least for those engaged in the "scientific" study of the Jewish Question, who were collecting material about ghettos (both pre- and post-1939), the prominent and crowded Jewish community of Salonika brought to mind the Jews of Poland, that is, the

Ghettos Outside the Occupied Soviet Union

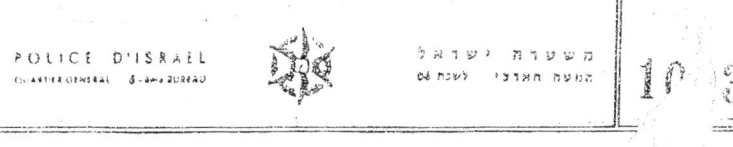

FIGURE 20 (*continued*)

Ostjuden.[50] This is what connects the case of Salonika to that of Amsterdam: in both places the local Jewish neighborhoods were reminiscent of the Jews of Eastern Europe – because of their long-established existence, size, and poverty, as well as the conspicuous differences between the Jews and their non-Jewish surroundings. It is true that it took *anti-Semitic Germans* to see these places in this light; but see them they did.

Hungary

The last wave of the use of the term "ghetto" began in April 1944, after the Germans had seized control of Hungary on March 19. During the planning for the deportation of all the Jews of Hungary – an operation that Adolf Eichmann and the senior echelons of the Hungarian Interior Ministry agreed to on April 4 – it was decided to carry out the deportation systematically, county by county.[51] With this in mind, starting in mid-April, approximately 180 detention facilities were established, all of them

---

[50] Photo collection of the Institut zur Erforschung der Judenfrage, at YIVO, New York. I would like to thank Nina Shpringer, the curator of photographs at Yad Vashem, for bringing this item to my attention.

[51] On the course of events in Hungary, see, at length, Randolph L. Braham, *The Politics of Genocide: The Holocaust in Hungary*, pp. 572–625; Christian Gerlach and Götz Aly, *Das letzte Kapitel: Realpolitik, Ideologie und der Mord an den ungarischen Juden 1944/1945*, pp. 139–40.

intended to serve as collection camps for Jews before their deportation by rail to Auschwitz. These places went by various names. The Interior Ministry order of April 7 refers to conveying the Jews to "collection camps" (*gyűjtőtábor*); but it also states that the Jews should be confined to "Jewish buildings" (*zsidóépület* and *zsidóház* – parallel terms that may imitate the Judenhäuser established in Germany at the start of the war) and "ghettos" (*gettó*) in the cities and towns.[52] A later order, dated April 28, 1944 – the government decree that students of the Holocaust in Hungary generally call the "Ghetto order" – referred to the confiscation of the Jews' homes and designation of a new domicile (*lakóhely*) for them, without using the word "ghetto."[53] In the field, the most common term employed in the provinces for the urban concentration and detention sites was "ghetto," but sometimes also "Jewish ghetto" (*zsidógettó*).[54] Other terms were used in rural areas, such as "collection place" (*gyűjtőhely*)[55] and "settlement" (*lakótelep*).[56] A clear distinction was made between all of these and the entrainment centers (*bevagonírozási központ*) to which the Jews were sent from the ghettos to board railcars when they were actually deported. Some of the ghettos, by whatever name, were not under Jewish administration. Many of them were established in brick factories on the outskirts of a city or town. The physical layout of many of these places was quite different from that of the ghettos in Poland in 1940–1941, although some resembled some of the later ghettos in the Soviet Union. However, in a study currently carried out by László Csősz on these ghettos and detention centers in the Hungarian countryside, the author shows that in a series of towns where the term ghetto was used (most of them in Trianon Hungary, that is, not in the newly annexed territories), the restricted area of the Jews was in the town, in traditional Jewish neighborhoods. These resembled more the earlier ghettos of the Nazi period, and the considerations of the local (collaborating) authorities played a role in the implementation of the short-lived ghettoization. In this context, it is important to emphasize that a discourse on ghettos for Jews

---

[52] See Order No. 6163/1944, in Ilona Benoschofsky and Elek Karsai, eds., *Vádirat a nácizmus ellen*, pp. 124–7. I would like to thank Dr. Kinga Frojimovics for the information about Hungary and the Hungarian terms used here.

[53] Order No. 1610/1944, in Benoschofsky and Karsai, *Vádirat*, pp. 244–50.

[54] This is the term that the local authorities allowed the Jews in the ghettos of Edelény and Szendrő (Borsod County) to use as their mailing address.

[55] This term is used in the order issued by Andor Thaisz, the subprefect of Fejér County, to set up ghettos in that county (ghettos were established in nine localities there).

[56] This term is used in the order issued by Sándor Neográdi Horváth, subprefect of Nógrád County (where ghettos were set up in five localities).

emerged in Hungarian anti-Semitic literature in the years preceding the German occupation.[57] But both the purpose and meaning of the concept changed when it was actually adopted in Hungary in 1944.

Admiral Miklós Horthy, the regent of Hungary, who had cooperated with the Germans over the years and did not resist them after their takeover of the country in March 1944, ordered a suspension of the deportations on July 7. By that time, however, only one large concentration of Jews remained in Hungary – in Budapest. There, since June 24, Jews had been housed in approximately 2,100 buildings scattered all over the city, marked with a yellow star ("star houses" – *csillagos házak*); this was understood as "ghettoization," that is, restriction to "mini-ghettos," and referred to as such by the Jews. Fundamentally, however, these buildings were more like the Judenhäuser in Germany. The authorities began planning the concentration of the Jews of Budapest in May and had initially spoken about resettling them in seven municipal districts – what Tim Cole refers to as "concentration within dispersion." But as in Warsaw and Amsterdam some years earlier, the plans were modified after they were submitted to the municipal authorities, who objected that a closed ghetto would interfere with the functioning of the city. "Jewish houses" offered an easy way around such problems.[58] On November 20, 1944, after the October coup that brought Ferenc Szálasi's Arrow Cross Party to power, what everyone called the "little ghetto" (*kisgettó*) was established, along with the "protected ghetto" (*vedett gettó*) or "international ghetto" (*nemzetközi gettó*) for Jews with documents issued by neutral diplomatic missions. On December 10, 1944, the ghetto in Pest (*Pesti gettó*), also known as the "large ghetto" (*nagygettó*), was sealed off, and all the Jews of Budapest who had been living in the "star houses" were moved into it.

The Budapest ghetto existed for only a few months, until the liberation of the city by the Red Army (January–February 1945). It was established after the end of the major wave of deportations, but not on the assumption that the treatment of the "Jewish problem" was complete. In a sense, the Budapest ghetto was a reprise of the ghettos in Poland in 1940 and 1941: a concentration of Jews in a Jewish neighborhood in anticipation of a new decision about what would be done with them. But the circumstances

---

[57] László Csősz, "Municipal Administration in Hungary and the Holocaust: Regional Patterns and Individual Responses," unpublished paper, presented at the Yad Vashem workshop on "Persecution and Murder of the Jews: Grassroots Perspectives," July 4–12, 2010.

[58] Tim Cole and Graham Smith, "Ghettoization and the Holocaust: Budapest 1944."

in Hungary in late 1944 and early 1945 were different: these were the twilight months of World War II, and the short-lived Arrow Cross regime in Hungary and German involvement produced great uncertainty and hideous scenes of murder.[59]

[59] For all these details, see Hava Baruch, "Ghetto Budapest. Ifyuno ve-Yihudo shel Tahalich ha-Ghetto'izatsiya veha-Kiyum ha-Yehudi be-Virat Hungariya beyn Yuni 1944 le-Yanuar 1945." Kinga Frojimovics, Géza Komoróczy, Viktória Pusztai, and Andrea Strbik, *Jewish Budapest: Monuments, Rites, History*, pp. 382–423.

12

Summary and Conclusions

> Antisemitism was one of the foundations of the platform of Nazism. It stemmed in practice from two outlooks: (1) the pseudo-scientific biological statements of Prof. Günther and (2) the mystical-religious view that the world is directed by forces of good and evil. According to this view, the principle of evil was embodied in the Jews.... This world of images is totally incomprehensible in logical or rational terms, [because] it is a form of religiosity that leads to sectarianism. Millions of people believed these things under the influence of this literature, something that can be compared only to similar phenomena from the Middle Ages, such as the mania of witches (*Hexenwahn*).
>
> Dieter Wisliceny, an official in Adolf Eichmann's Department of Jewish Affairs IVB4 in the Reich Security Main Office, in a 1946 affidavit

> An antisemitism based on purely emotional grounds will find its ultimate expression in the form of progroms [sic]. An antisemitism based on reason, however (*jedoch*), must lead to systematic legal combatting and elimination of the special privileges which the Jew holds, in contrast to the other aliens who live among us (aliens' legislation). But (*aber*) its ultimate objective (*sein letztes Ziel*) must unswervingly be the irrevocable removal of the Jews altogether (*Entfernung der Juden überhaupt*).
>
> Adolph Hitler, letter to Gemlich, September 1919

In this book I have endeavored to answer fundamental questions that had never been addressed in studies of the ghettos of the Nazi era: precisely where and when did the idea for the ghettos originate? How are we to explain the protracted duration of the period over which they were established, the clear limits to their distribution, the fact that the "ghetto system" was not total and certainly not consistent, and the very different characters of many ghettos? While considering all this, I faced another enigma – the fact that we have never found a single comprehensive directive about ghettos, one that includes an explanation of their objective and the principles for their design and administration.

The starting point of our investigation was linguistic and cultural, an orientation that I contrasted to the dominant approach in ghetto studies (and to a large extent in Holocaust studies in general), followed notably by Raul Hilberg and Christopher Browning, which seeks to understand the ghettos from an administrative and planning perspective and looks for organizational and bureaucratic rationales. The fact that the Nazis employed a term that already had a history of some 400 years requires us to discover why the term was adopted, by whom and when, and in what sense, and not to accept its inclusion unquestioningly in the Nazi lexicon as self-evident and of merely technical significance. What is more, the linguistic and cultural perspective entails a close scrutiny of the uses of the term over the course of the Nazi regime. The historiographical analysis with which I began revealed the decisive influence of our extensive knowledge about a few ghettos in Poland on the dominant understanding of the term "ghetto" in the research literature and popular image of the Holocaust. To counter this I emphasized the large number of ghettos we now know existed (hundreds, in fact more than a thousand), the fact that many of them were in countries other than Poland, and the fact that even in Poland many of them were established relatively late in the process (in and after 1941, and not in 1939 or 1940).

Let us review the conclusions that were arrived at from this discussion.

1. It was Fear of the Ostjuden Peril that Produced the First Nazi Ghettos in 1939 and 1940

The factors that motivated the Nazis to create ghettos – that is, clearly segregated and overcrowded Jewish neighborhoods with unbearable living conditions – were psychological rather than bureaucratic: fear of the cultural stereotype of the Ostjuden as the source of Jewish power, and fear of the crowded Jewish neighborhoods of Eastern Europe ("ghettos"), the crucible of this dangerous type of Jew. This derogatory and ominous image of the Ostjuden was endowed with strong quasi-scientific backing by the work of a respected scholar, Professor Peter-Heinz Seraphim, whose *Das Judentum im osteuropäischen Raum* (Jewry in the Territory of Eastern Europe) was published at a fateful juncture in the history of the Third Reich: after the Nazi regime had developed deep roots (1933–1937) and was able to begin planning its campaign of expansion, and specifically in the fateful year (1938) when its anti-Jewish policy escalated rapidly and it was feverishly searching for new ways to deal with the Jews. The ideologues of Nazism saw themselves as "rational" anti-Semites (as Hitler defined his own brand of anti-Semitism in his first written tract, *Antisemitismus der Vernunft* [1919])[1] and were open to the influence of such a "scholarly" work and author. From the perspective of active anti-Semitism, the face-to-face encounter with the Eastern European ghetto and the Eastern European Jew in the immediate aftermath of the invasion of Poland in September 1939 required the German administrators in the field to actually deal with what was perceived to be an existential threat. In the absence of a decision about a comprehensive solution to the Jewish question, measures of some sort had to be taken. It must be emphasized again and again that the ghetto itself was not an essential component of an anti-Jewish policy – this had already been demonstrated in Germany during the 1930s and would be shown later in other occupied countries. Thus the account given here refutes the functionalist explanations that cite organizational and bureaucratic exigencies and maintain that the ghetto was essential for dealing with real problems that emerged on the ground. Those theories do not account for several facts: the drawn-out period during which ghettos were established, the delayed establishment of most of them, the absence of clear directives for creating them, the fact that the phenomenon was far from universal even in Eastern Europe, and the changes in their functions. What is more, I do not believe that they deal with the fact that the ghettos created huge practical problems for the Germans with regard to efficient administration of the cities, not to mention of the Jewish population, and were quite unnecessary from the perspective of "logical" anti-Semitism. But Nazi anti-Semitism, like earlier versions, and despite its self-image as "rational," was nurtured by images and fears that were strong enough to motivate action. Dieter Wisliceny, Eichmann's deputy, described this insightfully soon after World War II:

Antisemitism was one of the foundations of the platform of Nazism. It stemmed in practice from two outlooks: (1) the pseudo-scientific biological statements of Prof. Günther and (2) the mystical-religious view that the world is directed by forces of good and evil. According to this view, the principle of evil was embodied in the Jews, who were assisted by the Church (the Jesuits), the Freemasons,

---

[1] The expression employed by Hitler in what is referred to as his first political text: Adolf Hitler to Adolf Gemlich, September 16, 1919, in Ernst Deuerlein, ed., *Der Aufstieg der NSDAP in Augenzeugenberichten*, p. 93.

and Bolshevism. The literature of this approach is well known; the oldest texts of the NSDAP [the Nazi party] are imbued with this world of images. *A direct link runs from the* Protocols of the Elders of Zion *to the* Myth [of the Twentieth Century], *by [Alfred] Rosenberg*.... This world of images is totally incomprehensible in logical or rational terms, [because] it is a form of religiosity that leads to sectarianism. Millions of people believed these things under the influence of this literature, something that can be compared only to similar phenomena from the Middle Ages, such as the mania of witches (*Hexenwahn*). To this world of evil, the racial mystics opposed the world of the good, of light, personified in blond blue-eyed people, the sole source of all the energy that creates civilization and builds states. These two worlds were of course in a perpetual battle and the war of 1939, which Hitler began, was the final confrontation between these two forces.[2]

This is also how we must understand the activity associated with ghettos: it was originally a reaction to an image that was deeply embedded in Nazi anti-Semitism and had older cultural roots. Only this can explain the hesitant first steps toward the establishment of ghettos, both their erratic geographic distribution (including why the first ghetto was in Piotrków-Trybunalski, of all places) and the chronology of their formation. As a direct consequence of this understanding, I would challenge in principle the idea that Heydrich's *Schnellbrief* of September 21, 1939, is the "founding order" of the ghetto phenomenon.

2. We should refer to "Nazi Ghettos" in the Plural, rather than to "the Nazi Ghetto" as a Single Uniform Phenomenon

By tracking its evolution through a semantic lens, it is evident that the term "ghetto," starting from its historical roots in the early modern era, underwent successive metamorphoses from the 16th century until the Nazi era, and then again during the much shorter period when it was used by the overseers and implementers of the anti-Jewish policies of the Third Reich and its satellites. We can make out six main stages:

1. The earliest of all is the tangible phenomenon of a separate Jewish neighborhood, sometimes walled off, created for religious and administrative reasons or to ensure the social isolation of the

---

[2] Dieter Wisliceny's affidavit (*Bericht*), Bratislava, November 18, 1946, YVA, M-5/162, p. 8ff. Emphasis in the original. On Wisliceny and the credibility of his statements, see Dan Michman, "Täteraussagen und Geschichtswissenschaft: Der Fall Dieter Wisliceny und der Entscheidungsprozess zur 'Endlösung,'" pp. 205–19. Emphases in the quote are in the original text.

Summary and Conclusions

Jewish "other" (known from the early modern era, though there were medieval precedents that went by other names).

2. Next came the metaphorical use, applied to a poor and crowded Jewish neighborhood, especially in Eastern Europe (in the 19th and early 20th centuries, especially with regard to Polish Jews in the first decades of the 20th century and once again under the Nazi regime, starting in 1938).
3. In parallel, it served as an abstract term for the social isolation of the Jews by means of societal norms or legislation (in the 19th and early 20th centuries, and under the Nazis mainly until 1938).
4. After the outbreak of World War II, ghettos were a practical measure – though not universally implemented – to restrict the Jews of Eastern Europe (the Ostjuden) to their "own" urban district (the "ghetto") and to send those who had moved away from it back to their "natural habitat" – as a temporary measure, decided on locally, in anticipation of the promulgation of a comprehensive Jewish policy that would determine the fate of the Jews once and for all. There were open ghettos and closed ghettos, but the main purpose was to restrict the Jews' freedom of movement (from the end of 1939 until the first weeks after the invasion of the Soviet Union in June 1941).
5. This was followed by a temporary form of domicile to serve diverse ad hoc needs, such as forced labor, for a limited number of Jews, while the killing operations of the Final Solution in the occupied Soviet Union raged all around – but not as a necessary condition for its implementation. The establishment of these ghettos was based on the entrenchment of the phenomenon between late 1939 and early 1941. In this version, too, there were open ghettos and closed ghettos. The ghettos became more like camps, especially in Romania, but also in Theresienstadt in its first stage (this stage lasted from the summer of 1941 until 1943).
6. Finally, in the years 1941 to 1944, the ghetto was a way station for the transports of the Final Solution – in practice a collection, concentration, and transit camp (this form can be found in some of the ghettos in the Soviet Union and Poland, Theresienstadt, Salonika, and Hungary); almost all of these were closed ghettos.

Because several of these senses of "ghetto" were used at the same time, it is impossible to speak of a single fixed concept. Nevertheless, what became frozen in historical consciousness as the "classic Nazi ghetto" is the fourth item on our list, which is based mainly on the ghettos of Łódź and Warsaw. These were also the examples from which German and other officials themselves learned during the Holocaust itself. Two additional meanings (5 and 6) emerged as the Final Solution proceeded.[3]

With regard to terminology, I have clearly demonstrated that not every place that has been considered a "ghetto" was referred to as such in official documents (German, Romanian, or Hungarian). Alongside the term "ghetto" we also find "Jewish quarter" (*Judenviertel*), "Jewish residential quarter" (*Jüdisches Wohnviertel*), "Jewish residential area" (*Jüdisches Wohnbezirk*), "Jewish Street" (*Judenstrasse*), "settlement," "collection point," and so on. Some of these terms, too, can be traced back to the Middle Ages (Jewish quarter, Jewish street), while others were new coinages during the Holocaust. They were frequently employed as synonyms, but sometimes various persons distinguished among them. Consider the relevant section in the order issued by the German Army High Command (OKH) with regard to the occupied Soviet Union, on August 19, 1941, as quoted in a directive by General von Schenckendorff:

Ghettos (enclosed Jewish quarters) are to be set up in larger places where Jews are a large part of the population, and especially in cities, if their establishment is relevant or necessary and feasible with regard to the auxiliary means available in the local conditions, without causing any delay to other more urgent tasks.[4]

---

[3] With regard to function, Martin Dean, a scholar affiliated with the Holocaust Museum in Washington, has proposed a distinction between, on the one hand, "open ghettos" (the majority) and "closed ghettos" – both types still existed in what he calls the "fourth period" – and, on the other hand, extermination ghettos (ghettos that were sealed for a brief period, in advance of an extermination operation, as in Tuczin), transit ghettos, and survivors' ghettos (*Restghettos* or remnant ghettos), which survived until the very last days of the Nazi regime, after most of the Jews had been murdered. This is an attempt at a functional distinction, but clearly there were conceptual changes over time. See Martin Dean, "Preparing an Encyclopedia of Ghettos: Numbers, Types, and Essential Characteristics of Ghettos under German Administration."

[4] "Die Einrichtung von Gettos (umzaeuhnte Judenviertel) ist in Ortschaften mit groesseren juedischem Bevoelkerungsteil insbesonders in Staedten durchzufuehren, wenn die Einrichtung sachdienlich oder notwendig ist, und wenn sie nach der örtlichen Lage mit den zur Verfuegung stehenden Hilfsmitteln ohne Vernachlaessigung dringender Aufgaben moeglich ist (Befehl des OKH, H.Q. vom 19.8.1941). Danach kommt die Einrichtung von Gettos im Befehlsbereich vor allem dann in Betracht, wenn eine eingehende Ueberwachung des Judenviertels wegen seiner Lage zu den nichtjuedischen Wohnvierteln notwendig ist und diese Ueberwachung durch andere Massnahmen (Streifen der Feldgendarmerie, des Ordnungsdienstes) nicht einwandfrei durchgefuehrt werden kann": Christian Gerlach, *Kalkulierte Morde: Die deutsche Wirtschafts- und Vernichtungspolitik in Weißrußland 1941 bis 1944*, p. 525.

That is, according to the author of this order (or perhaps, more precisely, one of his subordinates), there was a difference between a ghetto, which was enclosed, and an open Jewish neighborhood (what scholars today refer to as an "open ghetto").

We should note, however, that the term "ghetto" spread in common parlance under the influence of the Germans and their collaborators. Following the gradual disappearance of the essential distinction between ghetto and camp, which existed in Poland in 1940 and 1941, the Jews themselves applied "ghetto" to places that the Germans considered to be camps in every respect. For example, in Germany itself more than a thousand Jews from Aachen and its environs were confined to a barracks camp (*Barrackenlager*) on Grüner Weg from early 1941 until late 1942,[5] but the Jews referred to the place as a ghetto.[6] Something similar took place in Munich.[7] Another example is Częstochowa, mentioned earlier. All of this points to another methodological problem, namely, identifying ghettos on the basis of Jewish or German documentation.

To make matters worse, scholars sometimes use the term "ghetto" to refer to places that neither the Germans, nor their collaborators, nor even the Jews ever called a ghetto. For example, some scholars consider the eviction of Budapest Jews from their homes immediately after the German takeover of Hungary to be a process of ghettoization, but there is absolutely no basis for this in the documentation.[8]

3. We must not Speak of "Ghetto" and "Judenrat" as if they were Conjoined Twins

"Ghetto" and "Judenrat" – two instruments of Nazi anti-Jewish policy – derived from different sources, began during different periods and

---

[5] Gedenktafeln "Wege gegen das Vergessen," www.aachen.de/DE/kultur_freizeit.
[6] Letter to the author from Mrs. Sylvia Mannes, Kibbutz Ein Hanatziv, March 7, 2007.
[7] In Else Behrend-Rosenfeld's diary, referring to events from March 1941 on, she writes of the requirement that the Jews leave their homes, referred to as "Jewish houses" (*jüdische Häuser*), and of the preparation of a barracks camp for them in Milbertshofen, a suburb of Munich. She writes: "Wir nehmen an, daß sie als künftige Unterkunft für die Münchner Juden dienen sollen, ein neues, echtes Ghetto!" See Else R. Behrend-Rosenfeld, *Ich stand nicht allein*, pp. 93–4 (and, also on Milbertshofen: pp. 95, 104–6, 110–11, 115–18, 158–9). The camp was in fact established; its inmates had an executive committee appointed by the camp overseers. See Peter Hanke, *Zur Geschichte der Juden in München zwischen 1933 und 1945*, pp. 261–85. I would like to thank Matthias Holzberg of Alfeld, Germany, who brought these sources to my attention.
[8] See Tim Cole, "Multiple and Changing Experiences of Ghettoization: Budapest 1944," p. 148. Cole refers to Bernard Klein's "The Judenrat," p. 32.

developed in different fashions, even though they overlapped in many respects. We have seen that the view that the ghetto and the Jewish council were intertwined is deeply rooted in the research literature and the popular conception of the Holocaust. It took firm shape there largely thanks to Hilberg's thesis that Heydrich's *Schnellbrief* of September 21, 1939, outlined a program whose second part ostensibly referred to "the concentration of the Jews in closed ghettos [*sic!*] [which] was intended to be no more than a makeshift device in preparation for the ultimate mass emigration of the victims" and that forcing the Jews to wear an identifying badge ("marking") and the establishment of Judenräte ("Jewish control organs") were "preliminary steps of the ghettoization process."[9] In keeping with this reading, the Judenrat has come to be understood as an integral component of the ghetto concept; the conjectured sequence is that the ghetto was invented first (at least as an idea) and that the Judenräte were then set up to manage Jewish affairs within them. That is, the Judenrat was the first step toward the establishment of the ghetto or was established at the same time or shortly after it.

The fact is that although there were Jewish councils in an overwhelming majority of ghettos,[10] there were also quite a few ghettos run by local non-Jewish auxiliary forces (militias, gendarmerie, the municipality) in the occupied Soviet Union and later in Hungary. The ghettos established by the Romanians in Transnistria did not always have a Jewish administration. Clearly, then, nothing in the nature of the ghetto required that it be run by a Jewish council. What is more, many Judenräte and parallel Jewish administrative bodies (*Judenvereinigungen* or "Jewish unions") – what I have called "headships" – were established in various places and countries for Jewish communities that were not confined to ghettos (in the Netherlands, Belgium, France, Germany, Vienna, Prague, Belgrade, the Hungarian countryside, and even in many small places in Poland). Most importantly, the emergence of Jewish "headships" can be observed long before the establishment of the first ghettos in Poland (as early as 1937 in Germany), as a device employed by the Jewish Affairs Department of the SD to enable the SS to control the Jews en masse.[11] In many places where

---

[9] Raul Hilberg, *The Destruction of the European Jews*, p. 144.
[10] In some places we even find the synonymous use of Ältestenrat or Judenrat and *Ghettoverwaltung* (ghetto administration) – as in Theresienstadt: see Margalit Shlain, *Ha-hanhaggah ha-yehudit be-ma'avakah le-hissaredut: Terezyenshtat 1941–1945*, esp. p. 76.
[11] See, at greater length, Dan Michman, *Holocaust Historiography: A Jewish Perspective*, pp. 159–75.

Summary and Conclusions 153

a ghetto was established, a significant amount of time elapsed between the appointment of the Judenrat and the enclosure of the ghetto.

Consequently, although both Judenrat and ghetto were tools for dealing with the Jews, they should not be seen as inseparable or as the products of a single policy aimed at segregating the Jews, even if both were means to isolate the Jewish collective from its surroundings. The Judenrat (or Jewish headship) was a tool of SS policy, imposed all over Europe; the ghetto was a means to concentrate Jews in one place and was implemented only – and even then partially – in Eastern Europe.

4. The Placement of Ghettos in Old Impoverished Neighborhoods was not an Accident but the Result of an Ideological and Historical Perspective

Understanding the ghetto phenomenon as the product of a pseudo-academic discourse associated with an ideology that fed on images of the Ostjuden peril – a discourse in which Seraphim played a key role – can also explain the conspicuous fact that the Holocaust-era ghettos were usually located in poor and underprivileged urban neighborhoods (Bałuty in Łódź, Slobodka/Viljampole in Kovno, Podgórze in Krakow, etc.). It was the stereotype of the ghetto Jew ("ghetto" in Seraphim's sense) that led to the selection of these neighborhoods, already home to the poorest strata of the Jewish community, by the German authorities, and later by the Romanians and Hungarians who followed their example, even when their enclosure caused major problems for the functioning of the city itself. (From a logical perspective it would have been better to relocate the Jews to the suburbs; this point was included in the deliberations preceding the establishment of the Theresienstadt ghetto.) This choice made the situation of the ghetto residents even worse and created fertile ground for epidemics, which increased Jewish mortality even before the start of the Final Solution. Thus an argument frequently advanced by German spokespeople as the "reason" for ghettoization was in fact a consequence of this measure.

5. As Ghettos were Established for Ostjuden only, and as they were Implemented in an Unsystematic Way, they should be seen as a Phenomenon Entirely Different from the Concentration Camps

Research on the concentration camp system in general and on the different camps in particular has developed considerably since the beginning of the 1990s.[12] This has led to some efforts to present comprehensive and analytical views of the phenomenon. In some of those recent comprehensive works, ghettos are included under this heading of "Camps."[13] Even though some hints or remarks are made as to the different character of the ghettos (the United States Holocaust Memorial project deals with ghettos in two separate volumes,[14] and the author of the chapter on ghettos in the German series *Der Ort des Terrors*, Dieter Pohl, explicitly states the difference[15]), the decision to put the ghettos together with the camps points to an understanding that they basically present one logic of incarcerating "enemies" of National Socialism in specially designated, separate territorial spaces.

Our study has shown that the development that led to the emergence of the ghettos was unique and entirely different from the concentration camp idea, which was implemented from the very beginning of the Nazi regime in 1933, following an idea invented in Cuba by the Spaniards and in South Africa by the British at the end of the 19th century.[16] Moreover, camps were administered from Berlin by a well-organized bureaucracy, had a closely monitored and hierarchical internal structure, and did not allow for semi-independent regular daily life.

Consequently, ghettos should be viewed as a separate phenomenon with unique features, which resulted from the history of anti-Semitism.

6. The Institution of Ghettos Represented a Sharp Escalation of the Nazis' anti-Jewish Policy but was not a Preliminary Stage of the Final Solution

The profound semantic shift in the meaning of "ghetto" from the third to the fourth sense in my list raises significant questions about the evolution of Nazism in general and can be used as a test case thereof: first, about the relationship between old and traditional elements, on the one hand, and modern elements, on the other hand, in Nazi anti-Semitism; and, second,

---

[12] Therkel Straede, *De nazistiske koncentrationslejre: studier og bibliografi*.
[13] Geoffrey Megargee, ed., *Encyclopedia of Camps and Ghettos, 1933–1945*; Wolfgang Benz and Barbara Distel, eds., *Der Ort des Terrors. Geschichte der nationalsozialistischen Konzentrationslager*, vol. 9.
[14] *Encyclopedia of Camps and Ghettos, 1933–1945*, vols. 2 and 4.
[15] Pohl writes as follows: "The ghettos for Jews ... contributed considerably to the isolation and murder of the Jews, but they cannot simply be counted as part and parcel of the Nazi incarceration sites"; Benz and Distel, eds., *Der Ort des Terrors*, vol. 9, p. 161.
[16] Pierre Rigoulot and Joël Kotek, *Le siècle des camps: emprisonnement, détention, extermination, cent ans de mal absolu*.

Summary and Conclusions

about the relationship between the field echelons and the higher echelons in the formulation of the anti-Jewish policy.

With regard to the relationship (and even tension) between old elements and modern elements in Nazi anti-Semitism and its results, we can say that the term "ghetto" derived from the Jewish and anti-Semitic lexicon created, as we have seen, in the early modern age. By taking over this term, Nazism linked itself to a very old anti-Semitic tradition. Within a very few years, though, in the late 1930s and early 1940s, the term underwent a radical transformation, until a new concept emerged, in late 1939 and over the next two years, of what a physical ghetto was and should be. This shift points to a more profound change – in fact, an escalation – in Nazi anti-Semitism at the end of the 1930s, catalyzed by the encounter with Eastern European Jewry. The Ostjuden were viewed as the source of the strength and vitality of "the Jews" – Jews in both the biological sense ("Jewry") and the spiritual sense ("Judaism"), for which German anti-Semitism employed different words (*Judenheit/Judentum* and *Judaismus*). The "ghetto" was a means to confine the physical Ostjuden, and also to arrest the spread of the noxious influence of the spirit of Judaism. The conflation of these two aspects of the Jewish peril exacerbated the activism of what Michael Wildt has designated the "Unfettered Generation" (*Generation des Unbedingten*).[17] The old sense of "ghetto" melted away and the term was reshaped, like soft clay, to carry different meanings and serve different goals. But in addition to the idea of a "spiritual ghetto" or "invisible ghetto" – expressions employed by the Jews in Germany and by German officials with regard to the anti-Jewish policy of the 1930s – the physical ghetto took on a psychological import, in which a traditional concept was charged with a new burden, even though this could not be discerned from its external morphology.

The second question deals with the causal or evolutionary link between the establishment of ghettos and the Final Solution and with the relationship between the activities of the field echelons and the direction sketched out by the anti-Jewish policymakers. The very revival and refurbishing of an old term like "ghetto" is evidence, as just noted, that Nazi anti-Semitism developed in a particular cultural and ideological space, whose main channel was determined by an age-old anti-Semitic tradition. For

---

[17] See Michael Wildt, *Generation des Unbedingten: Das Führungskorps des Reichssicherheitshauptamtes*; for an English summary, see *Generation of the Unbound: The Leadership Corps of the Reich Security Main Office*.

all that, this anti-Semitism was modern; it had religious and ecstatic characteristics, as Dieter Wisliceny described with great precision.

It was this anti-Semitic ecstasy, the energy and ingenuity of the minions of the Nazi regime who were given unlimited room for maneuver, that turned the traditional pre-Holocaust Eastern European Jewish ghetto into a new form of quarantine for the ominous masses of Ostjuden, perceived as a threat to the Germans and to human existence in general. But despite the change in the meaning of the concept of a ghetto – the new sense it received and its expansion far beyond anything ever meant by "ghetto" in the past, including the appalling living conditions – it remained within the conceptual space of traditional anti-Semitism. Did this tradition also lead to the systematic and comprehensive campaign to exterminate the Jews?

In his first political tract, a letter composed in September 1919, Hitler wrote that

> An antisemitism based on purely emotional grounds will find its ultimate expression in the form of progroms [sic!]. An antisemitism based on reason, however (*jedoch*), must lead to systematic legal combatting and elimination of the special privileges which the Jew holds, in contrast to the other aliens living among us (aliens' legislation). *But* (*aber*) its ultimate objective (*sein letztes Ziel*) must unswervingly be the irrevocable removal of the Jews altogether (*Entfernung der Juden überhaupt*).[18]

At the very start of his career, as this demonstrates, Hitler distinguished "emotional antisemitism" from "rational antisemitism," which he identified with his own brand. But even within rational anti-Semitism he distinguished a deliberate struggle based on legislation from the "ultimate objective," which went further – a distinction indicated by the disjunctive "but."

The functionalist criticism of the intentionalist approach in Holocaust historiography – specifically, that one must not draw a direct line between Hitler's early statements and events that took place more than 20 years later – is valid. Hitler's early notion was vague and inchoate; it took

---

[18] "Der Antisemitismus aus rein gefühlsmäßigen Gründen wird seinen letzten Ausdruck finden in der Form von Progromen [sic]. Der Antisemitismus der Vernunft jedoch muß führen zur planmäßigen gesetzlichen Bekämpfung und Beseitigung der Vorrechte des Juden, die er nur zum Unterschied der anderen zwischen uns lebenden Fremden besitzt (Fremdengesetzgebung). Sein letztes Ziel aber muß unverrückbar die Entfernung der Juden überhaupt sein": Hitler to Gemlich, September 16, 1919, in Deuerlein, *Der Aufstieg der NSDAP*, p. 93; also in Eberhard Jäckel, ed., *Hitler. Sämtliche Aufzeichnungen 1905–1924*, pp. 88–90.

Summary and Conclusions

the contributions of many individuals and institutions that, to borrow Kershaw's phrase, were "working towards the Führer," all of them with their own specific ideas and background, to give shape and reality to the anti-Semitic program that began when Hitler came to power and to support a broad and intensive anti-Semitic policy. Nevertheless, we should not go to the other extreme and ignore Hitler's early dreams and visions, which, according to all scholars, motivated him and his activity. We must also accept the view, corroborated since the 1980s by a long line of prominent scholars – David Bankier, Ian Kershaw, Christopher Browning, Konrad Kwiet, Peter Longerich, and others[19] – that "without Hitler there would not have been a Holocaust"; that is, it was Hitler's decisions at various junctures that determined the objectives to be pursued, and these decisions were guided by his rabid ideology. The documentation we have regarding these junctures clearly points to Hitler's essential role. But Hitler's voice is not heard in theoretical or practical discussions of ghettos, and certainly not in actual orders to establish them; the only mention of a *Ghetto-Gedanke* in relation to Hitler comes from the Hitler-Brauchitsch consultation of September 20, 1939; but not even there do we find any suggestion that Hitler ordered some action or expressed his views regarding this issue (it was apparently Brauchitsch who raised the issue of the ghettos that were encountered by the troops in Poland and what to do with them). We should compare this to other policy-shaping junctures in which Hitler was involved, whether as initiator or by giving his consent to initiatives from below, notably the promulgation of the Nuremberg Laws in September 1935 and the unleashing of the first stages of the Final Solution in July 1941. In both cases the practical results of his approval or decisions were seen and felt within days or weeks (definitely less than a month) after the meeting in question, and their further development was marked by a clear pattern.[20]

---

[19] The works by Kershaw, Browning, Kwiet, and Longerich have been referred to already; for Bankier's approach to the subject, see David Bankier, "Hitler and the Policy-Making Process on the Jewish Question."

[20] The Nuremberg Laws regarding the citizenship of Jews (and others) and intermarriage with Jews, promulgated on September 15, 1935, had been on Hitler's mind from 1933, but were pressed for from below, by party members and state officials, since the beginning of 1935; Hitler became fully involved in the decision to proceed with them on September 9, and gave his final consent on September 13. See Kershaw, *Hitler (I) – 1889–1936: Hubris*, pp. 559–71; Saul Friedländer, *Nazi Germany and the Jews*, vol. 1: *The Years of Persecution 1933–1939*, pp. 146–9 (the two differ on some aspects of the development; mine is a synthesis of the two approaches). Historians still disagree about the moment of the "turning point" decision to go forward with what would crystallize

So it was not Hitler who revived the term "ghetto" or indicated a direction of action in this domain.

As opposed to the term "ghetto," with its long-standing tradition, the "Final Solution of the Jewish question" – meaning genocide of the Jews – was a totally new idea. The latter phrase has not yet been the object of a linguistic or semantic study of the type conducted here for "ghetto." Although there are ample references to it in the literature, and a broad consensus that it was added to the Nazi lexicon in 1941, it does not seem to have originated with Hitler. Nevertheless, and without expanding on the point here – though this should definitely be done – we can say that this concept sprouted and grew in the ideology with which Hitler endowed Nazism and which made Nazi anti-Semitism distinct from earlier forms of this phenomenon.

Lucy Dawidowicz tried to explain this concept as follows:

"The final solution of the Jewish question" was the code name assigned by the German bureaucracy to the annihilation of the Jews. The very composition of the code name, when analyzed, reveals its fundamental character and meaning to the Germans who invented and used it. The term "Jewish question," as first used during the early enlightenment/emancipation period in western Europe, referred to the "question" or "problem" that the anomalous persistence of the Jews as a people posed to the new nation-states and the rising political nationalisms. The "Jewish question" was, at bottom, a euphemism whose verbal neutrality concealed the user's impatience with the singularity of this people that did not appear to conform to the new political demands of the state.

Since a question demands an answer and a problem a solution, various answers and solutions were propounded to the "Jewish question," by foes and even friends, that entailed the disappearance of the Jews as such – abandonment of the Jewish religion or its essential elements, of the Jewish language, Yiddish, of Jewish

---

as the Final Solution. However, mainstream historians do agree today that there was no "single moment," but that the first step in a series of decisions was apparently taken in mid-July 1941. The ideas expressed by Hitler during a policymaking meeting with Göring, Rosenberg, Lammers, Bormann, and Keitel on July 16, together with Hitler's signing of a series of orders the next day, signaled that shift. Its results could be seen in the change in the modalities of murder in the East from the beginning of August (first applied in the Baltic states): from killing mostly males to murdering women and children as well, and from multiple but still scattered massacres to the systematic cleansing of entire areas. On this, see Jürgen Matthäus in Christopher Browning, with contributions by Jürgen Matthäus, *The Origins of the Final Solution: The Evolution of Nazi Jewish Policy, September 1939–March 1942*, pp. 253–94; Friedländer, *Nazi Germany and the Jews 1939–1945*, vol. 2: *The Years of Extermination*, pp. 199–251; Peter Longerich, *Policy of Destruction: Nazi Anti-Jewish Policy and the Genesis of the "Final Solution"*; Gerhard L. Weinberg, *Germany's War for World Conquest and the Extermination of the Jews*.

Summary and Conclusions

culture, Jewish uniqueness and separatism. The histories of Jewish emancipation and of European antisemitism are replete with proffered "solutions to the Jewish question."...

To this concept that the national socialists adopted they added one new element, embodied in the word "final." It means definitive, completed, perfected, ultimate. "Final" reverberates with apocalyptic promise, with speaking the last judgement, the end of days, the last destruction before salvation, Armageddon. "The final solution of the Jewish question" in the national socialist conception was not just another antisemitic undertaking, but a meta-historical program devised with an eschatological perspective. It was part of a salvationist ideology that envisioned the attainment of heaven by bringing hell on earth.[21]

Much of what Dawidowicz writes is on the mark, especially her emphasis on the word "final." She would see everything exclusively in the context of anti-Semitism, however. In my opinion, the "*Final* Solution of the Jewish Question" comes from a broader Hitlerian lexicon that refers to "ultimate," "absolute," and "final" solutions that can be promulgated to produce an absolute, static, and final situation – the apocalypse of the final redemption at the end of days. In this sense, Hitler's thought was ahistoric, or, more precisely, aimed at putting an end to history and achieving the stage of post-history. This language of total consummation is common. We saw in his 1919 letter the expressions "ultimate [or final] objective" and "irrevocable removal of the Jews." In a situation report composed after *Kristallnacht*, a middle-ranking official, the prime minister of Swabia and Neuberg, wrote of the need for a "solution without compromise" [*kompromißlosen Lösung*] of the "Jewish question."[22] There are many other examples of this, from the period before the start of the systematic campaign of extermination and especially after it was launched. But "final solutions" were not limited to the Jews. In September 1941, just when the Final Solution of the Jewish Question was being crystallized, SS officials were also saying that "our final goal is the elimination, with nothing left, of Christendom in its entirety."[23] The Nazi vision of Europe, too, was of a radically new order (*Neuordnung*), to be

---

[21] Lucy S. Dawidowicz, *The War Against the Jews, 1933–1945*, pp. xxi–xxiii.

[22] "Deutlich erkennbar für alle unterstrich dieser Mord [an vom Rath] die weltgeschichtliche Bedeutung der Judenfrage und die Notwendigkeit ihrer kompromißlosen Lösung": Regierungspräsident Schwaben und Neuburg. Bericht für November 1938 ("Lagebericht [Monatsbericht]"), Augsburg 07.12.1938, in Otto Dov Kulka and Eberhard Jäckel, *Die Juden in den geheimen NS-Stimmungsberichten 1933–1945*, CD, dok. 2588.

[23] "*Unser Endziel ist die restlose Zerschlagung des gesamten Christentums*": Bericht über die Arbeitstagung der Kirchensachbearbeiter beim RSHA, 22–23.9.41, IfZ, AkZ 4920/72, Fa 218, p. 6.

imposed unilaterally by Germany; the *Generalplan Ost* (general plan for the East) was devised to implement this new order in Eastern Europe. All these examples – and many others could be provided – indicate that the apocalyptic worldview preached by Hitler was totally different from old ways of thinking, both anti-Semitic and racist. This apocalyptic energy burst forth with the invasion of the Soviet Union, which was the ultimate war of the force representing the hierarchical principle of nature (Nazism) against the "Jewish" principle of equality, in all its manifestations (both Communism-Bolshevism and capitalism, both "popular democracy" and liberal democracy, and even Christianity, which disseminated Jewish ideas in the modern world). In *Mein Kampf*, Hitler observed that "the Jewish doctrine of Marxism repudiates the aristocratic principle of Nature and substitutes for it the eternal privilege of force and energy, numerical mass and its dead weight."[24] The "Final Solution of the Jewish Question" was meant to put an end to this distortion once and for all; it was an utterly new concept spawned by an apocalyptic worldview.

The term "ghetto," for all its importance, was revived by the executive echelons in the field, men devoted to the regime and faithful to the anti-Semitic creed, who were allowed broad room for action by their superiors. But the introduction of ghettos was not a "final" step; on the contrary, it was hesitant, geographically limited, and incomplete in its distribution. As noted, there is not the slightest hint that Hitler was involved in their conception or design. The case of the "Final Solution of the Jewish Question" is precisely the opposite: it was a profound and radical new departure in the history of anti-Semitism. The decision to implement it was taken at the very highest levels – by Hitler himself – as part of the decisive apocalyptic battle. It was an ideological and strategic measure that had no need for ghettos. This is why we must not see the emergence of the ghetto as a step on the road to the Final Solution, but as something on quite a different plane – even if, for the Jews at that time and scholars since, it is extremely difficult to distinguish this.[25]

[24] Adolf Hitler, *Mein Kampf* (My Struggle), p. 46.
[25] Tucked away in his discussion of mortality in the Warsaw ghetto is an important comment by Gutman that points in the same direction: "At that very time [1942] of growing immunity and adjustment to the appalling conditions, the Germans initiated the mass deportation and physical extermination of Warsaw Jewry. Thus the annihilation of the ghetto was not a corollary of the slow or rapid decline of the Jews. It was initiated as the manifestation of a comprehensive political and ideological creed and was not restricted to the Jews of Warsaw or the Generalgouvernement alone, but was part of the overall initiative to annihilate the Jewish people wherever the rule of Nazi Germany and its satellites had reached." See Gutman, *The Jews of Warsaw*, p. 65. For the ghettos, the

Summary and Conclusions

Our discussion and conclusions concerning the emergence of the ghetto during the Holocaust reopen many questions related to the development of various components of Nazi anti-Jewish policy and the relations among them, as well as the manner in which the destiny of individual ghettos has been interpreted. I have not addressed them here, seeking only to investigate a set of basic postulates that had been accepted without serious inquiry and to offer a new explanation. I leave the rest for my readers.

Judenräte, and the Final Solution as three separate items in the Nazis' anti-Jewish policies, see also Dan Michman, "Judenräte, Ghetti, Endlösung: tre componenti correlate di una politica antiebraica o elementi separati?" *Ventunesimo Secolo* 17 (October 2008), pp. 109–17.

Bibliography

A. Primary Sources

1. Archives

BAB Bundesarchiv, Berlin
BA-FA Bundesarchiv-Filmarchiv, Koblenz
BA-MA Bundesarchiv-Militärarchiv, Freiburg im Breisgau
BDC Berlin Document Center (now in Bundesarchiv Berlin, Berlin)
CDJC Centre de Documentation Juive Contemporaine (in Mémorial de la Shoah), Paris
Central State Archive, Riga
IfZ Institut für Zeitgeschichte, Munich
NIOD Nederlands Instituut voor Oorlogsdocumentatie
SAA Stadsarchief Amsterdam, Amsterdam
Tsahor, Dov, private collection, Tel Aviv
USHMM United States Holocaust Memorial Museum, Washington, DC
YVA Yad Vashem Archives, Jerusalem
www.diplomatiedervervolging.nl

2. Printed Sources, Diaries, Memoirs, and Belles-Lettres

Agnon, Shmuel Joseph, *Me-atzmi el atzmi* (From Myself to Myself). Jerusalem and Tel Aviv: Schocken, 2000 (Hebrew).
Akten zur deutschen auswärtigen Politik 1918–1945, Series D (1937–1945), vol. V, Baden-Baden, 1953.
Ancel, Jean, *Transnistria 1941–1942: The Romanian Mass Murder Campaigns* vols. 1–3, Tel Aviv: Goldstein-Goren Diaspora Research Center, Tel Aviv University, 2003.
Arad, Yitzhak, Yisrael Gutman, and Abraham Margaliot, eds., *Documents on the Holocaust*. Jerusalem: Yad Vashem, 1981.

Arad, Yitzhak, Shmuel Krakowski, and Shmuel Spector, eds., *The Einsatzgruppen Reports: Selections from the Dispatches of the Nazi Death Squads' Campaign Against the Jews, July 1941–January 1943*. New York: Holocaust Library, 1989.
Baron, Salo Wittmayer, *The Jewish Community: Its History and Structure to the American Revolution*. Philadelphia: Jewish Publication Society of America, 1948.
Behrend-Rosenfeld, Else R., *Ich stand nicht allein*. Cologne and Frankfurt am Main: EVA, 1949.
Benoschfsky, Ilona, and Elek Karsai, eds., *Vádirat a nácizmus ellen*. Budapest: I. MIOK, 1958.
Benz, Wolfgang, Konrad Kwiet, and Jürgen Matthäus, eds., *Einsatz im "Reichskommissariat Ostland". Dokumente zum Völkermord im Baltikum und in Weißrußland 1941–1944*. Berlin: Metropol, 1998.
Berenstein, Tatiana, Artur Eisenbach, and Adam Rutkowski, *Faschismus – Getto – Massenmord. Dokumentation über die Ausrottung der Juden in Polen während des zweiten Weltkrieges*. Frankfurt am Main, 1961.
Blumenthal, Nachman, *Darko shel Judenrat: Te'udot mi-Ghetto Bialystok* (Conduct and Actions of a Judenrat: Documents from the Bialystok Ghetto). Jerusalem: Yad Vashem, 1962 (Hebrew).
———, *Te'udot mi-geto Lublin: Judenrat lelo Derech* (Documents from the Lublin Ghetto: Judenrat Without Direction). Jerusalem: Yad Vashem, 1967 (Hebrew).
Burdick, Charles, and Hans-Adolf Jacobsen, eds., *The Halder War Diary 1939–1942*. Novato, CA: Presidio Press, 1988.
Carpi, Daniel, ed., *Italian Diplomatic Documents on the History of the Holocaust in Greece (1941–1943)*. Tel Aviv: Diaspora Research Center, Tel Aviv University, 1999.
Deuerlein, Ernst, ed., *Der Aufstieg der NSDAP in Augenzeugenberichten*. Munich: DTV, 1978.
Dokumentensammlung, vol. 1. Frankfurt am Main: United Restitution Organization, 1958.
Dublon-Knebel, Irith, comp. and trans., *German Foreign Office Documents on the Holocaust in Greece (1937–1944)*. Tel Aviv: Chair for the History and Culture of the Jews of Salonika and Greece, Goldstein-Goren Diaspora Research Center, Tel Aviv University, 2007.
Documentae Occupationis Teutonica, vol. VIII. Poznan, 1949.
Eschwege, Helmut, ed., *Kennzeichen J. Bilder, Dokumente, Berichte zur Geschichte der Verbrechen des Hitlerfaschismus an den deutschen Juden 1933–1945*. East Berlin: VEB Deutscher Verlag der Wissenschaften, 1966.
Evreii din Romania 1940–1944: Legislatia anti-Evreiasca, vol. 1. Bucharest: Hasefer, 1993.
Goebbels, Joseph, *Die Tagebücher von Joseph Goebbels: Sämtliche Fragmenten*, Teil I: Aufzeichnungen 1923–1941, vol. 7: July 1939–March 1940. Munich: K. G. Saur, 1998.
Gregorovius, Ferdinand, *Der Ghetto und die Juden in Rom*. Berlin: Im Schocken Verlag, 1935.

Haastert, N., "Rechtspflege und Rechtspolitik," *Deutsche Justiz*, August 2, 1935, pp. 1090–1.
Hapgood, Hutchins, *The Spirit of the Ghetto. With an introduction by Harry Golden*. New York: Schocken, 1966 (also: Cambridge, MA: Belknap Press of Harvard University Press, 1983; first published: New York, 1902).
Hatzofeh (Tel Aviv).
Heijermans, Herman, *Ghetto*. Amsterdam, 1898. English edition, *The Ghetto: A Drama in Four Acts* (1899), trans. Chester Baily Fernald. Whitefish, MT: Kessinger Publishing Company, 2008.
Herzl, Theodor, *Der Judenstaat*. Leipzig and Vienna: M. Breitenstein, 1896. English edition, *The Jewish State*, trans. Sylvie D'Avigdor. London: Pordes, 1967.
_____, *Das neue Ghetto*. Vienna: Verlag der Welt, 1897. English edition, *The New Ghetto*, trans. Heinz Norden. New York: The Theodor Herzl Foundation, 1955.
Hinkel, Hans, *Judenviertel Europas: Die Juden zwischen Ostsee und schwarzem Meer*. N.p., n.d. [summer 1939].
Hitler, Adolf, *Mein Kampf*. Munich, 1925. English edition, *Mein Kampf*, trans. James Murphy. London: Hurst and Blackett, n.d. (repr. of the 1942 reset version; original translation: 1939).
Jacobsen, Hans-Adolf, ed., *Generaloberst Halder. Kriegstagebuch*, vol. 1. Stuttgart: W. Kohlhammer, 1962.
Jäckel, Eberhard, ed., *Hitler. Sämtliche Aufzeichnungen 1905–1924*. Stuttgart: Deutsche Verlags-Anstalt, 1980.
Klein, Peter, ed., *Die Einsatzgruppen in der besetzten Sowjetunion 1941/42: Die Tätigkeits- und Lageberichte des Chefs der Sicherheitspolizei und des SD*. Berlin: Haus der Wannsee-Konferenz, 1997.
Kulka, Otto Dov, *Deutsches Judentum unter dem Nationalsozialismus*, vol. I. Tübingen: Mohr-Siebeck, 1997.
Kulka, Otto Dov, and Eberhard Jäckel, eds., *Die Juden in den geheimen NS-Stimmungsberichten 1933–1945*. Düsseldorf: Droste, 2004.
Krannhals, H. von, ed., *Die Berichte der Einsatzgruppen der Sicherheitspolizei in Polenfeldzug 1939* (1.9.1939–31.10.1939). Lüneburg: 1965.
Kruk, Herman, *The Last Days of the Jerusalem of Lithuania: Chronicles from the Vilna Ghetto and the Camps 1939–1944*, ed. and intro. Benjamin Harshav, trans. Barbara Harshav. New Haven and London: Yale University Press, 2002. Original Yiddish version: *Togbukh fun Vilner Ghetto*, New York, 1961.
Lau-Lavie, Naphtali, *Balaam's Prophecy*. New York: Cornwall Books, 1997.
Litzmanstädter (Lodzer/Lodscher) Zeitung.
Leschtschinski, Jacob, "Getto un wanderung in yiddisher leben," *Yivobletter* 5/1 (January 1933), pp. 1–6 (Yiddish).
Manoschek, Walter, ed., *"Es gibt nur eines für das Judentum: Vernichtung" – Das Judenbild in deutschen Soldatenbriefen 1939–1944*. Hamburg: Hamburger Edition: 1995.
Mendes-Flohr, Paul R., and Jehuda Reinharz, eds., *The Jew in the Modern World: A Documentary History*. New York: Oxford University Press, 1995.

Müller, Norbert, ed., *Deutsche Besatzungspolitik in der UdSSR. Dokumente.* Cologne: Pahl-Rugenstein, 1982.

Pentateuch, The, translated and explained by Samson Raphael Hirsch, rendered into English by Isaac Levy (2nd edn., completely revd.), vol. 1, *Genesis.* New York: Judaica Press, 1971. Original German edition, *Der Pentateuch,* übersetzt und erläutert von Samson Raphael Hirsch, vol. 1. *Die Genesis.* Frankfurt am Main: J. Kauffmann, 1899 (first print.: 1867).

Poliakov, Léon, and Josef Wulf, *Das Dritte Reich und die Juden: Dokumente und Aufsätze.* Berlin-Grünewald: Arani, 1955.

Präg, Werner, and Wolfgang Jacobmeyer, *Das Diensttagebuch des deutschen Generalgouverneurs in Polen 1939–1945.* Stuttgart: Deutsche Verlags-Anstalt, 1975.

Prager, Moshe, *Yeven-metsulah he-hadash* (The New Miry Pit). Tel Aviv: Masada, 1941 (Hebrew).

Prinz, Joachim, "Das Leben ohne Nachbarn. Versuch einer erste Analyse. Ghetto 1935," *Jüdische Rundschau,* April 1935

———, *Das Leben im Ghetto. Jüdisches Schicksal in fünf Städten.* Berlin: Erwin Löwe, 1937.

Redeker, Dietrich, "Deutsche Ordnung kehrt ins Ghetto ein," *Warschauer Zeitung,* March 13, 1940, and *Krakauer Zeitung,* March 21, 1940.

Reichsgesetzblatt, 1938.

Rosenberg, Alfred, "Nationalsozialismus und Wissenschaft," *Der Weltkampf* 1 (1941), pp. 3–6.

Samelson, William, "Piotrków-Trybunalski: My Ancestral Home," in Eric J. Sterling, ed., *Life in the Ghettos During the Holocaust.* Syracuse, NY: Syracuse University Press, 2005, pp. 1–16.

Das Schwarze Korps.

Seifert, Hermann Erich, *Der Jude an der Ostgrenze.* Berlin: Zentralverlag der NSDAP, 1941.

Seraphim, Peter-Heinz, "Bevölkerungs- und wirtschaftliche Probleme einer europäischen Gesamtlösung der Judenfrage," *Der Weltkampf* 1 (1941), pp. 43–4.

———, *Das Judentum im osteuropäischen Raum.* Essen: Essener Verlagsanstalt, 1938.

[Seyss-Inquart, Arthur], *Rede van den Rijkscommissaris Rijksminister Dr. Seyss-Inquart gehouden op Woensdag 12 Maart 1941 in het Concertgebouw te Amsterdam voor het Arbeitsbereich der N.S.D.A.P. in de Nederlanden.* N.p., n.d. [Amsterdam, 1941].

Seyss-Inquart, Arthur, *Vier Jahre in den Niederlanden: Gesammelte Reden.* Amsterdam: Volk und Reich, 1944.

Singer, Bernard, *Moje Nalewki.* Warsaw: Czytelnik, 1959.

Sombart, Werner, *Die Juden und das Wirtschaftsleben.* Leipzig: Duncker und Humblot, 1911. English edition, *The Jews and Modern Capitalism,* trans. M. Epstein. New Brunswick, NJ: Transaction Books, 1982.

Statistiek der Bevolking van Joodschen Bloede in Nederland. The Hague: Algmeene Landsdrukkerij, 1942.

Tory, Avraham, *Surviving the Holocaust: The Kovno Ghetto Diary,* ed. and intro. Martin Gilbert, annot. Dina Porat. Cambridge: Cambridge University Press, 1990.

Bibliography

Treitschke, Heinrich von, *Ein Wort über unser Judenthum*. Berlin, 1879–1880. First published in "Unsere Aussichten," *Preußische Jahrbücher*, 44 (1879), pp. 559–76; English translation: *A Word About Our Jewry*, ed. Ellis Rivkin, trans. Helen Lederer, in Paul R. Mendes-Flohr and Jehuda Reinharz, eds., *The Jew in the Modern World: A Documentary History*, pp. 343–5.

Trial of the Major War Criminals before the International Military Tribunal, Nuremberg, 14 November 1945–1 October 1946. Nuremberg: 1947–1949.

Verfolgung und Ermordung der europäischen Juden durch das nationalsozialistische Deutschland 1933–1945 (VEJ), vol. 1, ed. Wolf Gruner: *Deutsches Reich 1933–1937*. Munich: R. Oldenbourg, 2008.

Verordnungsblatt für das Generalgouvernement, 1942.

Weltkampf, Der.

Wildt, Michael, ed., *Die Judenpolitik des SD 1935 bis 1938: Eine Dokumentation*. Munich: Oldenbourg, 1995.

Wulf, Joseph, *Theater und Film im Dritten Reich: Eine Dokumentation*. Frankfurt, Berlin, and Vienna: Ullstein, 1983.

Zangwill, Israel, *Children of the Ghetto*. London: 1892.

B. Scholarly Literature

Adler, Hans Guenther, *Theresienstadt 1941–1945: Das Antlitz einer Zwangsgemeinschaft*. Tübingen: J. C. B. Mohr (Paul Siebeck), 1955.

Alberti, Michael, "'Exerzierplatz des Nationalsozialismus': Der Reichsgau Wartheland 1939–1941," in Klaus-Michael Mallmann and Bogdan Musial, eds., *Genesis des Genozids: Polen 1939–1941*. Darmstadt: Wissenschaftliche Buchgesellschaft, 2004, pp. 111–26.

Aly, Götz, *"Endlösung": Völkerverschiebung und der Mord an den europäischen Juden*. Frankfurt am Main: S. Fischer, 1995. English edition, *"Final Solution": Nazi Population Policy and the Murder of the European Jews*, trans. Belinda Cooper and Allison Brown. London: Arnold; New York: Oxford University Press, 1999.

———, *Hitlers Volksstaat: Raub, Rassenkrieg und Nationaler Sozialismus*. Frankfurt am Main: Fischer, 2005. English edition: *Hitler's Beneficiaries: Plunder, Racial War, and the Nazi Welfare State*, trans. Jefferson Chase. New York: Metropolitan, 2007.

Aly, Götz, and Susanne Heim, *Vordenker der Vernichtung: Auschwitz und die deutschen Pläne für eine neue europäische Ordnung*. Frankfurt am Main: S. Fischer, 1993. English edition (with considerable changes), *Architects of Annihilation: Auschwitz and the Logic of Destruction*, trans. A. G. Blunden. London: Weidenfeld and Nicolson, 2002.

Ancel, Jean, *Toledot ha-Sho'ah: Romania* (History of the Holocaust: Romania). Jerusalem: Yad Vashem, 2002 (Hebrew).

Angrick, Andrej, and Peter Klein, *Die "Endlösung" in Riga: Ausbeutung und Vernichtung 1941–1944*. Darmstadt: Wissenschaftliche Buch-Gesellschaft, 2006.

Arad, Yitzhak, *Ghetto in Flames: The Struggle and Destruction of the Jews in Vilna in the Holocaust*. Jerusalem: Yad Vashem, 1980.

———, *Toledot ha-Sho'ah: Berit ha-mo'atsot ve-ha-shetahim ha-mesuppahim* (History of the Holocaust: Soviet Union and Annexed Territories). Jerusalem: Yad Vashem, 2004. English edition: *The Holocaust in the Soviet Union*, Jerusalem and Nebraska: Yad Vashem and University of Nebraska Press, 2009.

Backhaus, Fritz, Gisela Enge, Robert Liberles, and Margarete Schlüter, eds., *Die Frankfurter Judengasse: Jüdisches Leben in der Frühen Neuzeit*. Frankfurt am Main: Societäts-Verlag, 2006.

Bajohr, Frank, "'The Folk Community' and the Persecution of the Jews," *Holocaust and Genocide Studies* 20 (2) (2006), pp. 183–206.

Bankier, David, "Hitler and the Policy-Making Process on the Jewish Question," *Holocaust and Genocide Studies* 3 (1988), pp. 1–20.

———, ed., *Probing the Depths of German Antisemitism: German Society and the Persecution of the Jews 1933–1941*. Jerusalem: Yad Vashem, 2000.

Bankier, David, and Dan Michman, eds., *Holocaust Historiography in Context: Emergence, Challenges, Polemics and Achievements*. Jerusalem: Yad Vashem, 2008.

Barkai, Avraham, "In a Ghetto Without Walls," in Avraham Barkai and Paul Mendes-Flohr, eds., *German-Jewish History in Modern Times, vol. 4: Revival and Destruction 1918–1945*. New York: Columbia University Press, 1998, pp. 333–59.

———, *"Wehr Dich!": Der Centralverein deutscher Staatsbürger jüdischen Glaubens (C.) 1893–1938*. Munich: C. H. Beck, 2002.

Baruch, Hava, "Ghetto Budapest: Ifyuno ve-Yihudo shel Tahalich ha-Ghettoizatsiya veha-Kiyum ha-Yehudi be-Virat Hungaria beyn Yuni 1944 le-Yanuar 1945" (The Budapest Ghetto: The Nature and Distinctiveness of the Ghettoization Process and Jewish Life in the Capital of Hungary, June 1944–January 1945), MA thesis, Hebrew University of Jerusalem, 1997 (Hebrew).

Bauer, Yehuda, "Sarny and Rokitno in the Holocaust: A Case Study of Two Townships in Wolyn (Volhynia)," in Steven Katz, ed., *The Shtetl: New Evaluations*. New York and London: New York University Press, 2007, pp. 253–89.

Bauer, Yehuda, with the assistance of Nili Keren, *A History of the Holocaust*. New York: Franklin Watts, 1982.

Bauman, Zygmunt, *Modernity and the Holocaust*. Ithaca, NY: Cornell University Press, 1993.

Bein, Alex, *The Jewish Question: Biography of a World Problem*, trans. Harry Zohn. Rutherford, NJ: Fairleigh Dickinson University Press, 1990. Original German edition, *Die Judenfrage: Biographie eines Weltproblems*. Stuttgart: Deutsche Verlags-Anstalt, 1980.

Ben, Joseph, *Yehudei Yavan ba-Sho'ah uva-hitnaggedut 1941–1944* (Greek Jewry in the Holocaust and the Resistance 1941–1944). Tel Aviv: Institute for the Study of the Jews of Saloniki, 1985 (Hebrew).

Bender, Sara, *The Jews of Białystok during World War II and the Holocaust*, trans. Yaffa Murciano. Hanover and London: University Press of New England, 2008. Original Hebrew version, *Mul Mavet Orev. Yehudei Bilaystok be-Milhemet ha-Olam ha-Sheniya* (Facing Death: The Jews of Bialystok in the Second World War, 1939–1943). Tel Aviv: Am Oved, 1997.

———, "Koder Be'eretz Oyev: Yehudei Kielce ve-Hasseviva Bemilchemet ha-Olam ha-Sheniya, 1939–1945" (Darkness in the Enemy's Territory: The Jews of Kielce and the Surroundings During WWII, 1939–1945), unpublished ms. (Hebrew).

Benz, Wolfgang, ed., *Dimension des Völkermords: Die Zahl der jüdischen Opfer des Nationalsozialismus*. Munich: Deutsche Taschenbuch Verlag, 1996.

Benz, Wolfgang, and Barbara Distel, eds., *Der Ort des Terrors. Geschichte der nationalsozialistischen Konzentrationslager*, vol. 9. Munichen: C. H. Beck Verlag, 2009.

Berg, Nicolas, and Dirk Rupnow, eds., "Schwerpunkt: 'Judenforschung' – Zwischen Wissenschaft und Ideologie," in *Jahrbuch des Simon-Dubnow-Instituts / Simon Dubnow Institute Yearbook* 5 (2006), pp. 303–598.

Bergmann, Werner, "The Jewish Council as an Intermediary System," in Yehuda Bauer et al., eds., *Remembering for the Future*. Oxford: Pergamon Press, 1989, vol. III, pp. 2830–50.

Blumenfeld, Tatiana, "Mahoz Rostov tahat ha-kibbush ha-Natsi 1941–1943" (The Rostov district under Nazi occupation, 1941–1943), MA thesis, University of Haifa, 2002 (Hebrew).

Böhler, Jochen, *Auftakt zum Vernichtungskrieg: Die Wehrmacht in Polen*. Frankfurt am Main: S. Fischer, 2006.

Bondy, Ruth, *Shorashim Aqurim: Peraqim be-Toledot Yahadut Chekhyah, 1939–1945* (Uprooted: Essays on the History of the Czech Jews, 1939–1943). Jerusalem: Yad Vashem, 2002.

Bonfil, Robert, *Jewish Life in Renaissance Italy*. Berkeley and London: University of California Press, 1994.

Botz, Gerhard, *Wohnungspolitik und Judendeportation in Wien 1938 bis 1945: Zur Funktion des Antisemitismus als Ersatz nationalsozialistischer Sozialpolitik*. Vienna and Salzburg: Geyer-Edition, 1975.

Brackmann, Karl-Heinz, and Renate Birkenhauer, *NS-Deutsch: Selbstverständliche Begriffe und Schlagwörter aus der Zeit des Nationalsozialismus*. Straelen: Straelener Manuskripte Verlag, 1988.

Braham, Randolph L., *The Politics of Genocide: The Holocaust in Hungary*. New York: Columbia University Press, 1994.

Browning, Christopher R., "Nazi Ghettoization Policy in Poland, 1939–1941," *Central European History* 19/4 (1986), pp. 343–68. Reprinted in Browning, Christopher R., *The Path to Genocide*, pp. 30–52.

———, *The Path to Genocide: Essays on Launching the Final Solution*. New York: Cambridge University Press, 1992.

———, "Before the 'Final Solution': Nazi Ghettoization Policy in Poland (1940–1941)," in Center for Advanced Holocaust Studies, *Ghettos 1939–1945: New Research and Perspectives on Definition, Daily Life, and Survival*. Washington, DC: United States Holocaust Memorial Museum, Center for Advanced Holocaust Studies, 2005, pp. 1–13.

———, "On My Book *The Origins of the Final Solution*: Some Remarks on Its Background and on Its Major Conclusions," in Bankier and Michman, eds., *Holocaust Historiography in Context: Emergence, Challenges, Polemics and Achievements.*, pp. 403–20.

Browning, Christopher R., with contributions by Jürgen Matthäus, *The Origins of the Final Solution: The Evolution of Nazi Jewish Policy, September 1939–March 1942*. Lincoln and Jerusalem: University of Nebraska Press and Yad Vashem, 2004.

Buchholz, Marlis, *Die hannoverschen Judenhäuser: Zur Situation der Juden in der Zeit der Ghettoisierung und Verfolgung 1941 bis 1945*. Hildesheim: A. Lax, 1987.

Buchler, Yehoshua Robert, ed., *Pinkas ha-Kehillot: Slovakia* (Encyclopedia of Jewish Communities: Slovakia). Jerusalem: Yad Vashem, 2003 (Hebrew).

Burleigh, Michael, *Germany Turns Eastwards: A Study of "Ostforschung" in the Third Reich*. Cambridge: Cambridge University Press, 1988.

Burleigh, Michael, and Wolfgang Wippermann, *The Racial State: Germany 1933–1945*. Cambridge: Cambridge University Press, 1991.

Cała, Alina, "The Discourse of 'Ghettoization': Non-Jews on Jews in 19th- and 20th-Century Poland," *Jahrbuch des Simon-Dubnow-Instituts / Simon Dubnow Institute Yearbook* 4 (2005), pp. 445–85.

Calabi, Donatella, "Venice: The Ghetto and the City, 1541–1797," in *Amsterdam and Venice*. Amsterdam: Jewish Historical Museum, 1991, pp. 46–66.

Center for Advanced Holocaust Studies, *Ghettos 1939–1945: New Research and Perspectives on Definition, Daily Life, and Survival*. Washington, DC: United States Holocaust Memorial Museum, Center for Advanced Holocaust Studies, 2005.

Centralny Komitet Żyów Polskich, *Instrukcje dla zbierania materiałów historycznych z okresu okupacji niemieckiej*. Łódź, 1945.

Cohen, Boaz, *Ha-Mehkar ha-Histori ha-Yisre'eli al ha-Shoah ba-Shanim 1945–1980: Me'afyenim, Megamot ve-Chivunim* ("Holocaust Research in Israel, 1945–1980: Trends, Characteristics, Developments,") Ph.D. dissertation, Bar-Ilan University, Ramat Gan, 2004 (Hebrew).

Cohen, Mark R., *Under Crescent and Cross: The Jews in the Middle Ages*. Princeton: Princeton University Press, 1994.

Cohen, Richard I., "Nostalgia and 'Return to the Ghetto': A Cultural Phenomenon in Western and Central Europe," in Jonathan Frankel and Steven J. Zipperstein, eds., *Assimilation and Community: The Jews in Nineteenth-Century Europe*. Cambridge: Cambridge University Press, 1992, pp. 130–55.

Cole, Tim, *Holocaust City: The Making of a Jewish Ghetto*. New York and London: Routledge, 2003.

―――, "Multiple and Changing Experiences of Ghettoization: Budapest 1944," in Eric J. Sterling, ed., *Life in the Ghettos During the Holocaust*. Syracuse, NY: Syracuse University Press, 2005, pp. 145–59.

Cole, Tim, and Graham Smith, "Ghettoization and the Holocaust: Budapest 1944," *Journal of Historical Geography* 21 (3) (1995), pp. 300–16.

Concinna, Enio, Donatella Calabi, and Ugo Camerino, *La Città Degli Ebrei: Il Ghetto di Venezia – Architettura e Urbanistica*. Venice: Albrizzi Editore, 1991.

Corni, Gustavo, *Hitler's Ghettos: Voices from a Beleaguered Society 1939–1944*. London: Arnold, 2002.

Corrsin, Stephen D., "Political and Social Change in Warsaw from the January 1863 Insurrection to the First World War," Ph.D. dissertation, University of Michigan, 1981. Later rewritten and published as *Warsaw Before the First World War: Poles and Jews in the Third City of the Russian Empire, 1889–1914*. Boulder, CO: East European Monographs, 1999.

Csősz, László, "Municipal Administration in Hungary and the Holocaust: Regional Patterns and Individual Responses," unpublished paper, presented at the Yad Vashem workshop on "Persecution and Murder of the Jews: Grassroots Perspectives," July 4–12, 2010.

Dąbrowska, Danuta, and Abraham Wein, eds., *Pinkas ha-Kehillot: Poland*, vol. 1, *Lodz veha-Galil* (Encyclopedia of Jewish Communities: The Communities of Łódź and the Region). Jerusalem: Yad Vashem, 1976 (Hebrew).

Dąbrowska, Danuta, Avraham Wein, and Aharon Weiss, *Pinkas ha-Kehillot: Poland*, vol. 2: *Galitziya ha-Mizrahit* (Encyclopedia of Jewish Communities: Eastern Galicia). Jerusalem: Yad Vashem, 1980 (Hebrew).

Datner, Szymon, *Walka i zagłada białostockiego getta*. Łódź: Centralna Żydowska Komisja, 1946.

Dawidowicz, Lucy S., *The War Against the Jews, 1933–1945*. New York: Bantam, 1976.

Dean, Martin, "Preparing an Encyclopedia of Ghettos: Numbers, Types, and Essential Characteristics of Ghettos under German Administration," paper read at the international conference on "Lessons and Legacies IX: Memory, History and Responsibility: Reassessments of the Holocaust, Implications for the Future," Claremont McKenna College, November 2–5, 2006 (publication forthcoming).

De Jong, Lou, *Het Koninkrijk der Nederlanden in de Tweede Wereldoorlog*, vol. 4/a–b. The Hague: Martinus Nijhoff, 1972.

———, *Het Koninkrijk der Nederlanden in de Tweede Wereldoorlog*, vol. 5/a–b. The Hague: Martinus Nijhoff, 1974.

Deletant, Dennis, "Ghetto Experience in Golta, Transnistria 1942–1944," *Holocaust and Genocide Studies* 18 (1) (2004), pp. 1–26.

Dieckmann, Christoph, "Das Ghetto und das Konzentrationslager in Kaunas 1941–1944," in Ulrich Herbert, Karin Orth, and Christoph Dieckmann, eds., *Die nationalsozialistischen Konzentrationslager: Entwickelung und Struktur*, vol. I. Göttingen: Wallstein, 1998, pp. 442–3.

Dieckmann, Christoph, and Sužiedėlis Saulius, *Lietuvos žydu persekiojimas ir masinės žudynės 1941 m. vasarą ir rudenį* (The Persecution and Mass Murder of Lithuanian Jews during Summer and Fall of 1941). Vilnius: Publications of the International Commission for the Evaluation of the Crimes of the Nazi and Soviet Occupation Regimes in Lithuania, vol. III, 2006.

Dworzecki, Mark, *Yerushalayim de-Lita ba-Meri uva-Shoa* (Jerusalem of Lithuania in Revolt and Holocaust). Tel Aviv: Mapai Press, 1951 (Hebrew).

Engelking-Boni, Barbara, and Jacek Leociak, *Getto Warszawskie: Przewodnik po nieistniejącym mieście*. Wrzesień: IFiS PAN, 2001.

Einat, Aharon, "Hahayim hapenimiyim begetto Vilna" (The internal life of the Vilna ghetto), Ph.D. dissertation, Hebrew University of Jerusalem, 2005 (Hebrew).

Eisenberg (Gotdiner), Mali, *Ed, maz'iq, meta'ed umantsiah: R. Moshe Prager ve-ha-Sho'ah, 1940–1984* (Witnessing, Protesting, Documenting and Commemorating: Moshe Prager and the Holocaust 1940-1984). Ramat Gan: Arnold and Leona Finkler Institute of Holocaust Research, 2006 (Hebrew).

Esh, Shaul, *Iyyunim be-Heqer ha-Sho'ah ve-Yahadut Zemanenu* (Studies in the Holocaust and Contemporary Jewry). Jerusalem: Hebrew University, 1973 (Hebrew).

Fatal-Knaani, Tikva, *Zo Lo Otah Grodna. Kehillat Grodna u-Sevivatah be-Milhama uve-Shoah 1939–1945* (*Grodno Is Not the Same: The Jewish Community in Grodno and Its Vicinity during the Second World War and the Holocaust, 1939–1943*). Jerusalem: Yad Vashem, 2001 (Hebrew).

Förster, Jürgen, "Die Sicherung des 'Lebensraumes'," in Horst Boog, *Der Angriff auf der Sowjetunion*. Stuttgart, Deutsche Verlags-Anstalt, 1983. English edition, *The Attack on the Soviet Union*, ed. Ewald Osers, trans. Dean S. McMurry, Ewald Osers, and Louise Willmot. Oxford: Clarendon Press, 1998.

Friedländer, Saul, *Die Jahre der Vernichtung: Das Dritte Reich und die Juden, II. 1939–1945*. Munich: Beck, 2007; English version: *Nazi Germany and the Jews 1939–1945*, vol. 2: *The Years of Extermination*. New York: HarperCollins, 2006.

———, *Nazi Germany and the Jews*, vol. 1: *The Years of Persecution 1933–1939*. London: Weidenfeld and Nicolson, 1997.

Friedman, Filip [Philip], *Zagłada żydów lwowskich*. Łódź: Centralna Żydowska Komisja, 1945.

Friedman, Philip, "Problems of Research on the Jewish Catastrophe," *Yad Vashem Studies*, 3 (1959), pp. 25–39; reprinted with slight changes as "Problems of Research on the Holocaust: An Overview" in Friedman, *Roads to Extinction: Essays on the Holocaust*, pp. 554–67.

———, "The Jewish Ghettos of the Nazi Era," *Jewish Social Studies* 16 (January 1954), pp. 61–88. Repr. in Friedman, *Roads to Extinction: Essays on the Holocaust*, pp. 59–87.

———, "The Messianic Complex of a Nazi Collaborator in a Ghetto: Moses Merin of Sosnowiec," in Friedman, *Roads to Extinction: Essays on the Holocaust*, pp. 353–64.

———, *Roads to Extinction: Essays on the Holocaust*. New York and Philadelphia: Jewish Publication Society, 1980.

Friedrich, Klaus-Peter, "Rassistische Seuchenprävention als Voraussetzung nationalsozialistischer Vernichtungspolitik: Vom Warschauer 'Seuchensperrengebiet' zu den 'Getto'-Mauern (1939/40)," *Zeitschrift für Geschichtswissenschaft* 53/7 (2005), pp. 609–36.

Frojimovics, Kinga, Géza Komoróczy, Viktória Pusztai, and Andrea Strbik, *Jewish Budapest: Monuments, Rites, History*. Budapest: Central European University Press, 1999.

Fuchs, Anne, and Florian Krobb, eds., *Ghetto Writing: Traditional and Eastern Jewry in German-Jewish Literature from Heine to Hilsenrath*. Columbia, SC: Camden House, 1999.

Gellately, Robert, *The Gestapo and German Society: Enforcing Racial Policy 1933–45*. New York: Oxford University Press, 1990.

Geller, Jacob, *Ha-Amidah ha-Ruhanit shel Yehudei Romania bi-Tequfat ha-Sho'ah (1940–1944)* (Spiritual Resistance of Romanian Jewry during the Holocaust (1940–1944)). Lod: Orot Yahadut ha-Magreb, 2003 (Hebrew).

Gerlach, Christian, *Kalkulierte Morde: Die deutsche Wirtschafts- und Vernichtungspolitik in Weißrußland 1941 bis 1944*. Hamburg: Hamburger Edition, 1999.

Gerlach, Christian, and Götz Aly, *Das letzte Kapitel: Realpolitik, Ideologie und der Mord an den ungarischen Juden 1944/1945*. Stuttgart and Munich: Deutsche Verlags-Anstalt, 2002.

Gitlis, Baruch, "'Redemption' of Ahasuerus: The 'Eternal Jew'" in *Nazi Film*, trans. Norman Berdichevsky. Astoria, NY: Holmfirth Books, 1991.

Glasenapp, Gabriele von, *Aus der Judengasse: Zur Entstehung und Ausprägung deutschsprachiger Ghettoliteratur im 19. Jahrhundert*. Tübingen: Niemeyer, 1996.

Golczewski, Frank, "Polen," in Wolfgang Benz, ed., *Dimension des Völkermords: Die Zahl der jüdischen Opfer des Nationalsozialismus*. Munich: DTV, 1996, pp. 411–97.

Gringauz, Samuel, "The Ghetto as an Experiment of Jewish Social Organization," *Jewish Social Studies* 11 (1) (1949), pp. 3–20.

———, "Some Methodological Problems in the Study of the Ghetto," *Jewish Social Studies* 12 (1950), pp. 65–72.

Gross, Konrad, "Schtetl und Ghetto im jüdisch-amerikanischen und -kanadischen Roman," in Annelore Engel-Braunschmidt and Eckhard Hübner, eds., *Jüdischen Welten in Osteuropa*. Frankfurt am Main: Peter Lang, 2005, pp. 231–47.

Gruner, Wolf, "'Lesen brauchen sie nicht zu können...' Die Denkschrift über die Behandlung der Juden in der Reichshauptstadt auf allen Gebieten des öffentlichen Lebens vom Mai 1938," *Jahrbuch für Antisemitismusforschung* 4 (1995), pp. 305–41.

———, "Die NS-Judenverfolgung und die Kommunen. Zur wechselseitigen Dynamisierung von zentraler und lokaler Politik 1933–1941," *Vierteljahrshefte für Zeitgeschichte* 48 (1) (2000), pp. 75–126.

Gutman, Israel, ed.-in-chief, *Encyclopedia of the Holocaust*. New York: Macmillan, 1990.

———, *The Jews of Warsaw, 1939–1943: Ghetto, Underground, Revolt*. Bloomington: Indiana University Press, 1983.

———, *Shoah ve-Zikkaron* (Shoah and Memory). Jerusalem: Merkaz Shazar and Yad Vashem, 1999 (Hebrew).

Gutman, Israel, and Chaim Schatzker, *The Holocaust and Its Significance*. Jerusalem: Zalman Shazar Center, 1984, pp. 69–84 (original Hebrew version: *Hashoah u-Mashma'utah*, 1983).

Haar, Ingo, *Historiker im Nationalsozialismus. Deutsche Geschichtswissenschaft und der "Volkstumskampf" im Osten*. Göttingen: Vandenhoeck und Ruprecht, 2000.

Hájková, Anna, "The Making of a Zentralstelle: Die Eichmann-Männer in Amsterdam," *Theresienstädter Studien und Dokumente* (2003), pp. 353–81.

Hanke, Peter, *Zur Geschichte der Juden in München zwischen 1933 und 1945*. Munich: Stadtarchiv, 1967.

Hart, Mitchell B., "'Let the Numbers Speak': On the Appropriation of Jewish Social Science by Nazi Scholars," *Jahrbuch des Simon-Dubnow-Instituts / Simon Dubnow Institute Yearbook* V (2006), pp. 281–99.

Heer, Hannes, "Killing Fields: The Wehrmacht and the Holocaust in Belorussia 1941–1942," *Holocaust and Genocide Studies* 11 (1) (1997), pp. 79–101.

Hekking, Veronica, and Flip Bool, *De illegale Camera 1940–1945. Nederlandse fotografie tijdens de Duitse bezetting*. Naarden: V+K Publishing/Immerc, 1995.

Herbert, Ulrich, Karin Orth, and Christoph Dieckmann, eds., *Die nationalsozialistischen Konzentrationslager: Entwickelung und Struktur*, vol. 1. Göttingen: Wallstein, 1998.

Heyde Jürgen, "The 'Ghetto' as a Spatial and Historical Construction – Discourses of Emancipation in France, Germany, and Poland," *Jahrbuch des Simon-Dubnow-Instituts / Simon Dubnow Institute Yearbook* IV (2005), pp. 431–44.

Heyde, Jürgen, and Katrin Steffen, "The 'Ghetto' as a Topographic Reality and Discursive Metaphor: Introduction," *Jahrbuch des Simon-Dubnow-Instituts / Simon Dubnow Institute Yearbook* IV (Göttingen: Vandenhoeck & Ruprecht, 2005), pp. 423–30.

Hilberg, Raul, *The Destruction of the European Jews*. Chicago: Quadrangle Books, 1961.

———, "The Ghetto as a Form of Government: An Analysis of Isaiah Trunk's Judenrat," *Annals of the American Academy of Political and Social Science* 450 (1) (1989), pp. 98–112.

Johnson, Eric A., *Nazi Terror: The Gestapo, Jews, and Ordinary Germans*. New York: Basic Books, 2000.

Katz, Jacob, *A State within a State: The History of an Anti-Semitic Slogan* (The Israel Academy of Sciences and Humanities Proceedings IV). Jerusalem: The Israel Academy of Sciences and Humanities, 1969/70, pp. 29–58.

———, "From Ghetto to Zionism, Mutual Influences," in Isadore Twersky, ed., *Danzig, Between East and West: Aspects of Modern Jewish History*. Cambridge, MA: Harvard University Press, 1985, pp. 39–48.

Keren, Nili, *Shoah: Masa' el ha-Zikkaron* (Shoah: A Journey to Memory). Tel Aviv: Tel Aviv Books, 1999, pp. 43–6 (Hebrew).

Kermisz, Józef, *Powstanie w getcie warszawskim (19 kwietnia–16 maja 1943)*. Łódź: Centralna Zydowska Komisja Historyczna w Polsce, 1946.

Kershaw, Ian, *Hitler (I) – 1889–1936: Hubris*. New York and London: Norton, 1998.

Klein, Bernard, "The Judenrat," *Jewish Social Studies* 22 (1) (1960), pp. 27–42.

Klein, Peter, *Die "Gettoverwaltung Litzmannstadt" 1940–1944. Eine Dienststelle im Spannungsfeld von Kommunalbürokratie und staatlicher Verfolgungspolitik*. Hamburg: Hamburger Edition, 2009.

Klemperer, Victor, *LTI – Notiz eines Philologen*. Stuttgart: Reclam, 2007 [Berlin, 1947]. English edition, *The Language of the Third Reich*. London: Continuum: 2006.

Koonz, Claudia, *The Nazi Conscience*. Cambridge, MA: Harvard University Press, 2003.
Kornberg, Jacques, *Theodor Herzl: From Assimilation to Zionism*. Bloomington and Indianapolis: Indiana University Press, 1993.
Kwiet, Konrad, *Reichskommissariat Niederlande. Versuch und Scheitern nationalsozialistischer Neuordnung*. Stuttgart: Deutsche Verlags-Anstalt, 1968.
_____, "Without Neighbors: Daily Living in Judenhäuser," in Francis Nicosia and David Scrase, eds., *Jewish Life in Nazi Germany: Dilemmas and Responses*. New York: Berghahn, forthcoming, chapter 5.
Levin, Dov, ed., *Pinkas Hakehillot: Lithuania* (Encyclopedia of Jewish Communities: Lithuania). Jerusalem: Yad Vashem, 1986 (Hebrew).
Levin, Itamar, *Lexicon ha-Shoah* (*Lexicon of the Holocaust*). Tel Aviv: Miskal, 2005 (Hebrew).
Levin, Judith, and Daniel Uziel, "Ordinary Men, Extraordinary Photos," *Yad Vashem Studies* 26 (1998), pp. 265–93.
Lewandowska, Stanisława, *Życie codzienne Wilna w latach II wojny Swiatowej*. Warsaw: Neriton, 1997.
Lifmann, Margot, "The Policy of the German Occupation in Holland during 1940–1945: The Impact of this Policy on Dutch Attitudes Towards this Policy as Reflected in German Reports (Stimmungs- & Lageberichte) and Dutch Newspapers," dissertation, Ramat Gan: Bar-Ilan University, 1994.
Longerich, Peter, *Policy of Destruction. Nazi Anti-Jewish Policy and the Genesis of the "Final Solution."* Washington, DC: United States Holocaust Memorial Museum, Center for Advanced Holocaust Studies, 2001.
_____, *Politik der Vernichtung: Eine Gesamtdarstellung der nationalsozialistischen Judenverfolgung*. Munich and Zurich: Piper, 1998.
Löwe, Andrea, *Juden im Getto Litzmannstadt, Lebensbedingungen, Selbstwahrnehmung, Verhalten*. Göttingen: Wallstein, 2006.
Lower, Wendy, "Facilitating Genocide: Nazi Ghettoization Practices in Occupied Ukraine 1941–1942," in Sterling, ed., *Life in the Ghettos During the Holocaust*, p. 120–44.
_____, *Nazi Empire-Building and the Holocaust in Ukraine*. Chapel Hill: University of North Carolina Press, 2005.
Mallmann, Klaus-Michael, Jochen Böhler, and Jürgen Matthäus, *Einsatzgruppen in Polen. Darstellung und Dokumentation*. Darmstadt: Wissenschaftliche Buchgesellschaft, 2008.
Mankowitz, Zeev W., *Life between Memory and Hope: The Survivors of the Holocaust in Occupied Germany*. Cambridge: Cambridge University Press, 2002.
Margaliot, Avraham, *Bein Hatzalah le'Avdan* (Between Rescue and Annihilation). Jerusalem: Institute of Contemporary Jewry and Leo Baeck Institute, 1990 (Hebrew).
Mason, Tim, "Intention and Explanation: A Current Controversy about the Interpretation of National Socialism," in Gerhard Hirschfeld and Lothar Kettenacker, eds., *Der Führerstaat: Mythos und Realität*. Stuttgart: Klett-Cotta, 1981, pp. 23–41.

Matthäus, Jürgen, "Die 'Judenfrage' als Schulungsthema von SS und Polizei: 'Inneres Erlebnis' und Handlungslegitimation," in Matthäus et al., *Ausbildungsziel Judenmord? "Weltanschauliche Erziehung" von SS, Polizei und Waffen-SS im Rahmen der "Endlösung,"* pp. 35–86.

———, "Konzept als Kalkül. Das Judenbild des SD 1934–1939," in Michael Wildt, *Nachrichtendienst, politische Elite und Mordeinheit: Der Sicherheitsdienst des Reichsführers SS.* Hamburg: Hamburger Edition, 2003, pp. 118–43.

Matthäus, Jürgen, Konrad Kwiet, Jürgen Förster, and Richard Breitman, *Ausbildungsziel Judenmord? "Weltanschauliche Erziehung" von SS, Polizei und Waffen-SS im Rahmen der "Endlösung."* Frankfurt am Main: S. Fischer, 2003.

Matthäus, Jürgen, and Klaus-Michael Mallmann, eds., *Deutsche, Juden, Völkermord: Der Holocaust als Geschichte und Gegenwart.* Hamburg: Wissenschaftliche Buchgesellschaft, 2006.

Megargee, Geoffrey P., *Inside Hitler's High Command.* Lawrence: University Press of Kansas, 2000.

———, ed., *Encyclopedia of Camps and Ghettos, 1933–1945,* vol. 1, Bloomington: University of Indiana Press and United States Holocaust Memorial Museum, 2009.

Mendelsohn, Ezra, *The Jews of East Central Europe Between the World Wars.* Bloomington: Indiana University Press, 1987.

Meyer, Michael A., ed., *Joachim Prinz, Rebellious Rabbi: An Autobiography. The German and Early American Years.* Bloomington and Indianapolis: Indiana University Press, 2007.

Michael, Robert, and Karin Doerr, *Nazi-Deutsch/Nazi German. An English Lexicon of the Language of the Third Reich.* Westport, CT, and London: Greenwood Press, 2002.

Michman, Dan, "Amsterdam, 1870–1940: Rapid Growth and the Creation of an Amsterdam Dutch-Jewish Sub-culture," *Encyclopaedia Judaica,* 2nd edn. Jerusalem: Macmillan Reference USA and Keter, 2006, vol. 1, pp. 113–15.

———, *Holocaust Historiography: A Jewish Perspective. Conceptualizations, Terminology, Approaches and Fundamental Issues.* London: Vallentine Mitchell, 2003.

———, "Hayey ha-Yehudim Tahat Shilton ha-Natzim – Shalosh Dugma'ot" (Jewish Life under Nazi Rule: Three Examples), *Bimey Shoah u-Fkuda* (Days of Holocaust and Reckoning), Unit 9. Tel Aviv: Open University, 1992, pp. 5–45 (Hebrew; Spanish version: "La vida judía bajo el domino nazi," *El Holocausto,* Unidad 4. Tel Aviv: Universidad Abierta, 1989, pp. 45–118).

———, "Judenräte, Ghetti, Endlösung: tre componenti correlate di una politica antiebraica o elementi separati?" *Ventunesimo Secolo* 17 (October 2008), pp. 109–17.

———, "Täteraussagen und Geschichtswissenschaft: Der Fall Dieter Wisliceny und der Entscheidungsprozess zur 'Endlösung,'" in Matthäus and Mallmann, eds., *Deutsche, Juden, Völkermord: Der Holocaust als Geschichte und Gegenwart,* pp. 205–19.

———, "Why Did Heydrich Write the *Schnellbrief*? A Remark on the Reason and on Its Significance," *Yad Vashem Studies* 32 (2004), pp. 433–47.

Michman, Dan, and David Bankier, eds., *Holocaust Historiography in Context: Emergence, Challenges, Polemics and Achievements*. Jerusalem: Yad Vashem, 2008.

Michman, Jozeph, Hartog Beem, and Dan Michman, *Pinkas. Geschiedenis van de joodse gemeenschap in Nederland*. Amsterdam and Antwerp: Contact, 1999.

Miller, Michael L., "Czech Holocaust or Holocaust in the Czech Lands?" *Yad Vashem Studies* 35 (1) (2007), pp. 214–15.

Miovic, Vesna, *The Jewish Ghetto in the Dubrovnik Republic (1546–1808)*. Zagreb-Dubrovnik: HAZU, Zavod za povijesne znanosti u Dubrovniku (Croation Academy of Sciences and Arts, Institute for Historical Sciences in Dubrovnik), 2005.

Miron, Guy, ed.-in-chief, *The Yad Vashem Encyclopedia of the Ghettos During the Holocaust*. Jerusalem: Yad Vashem, 2009.

Młynarczyk, Jacek, "Der Holocaust in Kielce/Distrikt Radom," master's thesis, Universität Essen, n.d. (c. 2000).

Molho, Michael, and Joseph Nehama, eds., *Sho'at yehudei Yavan 1941–1944* (The Destruction of Greek Jewry, 1941–1944). Jerusalem: Yad Vashem, 1965 (Hebrew). First published as *In Memoriam: hommage aux victimes juives des Nazis en Grèce*. Saloniki: N. Nicolaidès, 1948.

Moore, Bob, *Victims and Survivors: The Nazi Persecution of the Jews in the Netherlands 1940–1945*. London: Arnold, 1997.

Mosse, George, *Germans and Jews: The Right, the Left, and the Search for a "Third Force" in Pre-Nazi Germany*. London: Orbach and Chambers, 1971.

Musial, Bogdan, *Deutsche Zivilverwaltung und Judenverfolgung im Generalgouvernement: Eine Fallstudie zum Distrikt Lublin 1939–1944*. Wiesbaden: Harrasowitz, 1999.

Muzzarelli, Maria Giuseppina, "Beatrice de Luna, vedova Mendes, alias Donna Gracia Nasi: una Ebreia influente (1510–ca. 1569)," in Ottavia Nicoli, ed., *Rinascimento al femminile*, Laterza: 1991, pp. 83–116.

Namysło, Alexandra, "The Situation of the Jewish Population in Eastern Upper Silesia Contrasted with the Situation of the Jews in the Other Polish Territories Incorporated into the Reich," unpublished paper, presented at the Yad Vashem scholars' seminar, January 8, 2009.

Neumann, Boaz, *Re'iyat ha-Olam ha-Natzit: Merhav, Guf, Safa* (*The Nazi Weltanschauung: Space, Body, Language*). Haifa and Tel Aviv: University of Haifa and Sifriyat Maariv, 2002 (Hebrew).

———, *Nazism*. Tel Aviv: MOD Publishing House, 2007 (Hebrew).

Nirenberg, David, *Communities of Violence: Persecution of Minorities in the Middle Ages*. Princeton: Princeton University Press, 1996.

Ober, Kenneth H., *Die Ghettogeschichte: Entstehung und Entwicklung einer Gattung*. Göttingen: Wallstein, 2001.

Ofer, Dalia, "Life in the Ghettos of Transnistria," *Yad Vashem Studies* 25 (1996), pp. 229–74.

Orfali, Moises, "Doña Gracia Mendes and the Ragusan Republic: The Successful Use of Economic Institutions in 16th Century Commerce," in Elliott Horowitz and Moises Orfali, eds., *The Mediterranean and the Jews: Society, Culture and*

Economy in Early Modern Times. Ramat Gan: Bar-Ilan University Press, 2002, pp. 175–202.

Peled, Yael (Margolin), *Krakow ha-Yehudit 1939–1943: Amidah, Mahteret, Ma'avaq* (Jewish Krakow 1939–1943: Resistance, Underground, Struggle). Tel Aviv: Hakibbutz Hame'uhad and Ghetto Fighters' House, 1992 (Hebrew).

Petersen, Hans-Christian, "Ein 'Judenforscher' danach – Zur Karriere Peter-Heinz Seraphims in Westdeutschland," *Jahrbuch des Simon-Dubnow-Instituts / Simon Dubnow Institute Yearbook* V (2006), pp. 515–35.

―――, *Bevölkerungsökonomie – Ostforschung – Politik: Eine biographische Studie zu Peter-Heinz Seraphim (1902–1979)*. Berlin: Fibre, 2007.

Pohl, Dieter, *Von der "Judenpolitik" zum Judenmord: Der Distrikt Lublin des Generalgouvernements 1939–1944*. Frankfurt am Main: Peter Lang, 1993.

Poliakov Léon, *Harvest of Hate: The Nazi Program for the Destruction of the Jews of Europe*. New York: Holocaust Library, 1979 [Syracuse University Press, 1954]. Original French edition, *Bréviaire de la Haine*. Paris: Calman-Lévy, 1951.

Porat, Dina, *Me'ever lagashmi. Parashat hayav shel Abba Kovner* (Beyond the Reaches of Our Souls (Hamlet I iv 55–56): The Life and Times of Abba Kovner). Tel Aviv: Am Oved, 2000 (Hebrew). English edition: *The Fall of a Sparrow: The Life and Times of Abba Kovner*. Stanford University Press: 2010.

Presser, Jacques, *Ondergang: De vervolging en verdelging van het nederlandse jodendom 1940–1945*. The Hague: Staatsuitgeverij, 1965. English (abridged) edition, *Ashes in the Wind: The Destruction of Dutch Jewry*, trans. Arnold Pomerans. London: Souvenir, 1968.

Prévot, Philippe, *Histoire du ghetto d'Avignon*, Avignon: Aubanel, 1975.

Ramme, Alwin, *Der Sicherheitsdienst der SS. Zu seiner Funktion im faschistischen Machtapparat und im Besatzungsregime des sogenannten Generalgouvernements Polen*. East Berlin: Deutscher Militärverlag, 1970.

Ravid, Benjamin, "Alle Ghettos waren jüdische Viertel, aber nicht alle jüdischen Viertel waren Ghettos," in Fritz Backhaus, et al., *Die Frankfurter Judengasse: Jüdisches Leben in der Frühen Neuzeit*. Frankfurt am Main: Societäts-Verlag, 2006, pp. 13–30, 289–91. English version: "All Ghettos Were Jewish Quarters but Not All Jewish Quarters Were Ghettos," *Jewish Culture and History* vol. 10, Nos. 2&3 (Autumn/Winter 2008), pp. 5–24.

―――, "Curfew Time in the Ghetto of Venice," in Ellen E. Kittell and Thomas F. Madden, eds., *Medieval and Renaissance Venice*. Urbana and Chicago: University of Illinois Press, 1999, pp. 237–75.

―――, "From Geographical Realia to Historiographical Symbol: The Odyssey of the Word Ghetto," in *Essential Papers on Jewish Culture in Renaissance and Baroque Italy*. New York: New York University Press, 1992, pp. 373–85.

―――, "Ghetto," in Richard S. Levy, ed., *Antisemitism: A Historical Encyclopedia of Prejudice and Persecution*. Santa Barbara, CA: ABC Clio, 2005, pp. 272–4.

―――, *Studies on the Jews of Venice 1382–1797*. Cornwall: Ashgate Variorum, 2003.

Redlich, Shimon, *Together and Apart in Brzezany: Poles, Jews and Ukrainians, 1919–1945*. Bloomington and Indianapolis: Indiana University Press, 2002.

Rigoulot, Pierre and Joël Kotek, *Le siècle des camps: emprisonnement, détention, extermination, cent ans de mal absolu.* Paris: JC Lattès, 2000.
Rivlin, Brachah, ed., *Pinkas ha-kehillot: Yavan* (Encyclopedia of Jewish Communities: Greece). Jerusalem: Yad Vashem, 1998 (Hebrew).
Roest, Friso, and Jos Scheren, *Oorlog in de stad: Amsterdam 1939–1941.* Amsterdam: Van Gennep, 1998.
Rossino, Alexander B., *Hitler Strikes Poland: Blitzkrieg, Ideology, and Atrocity.* Lawrence: University Press of Kansas, 2003.
Roth, Markus, "The County Chiefs (Kreishauptleute) in the General Government Before and After 1945," paper at joint workshop of German and Israeli doctoral students, Yad Vashem, October 9, 2007.
_____, *Herrenmenschen. Die deutschen Kreishauptleute im besetzten Polen – Karrierewege, Herrschaftspraxis und Nachgeschichte.* Göttingen: Wallstein, 2009.
Rothkirchen, Livia, *The Jews of Bohemia and Moravia: Facing the Holocaust.* Lincoln: University of Nebraska Press; Jerusalem: Yad Vashem, 2005.
Ruderman, David B., *De culturele betekenis van het getto in de joodse geschiedenis.* Amsterdam: Vossiuspers en Universiteit van Amsterdam, 2003. English version "The Cultural Significance of the Ghetto in Jewish History," in David N. Myers and William V. Rowe, eds., *From Ghetto to Emancipation.* Scranton, PA: University of Scranton Press, 1997, pp. 1–16.
Rupnow Dirk, "'Heqer ha-Yehudim' ba-Reikh ha-Shelishi: Ha-arizatsiyah shel ha-historiyah ha-yehudit bi-tqufat ha-mishtar ha-Natsi" ("Jewish Studies" in the Third Reich: The Aryanization of Jewish History under the Nazi Regime), *Dappim le-heqer tequfat ha-Shoah* 21 (2007), pp. 7–33 (Hebrew).
_____, "Radicalizing Historiography: Anti-Jewish Scholarship in the Third Reich," *Patterns of Prejudice* 42: (1) (2008), pp. 27–59.
Saerens, Lieven, *Vreemdelingen in een wereldstad: Een geschiedenis van Antwerpen en zijn joodse bevolking (1880–1944).* Tielt: Lannoo, 2000.
Salamander, Rachel, *Die jüdische Welt von Gestern: Text- und Bild-Zeugnisse aus Mitteleuropa 1860–1938.* Vienna: Christian Brandstätter, 1990.
Sandkühler, Thomas, *"Endlösung" in Galizien: Der Judenmord in Ostpolen und die Rettungsinitiativen von Berthold Beitz 1941–1944.* Bonn: J. H. W. Dietz Nachfolger, 1996.
Schachar, David, *Am ve-Olam: Perakim be-Toledot Yisrael veha-Amim 1870–1970* (A People and the World: Chapters in the History of the Jews and Other Peoples 1870–1970), Vol. B: 1920–1945. Rehovot: Idan, 1998, pp. 318–20 (Hebrew).
Scheffler, Wolfgang, "Zur Organisation der Judendeportation unter besonderer Berücksichtigung des Schicksals der Juden in Bialystok (1941–1943)," historical report, 8 July 1966, given before the Bielefeld regional court, unpublished manuscript, Bundesarchiv Berlin, B 162/153.4063.
Schreiber, Jean-Philippe, and Rudi van Doorslaer, eds., *Les Curateurs du Ghetto: L'Association des Juifs en Belgique sous l'occupation nazie.* Brussels: Labor, 2004.
Schulze, Winfried, and Otto Gerhard Oexle, eds., *Deutsche Historiker im Nationalsozialismus.* Frankfurt am Main: S. Fischer, 1999.

Shachan, Avigdor, *Burning Ice: The Ghettos of Transnistria*, trans. Shmuel Himelstein. Boulder, CO: East European Monographs, 1996.

Shalem, Chaim, *Et la-asot le-Hatzalat Yisrael. Agudat Yisrael be-Eretz Yisrael lenochach ha-Shoah 1942–1945* (A Time to Take Action to Rescue Jews: Agudat Yisrael in Eretz Israel Confronting the Holocaust 1942–1945). Beer Sheva: Ben-Gurion Research Institute and Ben-Gurion University of the Negev Press, 2007 (Hebrew).

Shlain, Margalit, *Ha-hanhaggah ha-yehudit be-ma'avakah le-hissaredut: Terezyenshtat 1941–1945* (Jewish Leadership in Theresienstadt: Struggle for Survival, 1941–1945. Tel Aviv: n.s. 2005 (Hebrew).

Siegmund, Stephanie B., *The Medici State and the Ghetto of Florence: The Construction of an Early Modern Jewish Community*, Stanford: Stanford University Press, 2005.

Silberklang, David, "Ha-Sho'ah bimhoz Lublin" (The Holocaust in the Lublin District of Poland), dissertation, Hebrew University of Jerusalem, 2004 (Hebrew).

Sijes, Ben A., *De Februaristaking: 25–26 Februari 1941*. The Hague: Martinus Nijhoff, 1954.

Skibińska, Alina, and Jakub Petelewicz, "The Participation of Poles in Crimes Against Jews in the Świętokrzyskie Region," *Yad Vashem Studies* 35 (1) (2007), pp. 5–48.

Spector, Shmuel, *The Holocaust of Volhynian Jews, 1941–1944*, trans. Jerzy Michalowicz. Jerusalem: Yad Vashem, 1990.

———, "Rostov-on-Don," *Encyclopedia of the Holocaust* (Israel Gutman, ed.-in-chief). New York: Macmillan, 1990, p. 1306.

———, "Getta'ot ve-Yudenrattim be-Shithei ha-Kibbush ha-Natsi bi-Vrit ha-Mo'atsot (bi-Gvulot September 1939)" (Ghettos and Judenräte in the Nazi-occupied Soviet Union [September 1939 borders])," *Shevut* 15 (1992), pp. 263–76 (Hebrew).

Stauber, Ronnie, "Philip Friedman and the Beginnings of Holocaust Historiography," in David Bankier and Dan Michman, eds., *Holocaust Historiography in Context: Emergence, Challenges, Polemics and Achievements*, pp. 83–102.

———, *Laying the Foundations for Holocaust Research: The Impact of Philip Friedman*, Search and Research Series 15. Jerusalem: Yad Vashem, 2009.

Steffen, Katrin, "Connotations of Exclusion: 'Ostjuden,' 'Ghettos,' and Other Markings," *Jahrbuch des Simon-Dubnow-Instituts / Simon Dubnow Institute Yearbook* IV (2005), pp. 459–79.

Steinweis, Alan, "Hans Hinkel and German Jewry, 1933–1941," *Leo Baeck Institute Year Book* 38 (1993), pp. 209–20.

———, *Studying the Jew: Scholarly Antisemitism in Nazi Germany*. Princeton: Princeton University Press, 2006.

Sterling, Eric J., ed., *Life in the Ghettos During the Holocaust*. Syracuse, NY: Syracuse University Press, 2005.

Stoley, Bernard, "Dubrovnik," in Zvi Locker, ed., *Pinkas ha-Kehillot: Yugoslavia* (Encyclopedia of Jewish Communities: Yugoslavia). Jerusalem: Yad Vashem, 1988, pp. 91–2 (Hebrew).

Stow, Kenneth R., *Alienated Minority: The Jews of Medieval Latin Europe*. Cambridge, MA: Harvard University Press, 1994.

_____, *Catholic Thought and Papal Jewry Policy 1555–1593*. New York: Jewish Theological Seminary, 1977.
_____, *Theater of Acculturation: The Roman Ghetto in the Sixteenth Century*. Seattle: University of Washington Press, 2001.
Straede, Therkel, *De nazistiske koncentrationslejre: studier og bibliografi*. Odense: Syddansk Universitetsforlag, 2009.
Tabibian, Ketzia, *Masa' el he-Avar. Ha-Meah ha-Esrim: Bizchut ha-Herut* (A Journey to the Past: The Twentieth Century: In Favor of Freedom). Tel Aviv: Center for Educational Technology, 1999 (Hebrew).
Taffet, Garszon, *Zagłada Żydów Żółkiewskich*. Łódź: Centralna Żydowska Komisja, 1946.
Toaff, Ariel, "Ghetto," *Enciclopedia delle Scienze Sociali*, vol. 4. Rome: Istituto della Enciclopedia Italiana, 1994, pp. 285–91.
Trunk, Isaiah, *Judenrat: The Jewish Councils in Eastern Europe under Nazi Occupation*. New York: Macmillan, 1972.
_____, *Łódź Ghetto: A History*, trans. and ed. Robert Moses Shapiro. Bloomington: Indiana University Press, 2006.
_____, *Lodzsher geto: a historishe un sotsyologishe shtudie mit dokumentn, tabeles un mape*. New York: YIVO, 1962.
Unger, Michal, *Lodz: Aharon ha-Getta'ot be-Polin* (Lodz: The Last Ghetto in Poland). Jerusalem: Yad Vashem, 2005 (Hebrew).
_____, *Reassessment of the Image of Mordechai Chaim Rumkowski*, Search and Research Series 6. Jerusalem: Yad Vashem, 2004.
Vinnitsa, Gennadiy, "The Nazi Policy of Genocide of the Jewish Population in the Eastern and Central Parts of Belarus, 1941–1944," unpublished thesis, chapter 2.1 (Russian; English translation of this chapter kept by this author).
Volkmer, G. F., "Die deutsche Forschung zu Osteuropa und zum osteuropäischen Judentum in den Jahren 1933–1945," *Forschungen zur osteuropäischen Geschichte* 42 (1989), pp. 109–214.
Wein, Abraham, ed., *Pinkas ha-Kehillot: Poland, vol. 7, Lublin ve-Kielce* (Encyclopedia of Jewish Communities: Poland, vol. 7: Lublin and Kielce). Jerusalem: Yad Vashem, 1999 (Hebrew).
Wein, Abraham, and Aharon Weiss, eds., *Pinkas ha-Kehillot: Poland, vol. 3, Galitsiya ha-Ma'aravit uShleziya* (Encyclopedia of Jewish Communities: Poland, vol. 3, Western Galicia and Silesia). Jerusalem: Yad Vashem, 1984 (Hebrew).
Weinberg, Gerhard L., *Germany's War for World Conquest and the Extermination of the Jews*. Washington, DC: United States Holocaust Memorial Museum, Center for Advanced Holocaust Studies, 1998.
Weinstein, Roni, "'Mevudadim Ach Lo Dehuyim': Hayehudim bacHevra ha'iTalkit biTkufat haReformatsiya haKatolit" ("'Segregated Though Not Repelled': The Jews in Italian Society in the Age of the Catholic Reformation"), in Shulamit Volkov, ed., *Mi'utim, Zarim ve-Shonim: Kvutzot Shulayim ba-Historiya* (Minorities, Strangers and the Different: Marginal Groups in History). Jerusalem: Merkaz Shazar, 2000, pp. 93–132 (Hebrew).
Wildt, Michael, *Generation des Unbedingten: Das Führungskorps des Reichssicherheitshauptamtes*. Hamburg: Hamburger Edition, 2002.
_____, *Generation of the Unbound: The Leadership Corps of the Reich Security Main Office*. Jerusalem: Yad Vashem, 2002.

Wilhelm, Hans-Heinrich, *Die Einsatzgruppe A der Sicherheitspolizei und des SD 1941/42*. Frankfurt am Main: Peter Lang, 1996.

Wirth, Louis, *The Ghetto* (with an introduction by Hasia Diner). New Brunswick and London: Transaction Publishers, 1997. (First edition: Chicago: University of Chicago Press, 1928.)

Wodak, Ruth, ed., *Language, Power and Ideology: Studies in Political Discourse*. Amsterdam: J. Benjamins, 1989.

Wolf Jasny, A., *Di geshikhte fun Yidn in Lodzsh: in di yorn fun der Daytsher Yidn-oysrotung*, 2 vols. Tel Aviv: Y. L. Perets, 1960–1966 (Yiddish).

Yahil, Leni, *The Holocaust: The Fate of European Jewry, 1932–1945*, trans. Ina Friedman and Haya Galai. New York: Oxford University Press, 1990.

Yeshurun, Shraga, "Ha-Hit'argenut ha'Atsmit Shel Yehudei Bukovina be-Geto Mogilev" (Self-organization of the Jews of Bukovina in the Moghilev Ghetto), MA thesis, University of Haifa, 1979 (Hebrew).

Zhits, Dan, *Geto Minsk ve-Toledotav le'Or ha-Te'ud he-Hadash* (The History of the Minsk Ghetto (in light of the new documentation). Ramat Gan: Brener Chair in the History of European Jewry During the Holocaust and Finkler Institute of Holocaust Research, Bar-Ilan University, 2000 (Hebrew).

Zimmerer, Katarzyna, *Zamordowany świat: Losy Żydów w Krakowie 1939–1945*. Kraków: Wydawnictwo Literackie, 2004.

C. Internet Sites

Gedenktafeln "Wege gegen das Vergessen," www.aachen.de/DE/kultur_freizeit.

"Ghetto," http://www.ushmm.org/wlc/article (the version quoted here is from 2007 and has since been removed from the United States Holocaust Memorial Museum website).

Simon Wiesenthal Center, http://motlc.learningcenter.wiesenthal.org/pages/t025/t02556.html.

http://www.nypl.org/research/chss/jws/yizkorbookonline.cfm.

http://zydziwpolsce.edu.pl/panel10.html.

Index

Note: recurring terms such as ghetto (except for special meanings); German/Germans; and Third Reich are not included.

Aachen, 151
Abramczik, Dov, 88, 88n85
Abramovici, Sloimu, 131
Acqui, 24n13
Adler, Hans Günther, 136n39
Agnon, Samuel Joseph, 30n17
Agudath Yisrael, 7n1
Alberti, Michael, 6, 12n19
Aleksiun, Natalya, 30n18
Alexandria, 39n9
Alexianu, Gheorghe, 132
Ältestenrat (Council of Elders), 65, 76, 110, 113n30, 134–5, 135n36, 152n10 (*see also Judenrat*)
Aly, Götz, 89, 89n86
Amburger, Andreas von, 103
Amstel, 100n28
Amsterdam, 29, 39n9, 62n4, 86, 91, 93n7, 94–101, 95n7, 96n8, 99n25, 100n27, 100n29, 115, 122, 125, 126–8, 128n18, 141, 143
Annihilation (or extermination) camps, 6, 12n19
Anschluss, 97n13
Anti-Jewish policy, 32n1, 36, 43, 62, 67, 71, 83, 90, 95, 123, 126, 129, 147, 151, 154, 155, 161

anti-Semitism
   emotional, 156
   modern, 49
   rational, 48n6
   traditional, 156
Antonescu, Ion, 129, 130, 134
Antonescu, Mihai, 130
Antwerp, 91
Arad, Yitzhak, 103, 104
Armageddon, 159
Army High Command (OKH – *Oberkommando des Heeres*), 114, 150, 150n4
Aryanization, 33, 43, 41n11, 87n83
Asia, 61
Assimilation, 48
Athens, 139n49
Auerswald, Heinz, 77n45
Auschwitz, 138, 142
Austria, 6, 32, 72, 89, 95, 139
Autonomy, Jewish, 2

Baeck, Leo, 40n9
Baltic states, 12, 14n23, 58n20
Bałuty, 153
Bankier, David, 157, 157n19
Bar, 115
Barbarossa, Operation, 102

183

Index

Barkai, Avraham, 91
Batz, Rudolph, 110
Bauer, Yehuda, 3n3, 69
Bauman, Zygmunt, 13n22
Behrend-Rosenfeld, Else R., 151n7
Belgium (Belgique), 7, 13n22, 72, 91, 95, 139, 152
Belgrade, 152
Belorussia (*Weißruthenien*), 102, 107, 112
Bełżec, 87n84
Ben, Joseph, 139n48
Bender, Sara, 18n40, 103n3
Benz, Wolfgang, 110n19
Berdychiv (Berditchev), 119
Bergmann, Werner, 13n22
Berlin, 17, 32, 39, 41–3, 57, 65, 75, 92, 96, 126, 128n18, 136, 154
Berlin Olympics, 39
Bershad, 133
Bessarabia, 129, 132
Beutel, Lothar, 75, 76n41
Białystok, 86, 103n3
Bible, 38
black ghettos, 30
Black Sea, 46, 63
Blumenthal, Nachman, 7, 7n4
Bobelis Jurgis, 106
Bohemia, 69, 122, 134 (*see also* Protectorate Bohemia and Moravia)
Böhler, Jochen, 73, 68n15, 70n23
Böhmcker, Hans, 95, 95n7, 96, 98, 99n20, 99n25, 100n27, 100n31, 126, 126n12, 127n14
Bolshevism, 102, 114, 148, 160
Bormann, Martin, 95, 158n20
Brackmann, Albert, 45n1
Brackmann, Karl-Heinz, 8n7
Braham, Randolph L., 141n51
Brauchitsch, Walther von, 68, 157
Breslau, Synod of, 11, 11n16, 21, 21n2
Browning, Christopher R., 16–8, 70–2, 77n45, 77n48, 82, 89, 96n8, 146, 157

Brünn (Brno), 122, 134, 135n36
Brussels, 91
Brzezany, 115n37
Bucharest, 128, 129
Buchholz, Marlis, 91
Büchler, Yehoshua Robert, 90n1
Budapest, 16, 143, 151
Bug, 64
Bukovina, 129, 132

Calabi, Donatella, 22
Cambrai, League of, 21, 21n4
capitalism, 160
carrière juif, 20
Casale Monferrato, 24n13
Caucasus, 115n35
Central Publication Office of the Nazi Party, 63n7
Centralverein deutscher Staatsbürger jüdischen Glaubens (Central Association of German Citizens of the Jewish Faith), 38
Charleroi, 91
Chicago, 29
Cohen, Mark R., 26n4
Cole, Tim, 16, 143, 151n8
Cologne, 37
Community memorial books (*Yizkor Bicher*), 1, 14, 14n29
concentration camps, 12n19, 133, 136, 153
Conegliano Veneto, 24n13
confidential situation reports (*Lage-und Stimmungsberichte*), 36
Corni, Gustavo, 13n22, 15, 15n32, 16
Correggio 24, 24n13
Corrsin, Stephen D., 29n13
Council of [Jewish] Elders (*see Ältestenrat*)
Creanga, Ion, 133n30
Crimea, 115, 115n35, 117
Croatia, 22n7
Csősz, László, 142, 143n57
Cum Nimis Absurdum (papal bull), 20
Czernowitz (Cernăuţi), 130

Index

Częstochowa (Tschenstochau), 125, 151

Dawidowicz, Lucy S., 158, 159
de Jong, Lou, 93n7
De Misthoorn, 96
Dean, Martin, 104n6, 150n3
Denmark, 7
Der ewige Jude (The Eternal Jew), 69, 97
Der Morgen, 38
Displaced Persons camps, 7n4, 8
Dniepropetrovsk, 120
Dniester, 131
Draft Law for Regulating the Status of the Jews (*Entwurf zu einem Gesetz zur Regelung der Stellung der Juden*), 32n6
Drancy, 139
Drexel, Hans, 78-9
Dreyfus-Ben-Sasson, Havi, 81n60
Dubienka, 87n84
Dubrovnik (=Ragusa), 22n7
Dumitru, Diana, 22n7
Dutch Nazis, 98-9
Dworzecki, Meir [Mark], 7, 7n5, 14
Dzhankoi, 115n35
Działoszyce, 87n84

Egypt, 27
Eichmann, Adolf, 9, 56, 69, 84, 84n71, 99, 99n23, 127, 134, 135, 136, 137, 139n48, 141, 145, 147
Einsatzgruppen
  Einsatzgruppe B (in USSR), 103, 113n30
  Einsatzgruppe D (in USSR), 129
  Einsatzgruppe III (in Poland), 71n25
Einsatzkommando 3 (in USSR), 107
Eisenbach, Artur, 84n73
Eisenberg (Gotdiner), Mali, 62, 63n4
Elista, 115n35
England, 20
Eretz Israel (Palestine), 7n1, 30n17, 62n4
Eshkoli, Hava, 88n85

Este, 24n13
Extermination, 11n18, 12n19, 13, 16, 103-4, 116, 150n3, 159, 160n25

Fefferman, Kiril, 115n35
Ferrara, 24n13
Feudalism, 27
Final Solution, 2, 6, 9, 11, 11n19, 17, 18, 102, 103-4, 112, 117, 120, 123, 126, 137, 149-50, 155, 157-60, 161p25
Fischer, Hans, 71, 71n25
Fischer, Ludwig, 76
Fischer, Ronit, 133n33
Florence, 24n11, 24n13
forced concentration, 69
forced labor, 120, 138n46
  camps, 125
  units, 104
Foreign Ministry (German), 32, 32n4, 69
Four-Year Plan, 42, 42n15
France, 7, 21n4, 21n14, 95, 152
Frank, Hans, 56n17, 75, 75n39, 76, 76n42, 83, 84, 86, 97, 97n12, 106, 123, 124
Frankfurt am Main, 39n9, 94n2, 105, 105n7
Freemasons, 147
Freiburg, University of, 116n38
Friedländer, Saul, 19, 157n20
Friedman, Philip, 1, 2n1, 3, 7n3, 13n22, 16n35, 62n4
Frojimovics, Kinga, 142n52
Functionalism, 147

Galicia, 102, 111, 115, 115n36, 115n37, 124, 125
Geller, Jacob, 133n32
Gemlich, Adolf, 145
Generalgouvernement, 10, 62n4, 75, 83, 84, 87, 97n12, 103, 106, 115, 115n36, 124, 124n3, 124n4, 160n25
Gennadiy, Vinnitsa, 116n40
Genocide, 6, 9, 9n11, 12n19, 116n40, 120, 158

Gestapo, 36, 40, 41, 42n13, 43, 56–8, 56n19, 93, 97n13, 126
Ghetto
  benches, 30
  black, 30
  closed, 14n23, 80, 82, 143, 149, 150n3, 152
  mediaeval, 1, 2
  Nuovo, 21
  open, 149, 150n3, 151
  social, 30, 41
  spiritual, 30, 37, 38, 155
  Vecchio, 21
  Warsaw, 7, 7n6, 15n30, 49, 77, 77n45, 82n61, 86, 89n86, 100n30, 125 136, 160n25
  Warsaw Ghetto uprising, 7
Ghetto Fighters' House (Beth Lohamei Hagettaot), 7n4
Goebbels, Joseph, 33, 69, 70, 74, 95
Golden, Harry, 29n10
Golta, 133
Göring, Hermann, 33–5, 42, 43, 58, 60, 61
Goshen, 27
Greece, 138
Gregorovius, Ferdinand, 40n9
Greiser, Arthur, 79, 81
Gringauz, Samuel, 7, 7n2, 8, 9n9
Grodno, 117n43
Gruenbaum, Itzhak, 7n1
Grüner Weg (*Barrackenlager*), 151
Gur, Rebbe of, 62n4
Gutman, Israel, 13–15, 14n23, 14n24, 72, 160n25
Gutterer, Leopold, 98n16
gypsies, 66

Hacohen, Aaron, 22n7
Hagen, Herbert, 56
Halder, Franz, 68
Hamburg, 16, 36, 37, 37n6
Hapgood, Hutchins, 29n10
Harster, Wilhelm, 97, 97n13, 126
Hashomer Hadati, 88
Haushofer, Albrecht, 69
Headships, 65, 65n8, 152

Hebron, 30n17
Heijermans, Herman, 29, 98n17
Heise, Karl August Hermann Ludwig, 116
Herzl, Theodor, 26, 26n3
Hess, Rudolf, 40, 42
Heyde, Jürgen, 12n19, 30n14
Heydrich, Reinhard, 9, 10n15, 17, 18, 31, 33–5, 33n9, 40, 40n10, 41, 44, 56, 56n19, 58, 60, 65, 66, 68, 69, 71, 74, 75, 110, 122, 134, 137, 148, 152
Higher School for National Socialism, 105
Hilberg, Raul, 6, 9–11, 10n14, 10n15, 11n16, 13, 21n2, 69, 89, 90, 110n19, 146, 152
Himmler, Heinrich, 42, 61, 75, 75n38, 124, 125n5
Hinkel, Hans, 63, 63n6, 63n7, 64
Hippler, Fritz, 69
Hirsch (Baron) camp, 138, 139
Hirsch, Samson Raphael, 25, 26
Hirschberg, Alfred, 38
Hirschfeld, Gerhard, 63n7
Hitler, Adolf, 54, 68, 68n16, 129, 145, 147, 147n1, 148, 156–60
Holocaust, 3, 3n7, 7n3, 8, 9, 10n14, 11, 11n19, 13, 13n22, 14n24, 16n35, 18, 19, 21n2, 29, 62n4, 79, 88, 90, 99, 100n29, 102, 104, 116n40, 123n2, 142, 146, 150, 152, 153, 156, 157, 161
  consciousness, 1–2
  historiography, 2n1, 156
  history, 2
Holzberg, Matthias, 151n7
Hoppe, Bert, 116n38
Horthy, Miklós, 143
Horváth, Sándor Neográdi, 142n56
Hrubieszów, 87n84
Hungary, 8, 46, 88, 122, 123, 139, 141–4, 141n50, 141n51, 142n52, 142n53, 142n54, 142n55, 142n56, 143n57, 143n58, 144n59, 149, 151, 152

Index

Innsbruck, 97n13
Institute of Contemporary History in Munich (*Institut für Zeitgeschichte*), 116n38
Intentionalism, 8n8, 31
Israel, 7, 7n4, 13, 14, 14n24, 15, 27, 30n17, 99n23, 136n39
Italy, 24, 23n10, 25, 139, 139n49
Izbica, 87n84

Jäger, Karl, 106
Jeckeln, Friedrich, 119
Jew Street (*Judenstrasse/Joodschestraat*), 20, 100
Jew Town, 20
Jewish Administration, 4, 142, 152
Jewish Affairs Department of the SD (SD-II 12), 37, 63, 152
Jewish courtyard, 20
Jewish cultural organizations (*jüdischen Kulturbunde*), 37
Jewish Department of the General Government (*Referat Judenwesen*), 84, 84n73
Jewish Historical Institute, Warsaw, 30n18
Jewish residential quarter (*Jüdisches Wohnviertel*), 58, 79, 113n30, 150
Jewish self-government, 2, 13
Judendorf (Jewish village), 20
Judengasse (Jewish alley), 20
Judenhäuser (Jewish houses), 4, 16n33, 43, 91, 142, 143
Judenheit (Jewry), 155
Judentum (Jewry), 5, 40n10, 45, 66n12, 72, 111, 116n39, 126n11, 146, 155
Judaismus (Judaism), 155
Judenhof (Jewish court), 20
Judensiedlung (Jewish settlement), 42
Judenpolitik (anti-Jewish policies), 2
Judenrat, 2, 12, 13, 13n22, 18, 19, 65, 69, 76, 83n64, 87, 98n16, 103, 110, 115n36, 117, 117n43, 118, 151, 152, 152n10, 153 (*see also* Ältestenrat)
Judenstadt (Jewish city), 20, 136
Judenviertel (Jewish quarter), 20, 63, 73, 95n7, 96n8, 99, 126n12, 128n18, 127, 139, 150, 150n4
Judeo-Bolshevism, 102
Judería, 20
Jüdische Ältestenräte (*see* Ältestenrät; Judenrat)
Jüdische Rundschau (newspaper), 39
Juiverie, 2

Keitel, Wilhelm Bodewin Johann Gustav, 158n20
Kershaw, Ian, 157
Kielce, Province of, 77, 79, 85n76, 87n84, 88, 123n2
Kiev, 120
Kirste, Arnold, 110
Kishinev (Chişinău), 130
Kovner, Abba, 103
Kovno (Kaunas, Kauen), 7, 49, 106, 107, 110, 118, 119, 121n51, 153
Krakow (Krakau), 7, 49, 71, 73, 75, 76, 82, 83, 85n76, 86, 97, 97n12, 97n13, 102, 106, 115n36, 123n2, 125, 153
Krasnik, 83n64
Kristallnacht, 31, 33, 42, 44, 159
Krone, Mosche, 88n85
Krüger, Friedrich Wilhem, 124
Kruk, Herman, 85n76
Kutno, 81
Kwiet, Konrad, 157

Labor camps, 87n84, 119, 122, 133, 135, 136 (*see also* Forced labor camps)
Lammers, Hans, 158n20
Lasch, Karl, 83, 102, 115n36
Lateran Council, Fourth, 21n2
Latvia (*Lettland*), 102, 111
Lau, Moshe Chaim, 78
Lebensraum, 6, 15, 61
Leczna, 87n84
Lemberg (Lwów), 30, 30n18, 49, 102, 115n36, 117n43
Lettland (*see* Latvia)
Levin, Yitzhak Meir, 7n1
Libau, 116

Liège, 91
Lithuania, 1, 5, 15n31, 102, 106
Litzmannstadt, 81, 81n59, 82n62 (see also Łódź)
Lodscher Zeitung, 61, 81n60
Łódź, 7, 7n6, 14, 49, 61, 70, 71, 75, 79–83, 81n56, 82n61, 85n75, 86, 86n77, 88, 89n86, 97, 125, 136, 150, 153 (see also Litzmannstadt)
Lohse, Hinrich, 112, 113, 116, 116n39
London, 27, 99
Longerich, Peter, 33n9, 157
Louis XII, 21n4
Lower, Wendy, 119, 119n47, 119n48
Łowicz, 82
Lublin, 7, 11n18, 69, 71, 82, 83, 83n64, 87n84, 106, 123n2, 125
Luchinetz, 133
Lübeck, 95
Lwów, 30, 30n18, 117n43 (see also Lemberg)
Lwów Polytechnic Institute, 30, 30n18

Madagascar Plan, 89n86, 106n8
Mährisch Ostrau (Moravská Ostrava), 134
Mantua, 24
Marr, Wilhelm, 54
Marxism, 160
Maskilim (enlightened Jews), 26
Matthäus, Jürgen, 57n20, p73n31
Maximilian I, Emperor, 21n4
Mechelen/Malines, 139
Meershoek, Guus, 96n8
Mein Kampf, 54, 160
Memel, 7n2
Michman (Melkman), Jozeph, 62n4
Miechov (Kielce Province), 88, 88n85
Migration, 33, 41, 43, 46
Mikoyanshakhar, 115n35
Milbertshofen, 151n7
Ministry of Propaganda, 63
Minsk, 110, 118, 118n45
Mirandola, 24n13
Mizrachi, 88n85
Modena, 24n13
Moghilev, 133, 133n33

Moncalvo, 24n13
Moravia, 69, 122, 134
Munich, 84n71, 116n38, 151, 151n7

National Socialism, 1, 8n8, 105, 154
National Union of Jewish Frontline Soldiers, 37
Naumann, Max, 37n2
Nazi
  bureaucracy, 4
  ideology, 95
  party, 63n7, 95, 148, 148n2
  regime, 6, 11n18, 31, 36, 46n2, 91, 146, 149, 150n3, 154, 156
Nebe, Arthur, 103
Neo-Orthodox Judaism, 27
Netherlands, The, 7, 72, 91, 93n7, 94–9, 125–7, 152
Neumann, Boaz, 6, 10n15, 15, 16, 16n33
Neumann-Neurode, Karl Ulrich von, 76
New York, 29n10
Nieuwe Kerkstraat, 100n28
Nisko Reserve (Reservat Lublin), 69, 84n71, 89n86
Nissenbaum, Rabbi, 88, 88n85
Norway, 7
Nuremberg, 65n10
  Laws, 32, 37, 39, 40, 157, 157n20
  Trial, 9

Odessa, 133
"Old Reich" (Altreich), 32, 82, 134, 135n36
Opole-Lubelski, 83
Ostjuden 29, 45, 53, 53n12, 63, 73, 74, 82, 88, 89, 94, 97, 119, 124, 141, 146, 149, 153, 155, 156 (see also Poland, Jews of)
Ostland, 106, 112, 114, 116, 116n39, 118
Ostrawa, 69

Padua, 24n13
Paris, 63
Pesaro, 24n13
Pest, 143

Index

Petelewicz, Jakub, 79n53
Piaski, 83
Piotrków-Trybunalski, 67, 71, 77–9, 83
Podgórze, 153
Pogrom, 30n17
Pohl, Dieter, 73n31, 154
Poland, 1, 6, 7n1, 8–10, 9n12, 10n15, 12n19, 13, 14n23, 15, 15n30, 15n31, 17, 18, 29, 30, 46, 49, 53, 56, 56n17, 61–89, 90, 94–7, 97n12, 100, 102–5, 107, 110, 115, 118, 120, 122–4, 123n2, 125n5, 129, 131, 134, 135, 142, 143, 146, 147, 149, 151, 152, 157
  invasion of, 10n15, 61, 63, 71, 88, 147
  Jews of, 29, 62, 67, 73, 84n71, 140
Poliakov, 7n6,
  Léon 9
Popes
  Julius II, 21n4
  Paul IV, 20, 22
Prager, Moshe, 62–3n4
Prague, 39n9, 122, 134, 136, 152
  Jewish community council, 136
Prais, Leah, 85n76
pre-emancipation period, 8, 32, 40, 66
Prinz, Joachim, 39, 39n9
Propaganda, 33, 63, 69, 74, 95, 136
Proszowice, 87n84
Protectorate Bohemia and Moravia, 69, 72, 122, 134, 135, 135n36
Przemyśl, 70

Racism
  ideology, 76
  law, 73
Radom, 71, 83, 85n76, 115, 123, 125
Ragusa (=Dubrownik), 22, 22n7
Rauter, Hanns Albin, 99
Ravid, Benjamin, 21, 24n15
Red Army, 143

Redeker, Dietrich, 87
Redlich, Shimon, 115n37
Reggio, 24n13
Reich Main Security Office (*RSHA*), 84n71, 112
Reich Ministry for Popular Information and Propaganda, 95
Reich Ministry for the Occupied Eastern Territories (*Reichsministerium für die besetzten Ostgebiete [RmfdbO]*), 111
Reichskommissar for the Strengthening of the German People, 75
resettlement (*Umsiedlung*), 89n86, 124
Rhodes, 7
Riga, 49, 93, 110, 111, 115, 116, 116n38, 118, 118n45, 137
Rivierenviertel, 127, 127n16
Romania, 122, 128–34, 150, 153
Rome, 22, 23, 24n13, 26, 40n9, 139n49
Roques, Franz von, 102, 113
Roques, Karl von, 111
Rosenberg, Alfred, 105, 105n7, 106, 111, 120, 148, 158n20
Rosenfeld, Morris, 28
Rostov on Don, 117
Rovigo, 24n13
RSHA (*see* Reich Main Security Office)
Rumkowsky, Mordechai Chaim, 86n77
Ruppin, Arthur, 46, 48
Russia, 117 (*see also* Soviet Union)

Sadova, 133
Sakowska Ruta, 15n30
Salonika (Thessaloniki), 97, 122, 123, 138–41, 149
Sammelghetto (Central Ghetto), 1, 2
Schenckendorff, Max von, 107, 110, 111, 150
Schicksalsjahr (year of destiny) 1938, 32
Schmidt, Fritz, 95, 96, 98, 99n24

Schnellbrief (of September 21, 1939), 3, 3n3, 9, 17–18, 65–8, 66n12, 67n14, 70–2, 74, 76, 110, 148, 152
Schocken Verlag, 40n9
Schocken, Zalman, 30n17
Schön, Waldemar, 76, 77n45, 100n30
Schwaben und Neuburg, 159n22
Schwarze Korps, Das, 44, 73
SD (*Sicherheitsdienst* – SS Security Service), 33, 36, 37, 40, 42n13, 56, 56n19, 57, 62, 63, 95, 97, 97n13, 138, 152
SD Main Office (*SD-Hauptamt*), 36, 57
Seifert, Hermann Erich, 63n7, 77n45
Senigallia, 24n13
Seraphim, Peter-Heinz, 5, 6n1, 45–7, 46n3, 49, 51–60, 53n12, 58n22, 62–3, 62n4, 65, 67, 69, 73–6, 78, 84, 87, 87n83, 94, 94n2, 98, 105–7, 106n8, 107n13, 111–12, 119, 139, 146, 153
Seyss-Inquart, Arthur, 94, 95, 97, 97n12, 99n25, 100, 100n31, 126, 127
Shargorod, 133
Shpringer, Nina, 141n50
Siena, 24n13
Silberklang, David, 82
Silesia, 83
Simferopol, 120
Singer, Bernard S., 25, 29
SIPO (*Sicherheitspolizei* – German Security Police), 33, 37, 95, 97
Slavnoye, 107
Slobodka (Viljampole), 107, 153
Slovakia, 90
Smolensk, 113n30
Sobibor, 87n84
Sombart, Werner, 51, 52
Sonderkommandos, 103
South Africa, 154
Soviet Union, 8, 10n15, 14n23, 46, 64, 102–21, 129–30
Spain, 20, 21n3, 21n4

SPD (*Sozialistische Partei Deutschlands* –West German Socialist Party), 63n4
Special Officer-in-Charge for the Monitoring of Non-Aryans (*Sonderbeauftragter für die Überwachung der Nichtarier*), 63
special processing (*Sonderbehandelung*), 103
Speer, Albert, 42, 43
SS (*Schutzstaffel*), 33, 42, 44, 64, 65, 69, 72, 73, 75, 76, 84, 88, 89, 106, 110, 114, 119, 124, 129, 134, 135n36, 153, 159, 159n23
SS Department of Jewish Affairs (*IVB4*; mentioned as "Eichmann's Department"), 145
Stahlecker, Franz, 106, 112
Steffen, Katrin, 12n19
Stow, Kenneth, 23
Survivors, 1, 6, 8, 150n3
Szálasi, Ferenc, 143

Taubert, 69
Tenant Protection Law (*Aufhebung der Mieterschutzes für Juden*), 41
Territorialism, 2
Teter, Magda, 23n10
Thadden, Eberhard von, 139n48
Thaisz, Andor, 142n55
Theresienstadt, 122, 123, 134, 135, 136, 137, 149, 152n10, 153
Tibulovca, 133, 133n32
Tolochin, 107
Transit camps, 136, 139
Transit-Ghetto, 1, 2
Transnistria, 122, 130–4, 152
Transvaalviertel, 127, 127n16
Treblinka, 87n84
Treitschke, Heinrich von, 49
Trianon, 142
Trunk, Isaiah, 11n19, 12, 13, 14, 80n55
Tsahor, Dov, 88n85
Tuczin, 150n3
Tuliskόw, 81

Turin, 24n13
Tuscany, Duchy of, 24n11

Uebelhör, Friedrich, 79, 80–2, 85n75
Ukraine, 102, 106, 112, 114, 115, 129, 131
United States, 24, 29n10
United States Holocaust Memorial Museum, Washington, DC, 4, 12n19, 104n6, 153n3, 154
Urbino, 24n13

van Doorslaer, Rudi, 13n22
Vatican, 24
Veneto, 23n13
Venice, 20, 21, 21n4, 22, 23, 24n13, 24n15
Verband nationaldeutschen Jüden (Union of Jewish German Nationalists), 37, 37n2
Vercelli, 24n13
Verhovka, 133
Verona, 24n13
Vienna, 28, 56, 69, 152
Viljampole, 107, 153
Vilna (Vilnius), 7, 14, 30, 49, 103, 115, 119 (*see also* Wilno)
Vinnitsa, 115, 120
Vitebsk, 107, 107n15
Voikovstat, 115n35
Volhynia, 115n37, 118

Wannsee Conference, 137
Warsaw, 7, 7n6, 14, 15n30, 17, 29, 29n13, 30n18, 49, 62n4, 67, 69, 70n23, 71, 75–8, 76n45, 82–4, 82n61, 85n76, 86, 88, 89n86, 97, 100–2, 100n30, 110, 115n36, 125, 130, 136, 139, 143, 150, 160n25

Warthegau (also *Wartheland*), 6, 71, 75, 77n48, 79, 81, 84
Wehrmacht, 19, 66n12, 70, 73, 102, 134, 135n36
Westerbork, 139
Western Europe, 2, 91, 95, 123, 158
Wiesenthal, Simon, 2n2
Wildt, Michael, 155
Wilno, University of, 30
Wisliceny, Dieter, 9, 84n71, 137, 138, 138n46, 145, 147, 148n2, 156
Wittmayer, Baron Salo, 27, 27n7
Wolf Jasny, Avraham, 14
Wolyn (Wolhynien/Volhynia), 115n37
World War I, 52
World War II, 8, 13, 12n19, 61, 102, 144, 147, 149

Yad Vashem, 7n4, 141n50
Yahil, Leni, 10n15, 104, 104n5
Yalta, 115n35
Yellow Star of David, 61, 81, 138
Yevpatoria, 117
Yizkor-bikher (*see also* community memorial books), 1
Yiddish, 14n29, 28, 48, 85n76, 88n85, 158

Zamboni, Guelfo, 139n49
Zamość, 83
Zangwill, Israel, 29
Zaporozhe, 120
Zentralstelle für jüdische Auswanderung (Central Office for Jewish Emigration), 127, 136
Zhytomyr, 119
Zueca, 20
Zygelbojm report, 7n1

Printed in Great Britain
by Amazon